TENDENCIES IN
MODERN AMERICAN POETRY

TENDENCIES
IN MODERN AMERICAN
POETRY

BY

AMY LOWELL, *1874-1925.*

1971

OCTAGON BOOKS
New York

Reprinted 1971

by special arrangement with Conrad W. Oberdorfer and G. d'Andelot Belin
as Trustees under the Will of Amy Lowell

OCTAGON BOOKS

A DIVISION OF FARRAR, STRAUS & GIROUX, INC.

19 Union Square West

New York, N. Y. 10003

LIBRARY OF CONGRESS CATALOG CARD NUMBER: 74-155814

ISBN 0-374-95133-0

Printed in U.S.A. by
NOBLE OFFSET PRINTERS, INC.
NEW YORK 3, N. Y.

PREFACE

It is impossible for any one writing to-day not to be affected by the war. It has overwhelmed us like a tidal wave. It is the equinoctial storm which bounds a period. So I make no apology for beginning a book of poetical essays with a reference to the war. In fact, the war and the subject of this volume are not so far apart as might at first appear.

The so-called "new movement" in American poetry is evidence of the rise of a native school. The welding together of the whole country which the war has brought about, the mobilizing of our whole population into a single, strenuous endeavour, has produced a more poignant sense of nationality than has recently been the case in this country of enormous spaces and heterogeneous population. Hyphens are submerged in the solid overprinting of the word "America." We are no more colonies of this or that other land, but ourselves, different from all other peoples whatsoever.

It is this realization of ourselves that has drawn us into an understanding sympathy with our allies hardly to be conceived of before. And let us make no mistake; such a result cannot be reached through a devotion to the teachings of materialism. The real truth is that at a time when most people were bewailing the growth of

v

materialism, already, beneath the surface, the seething of a new idealism was in process.

Long before the shadow of battle flung itself over the world, the travail of this idealism began. Slowly, painfully, it took on a shape, hidden away in the dreams and desires of unknown men.

Literature is rooted to life, and although a work of art is great only because of its æsthetic importance, still its very æstheticism is conditioned by its sincerity and by the strength of its roots. Posterity cares nothing for the views which urged a man to write; to it, the poetry, its beauty as a work of art, is the only thing which matters. But that beauty could not exist without the soil from which it draws its sustenance, and it is a fact that those works of art which are superficial or meretricious do certainly perish remarkably soon. This is why time alone can determine a man's fate. Tinsel can be made to look extraordinarily like gold; it is only wear which rubs off the plating.

To a certain extent, the change which marks American poetry has been going on in the literature of other countries also. But not quite in the same way. Each country approaches an evolutionary step from its own racial angle, and they move alternately, first one leads and then another, but all together, if we look back a century or so, move the world forward into a new path. At the moment of writing, it is America who has taken the last, most advanced step.

It is not my intention, here, to combat the opinions of the conservatives. Conservatives are always with us, they have been opposing change ever since the days of the cave-men. But, fortunately for mankind, they agitate in vain. Already the more open minded see that the change going on in the arts is not a mere frivolous interest in experiment. Already the reasons for difference begin to stand out clearly. We who watch realize something of the grandeur of conception toward which this evolution is working.

The modern poets are less concerned with dogma and more with truth. They see in the universe a huge symbol, and so absolute has this symbol become to them that they have no need to dwell constantly upon its symbolic meaning. For this reason, the symbol has taken on a new intensity, and is given much prominence. What appear to be pure nature poems are of course so, but in a different way from most nature poems of the older writers; for nature is not now something separate from man, man and nature are recognized as a part of a whole, man being a part of nature, and all falling into a place in a vast plan, the key to which is natural science.

In some modern American poets this attitude is more conscious than in others, but all have been affected by it; it has modified poetry, as it is more slowly modifying the whole of our social fabric.

What sets the poets of to-day apart from those of the Victorian era is an entire difference of outlook. Ideas believed to be fundamental have disappeared and given place to others. And as poetry is the expression of the heart of man, so it reflects this change to its smallest particle.

It has been my endeavour in these essays to follow this evolution, in the movement as a whole, and also in the work of the particular poets who compose it. I have tried to show what has led each of these men to adopt the habit of mind which now characterizes him, why he has been forced out of one order into another; how his ideas have gradually taken form in his mind, and in what way he expresses this form in his work. I have pointed out his ancestry, physical as well as mental, and have noted where atavism has held him back, where pushed him forward.

I wish I had space to consider all the men and women whose work has aided to make this movement vigorous and important. But that must be left to future literary historians. Still, it is with regret that I pass by the work of Mr. Louis Untermeyer and Mr. James Oppenheim, of Mr. Ezra Pound and Mr. Vachel Lindsay, of Mr. William Rose Benét and Mrs. Eunice Tietjens, and others as well, but the main tendencies of which they are a part have been considered under other names. It is true that at a first glance Mr. Lindsay does not seem to fall very readily into any of these groups, but I think a closer attention will find him to be rather popularizing the second stage of the movement than heading a completely new tendency of his own.

As to those poets who still cling to an older order, of course, in such a volume as this, their work can find no place however excellent it may be in itself.

How shall one write a book of literary criticism? What weight shall one lay on biography; what on æsthetics? I quite agree with that brilliant disciple of Signor Benedetto Croce, Mr. J. E. Spingarn, that the criticism of art should be first, foremost, and all the time, æsthetic. As I have already said, its æsthetic value is, in the final summing up, the only value of a work of art, as such. But life, too, has a right to its criticism, and to the lover of poetry the life which conditioned the poems also has its charm. Therefore I have considered these poets as men and artists.

It is my good fortune to know all these poets, but I have tried not to let friendship interfere with opinion. Still it is possible that personal intercourse may have led to a closer understanding of aims and motives than I realize. That it has enabled me to round out the brief biographies submitted to me by the poets themselves, I am well aware. The facts of a man's life tell very little, unless one also knows the man; and a couple of pages of dates and occupations alone would certainly not have enabled me to write as I have done, had not the memory of many conversations come to my aid.

My thanks, therefore, are chiefly due to the poets themselves, who have helped me with all the information they had to give and with outlines of the events of their lives. The photographs here reproduced I owe to their kindness. I am also indebted to the courtesy of various publishers for permission to reprint the poems which appear in the text. To The Macmillian Company for extracts from Mr. Robinson's volumes, "Captain Craig," "The Man Against the Sky," and "Merlin," and from Mr. Masters' volumes, "The Spoon River Anthology," "Songs and Satires," and "The Great Valley"; to Messrs. Henry Holt and Company for poems reprinted from Mr. Frost's books, "A Boy's Will," "North of Boston," and "Mountain Interval," and from Mr. Sandburg's volume, "Chicago Poems"; to Messrs. Houghton, Mifflin and Company for the quotations from "H. D."'s "Sea

Garden," and Mr. Fletcher's "Irradiations — Sand and Spray" and "Goblins and Pagodas"; to Messrs. Charles Scribner's Sons for the poems, "The Children of the Night," "John Evereldown," "Richard Cory," and "Cliff Klingenhagen," from Mr. Robinson's "The Children of the Night," and "The Master," "Doctor of Billiards," and "How Annandale Went Out," from the same author's "The Town Down the River"; to The New Republic Company for Mr. Fletcher's "Clipper-Ships;" and to The Four Seas Company for the same author's Japanese poems. I should also add that certain parts of these essays have appeared in "The New Republic," "The Poetry Journal," and "The Poetry Review," and that the nucleus of the volume was a course of lectures delivered at the Brooklyn Institute of Arts and Sciences in January, 1917.

It is impossible for the judgment of any one critic to be final. In fact, no contemporary criticism can make any such pretence. Hitherto, American students have felt this so strongly that practically no serious consideration of contemporary work has been attempted. Other countries, however, are not so modest. France, particularly, delights in analyzing the art of the time. The French realize that a contemporary can often reveal facets in an author's work which may be hidden from posterity, that certain *nuances* can only be apprehended by a person living under the same conditions. This must be my excuse for attempting a study of living authors. Also, that they are poets. For, recently, in England and America, a movement has started which has taken form in various little booklets, monographs of this and that novelist for the most part. Poetry has not been touched upon; and this is strange, for poetry, far more than fiction, reveals the soul of humanity. Poets are always the advance guard of literature; the advance guard of life. It is for this reason that their recognition comes so slowly.

AMY LOWELL.

BROOKLINE,
July 1, 1917.

CONTENTS

LIST OF ILLUSTRATIONS

EDWIN ARLINGTON ROBINSON

EDWIN ARLINGTON ROBINSON

WHEN people speak of the "New Poetry," they generally mean that poetry which is written in the newer, freer forms. But such a distinction is misleading in the extreme, for, after all, forms are merely forms, of no particular value unless they are the necessary and adequate clothing to some particular manner of thought.

There is a "New Poetry" to-day, and the new forms are a part of its attire, but the body is more important than the clothing and existed before it. All real changes are a matter of slow growth, of evolution. The beginnings of a change are almost imperceptible, the final stages, on the other hand, being so radical that everyone remarks them, and with such astonishment that the cry of "freak," "charlatan," is almost sure to be raised by ignorant readers.

A great artistic movement is as inevitable a thing as the growth of a race. But, as in races, individuals possess differing characteristics, so the various artists whose work represents a revolt may differ most widely one from another, and yet, in varying still more widely from artists of other epochs, they create what critics call a "movement."

In this book, I have attempted no catalogue of present-day American poets. There are excellent poets whose work I am not going to touch upon. I shall only consider those few poets who seem most markedly to represent a tendency. A poetic movement may be compared to a braid of woven strands. Of the six poets of whom I shall speak, each is an exemplar, and I think the most typical exemplar, of a strand. But one particular tinge is peculiar to all the strands, and that particular tinge is revolt against the immediate past.

We shall see these poets revolting against stilted phrases and sentimentality; we shall see them endeavouring to express themselves, and the new race which America is producing; we shall see them stepping boldly from realism to far flights of imagination. We shall see them ceding more and more to the influence of other, alien, peoples, and fusing exotic modes of thought with their Anglo-Saxon inheritance. This is indeed the melting pot, and its fumes affect the surrounding company as well as the ingredients in the crucible.

To understand the change which is going on in American poetry, it is necessary to glance back for a moment to earlier conditions.

If we examine the state of American poetry from,
let us say, 1830 until the Civil War, we shall be
struck with one thing. That is, with the racial
homogeneity of our poets. They are all of good
English stock, in their work, I mean. It is true that
two great geniuses flung themselves up out of this
mass of cultivated endeavour. But that is no exception to the Anglo-Saxon rule, for no literature is
richer in geniuses than is the English. But these
two geniuses, Edgar Allan Poe and Walt Whitman,
were too far ahead of their times to have much effect
upon their contemporaries. They are better understood, and have more followers, in the America of
to-day. Wordsworth on the one hand, Byron on
the other, were the main springs of American poetry.

Good poetry, if not strikingly great poetry,
marked the epoch of Whittier, Bryant, Emerson,
Lowell, Longfellow, and Holmes. They were English provincial poets, in the sense that America was
still a literary province of the Mother Country.

But from the Civil War until almost the present
day, the literary sponsors of American verse were
much less worthy of disciples. The robustness of
Byron gave place to the sugared sentimentality of
Tennyson; the moral strength of Wordsworth made
way for the frozen didacticism of Matthew Arnold.
But worse was to follow, for technique usurped the
place of emotion, and words, mere words, were
exalted out of all due proportion. Swinburne and

Rossetti are not good masters to follow, no matter with what skill they themselves wrought. Only those of our poets who kept solidly to the Shakespearean tradition achieved any measure of success. But Keats was the last great exponent of that tradition, and we all know how thin, how lacking in charm, the copies of Keats have become. No matter how beautiful a piece of music may be, we cannot hear it indefinitely without satiety, and the same piece rendered by a phonograph soon becomes unbearable. Our poets were largely phonographs to greater English poets dead and gone, as the pages of our magazines of twenty years ago will abundantly prove.

Art is like politics. Any theory carried too far ends in sterility, and freshness is only gained by following some other line. Faultless, flowing verses, raised about a worn-out, threadbare idea — fine moral sentiments expressed in the weak, innocuous language of the hymn-books — had no resemblance to the temper of modern American life. Publishers still printed poetry, but not with any idea of its answering a demand; editors accepted it to round out short pages, but they hardly expected to have more attention accorded it than an ornamental scroll would have received. Readers found more sustenance in Browning, and bewailed the fact that he was dead, and, alas, English! America was not a country for poets, said the wiseacres, it was given over to materialism, and materialism could never produce art.

This was tantamount to saying that art was an artificial thing, whereas making steel harrows was a natural thing. Of course, that is a ridiculous point of view. Art, true art, is the desire of a man to express himself, to record the reactions of his personality to the world he lives in. Great emotion always tends to become rhythmic, and out of that tendency the forms of art have been evolved. Art becomes artificial only when the forms take precedence over the emotion.

Now here was a great country practically dumb. Here was a virile race, capable of subduing a vast continent in an incredibly short time, with no tongue to vent its emotion. How should such a race express itself by the sentiments appropriate to a highly civilized country no bigger than New York State, and of that country some fifty years earlier, to boot?

I would not be construed into saying that the larger the country, the more profound the emotions. That would be absurd. I only mean that the material conditions under which Americans lived — the great unoccupied spaces, the constant warring and overcoming of nature, the fluid state of the social fabric — all made a different speech necessary, if they were really to express the thoughts that were in them.

There was one other element in the constitution of the American people, quite as important as these I have mentioned. That element was, and is, the ingrained Puritanism which time and place do so little to eradicate. Of course, the dwellers in large cities, worked upon from their earliest childhood by modern conditions, were able to modify the Puritan sentiment, to cast out what of poison remained in it. For Puritanism, at this late day, has resolved itself into a virulent poison which saps vitality and brings on the convulsions of despair.

Puritanism was always a drastic, soul-searching, joyless religion. It was itself a revolt against a licence that had become unbearable. But no student of history can fail to be struck with the vigour and healthy-mindedness of a race which can live under such an incubus and retain its sanity. There is no more horrible page to the student than that of the early times in New England, when nervous little children were tortured with exhortations to declare their faith and escape the clutches of the devil, and senile old women were hanged for witches. Moloch and his sacrifices of human victims is no more revolting. Yet, in spite of much infant mortality, and many of the weaker members of a community going insane, the people as a whole lived and throve under this threatening horror, with the vitality of a race born to endure.

Indeed, my simile of a drug is no idle comparison.

For Puritanism undoubtedly did much to strengthen the fibre of the early settlers, but its prolonged effect has been to produce anæmia and atrophy, and where these do not follow, where the strength of the individual keeps him fighting for the cause of individuality against the composite thought of a race, the result is an innate cynicism, a dreadful despair which will not let him be.

The age of Bryant and Longfellow was singularly free from these negative, but powerful, results of the Puritanic poison. Didactic and moral these poets undoubtedly were, but with them the paternal tradition was diluted by nothing more violent than time. They were in sympathy with its main trend only; like fruits set in the sun, the substance itself had mellowed and sweetened. Living in a highly educated community, they modified with it, and only so far as it, too, modified. They were not at war with their times, their surroundings, or their fellow citizens.

In the case of smaller places, the result is very different. Here, Puritanism held sway quite out of time. It persisted long after it had become an anachronism to New England at large. An individual brought up in one of the small towns scattered over the country was therefore obliged to reproduce suddenly in himself the evolution of three hundred years. In so far as he was advanced mentally beyond his fellows, he suffered the pangs of growth and misunderstanding. And his evolution carried with it the farther torture of consciousness. Sudden change can never accomplish the result of a long, slow process. What large cities like Boston lived into, the clever youths of smaller towns were thrust violently upon.

We must never forget that all inherited prejudice and training pulls one way, in these unfortunate cases; the probing, active mind pulls another. The result is a profound melancholy, tinged with cynicism. Self-analysis has sapped joy, and the impossibility of constructing an ethical system in accordance both with desire and with tradition has twisted the mental vision out of all true proportion. It takes the lifetime of more than one individual to throw off a superstition, and the effort to do so is not made without sacrifice.

Unless one understand this fact, one cannot comprehend the difficult and beautiful poetry of Edwin Arlington Robinson.

Mr. Robinson, as his name implies, comes of good Anglo-Saxon stock. His father, Edward Robinson, was a grain merchant in the village of Head Tide, Maine, where his son was born on December 22, 1869.

Head Tide is a picturesque little village on the Sheepscott River, some miles east of the Kennebec. Time has moved slowly at Head Tide, and customs have moved as slowly. There is still the village inn with a ball-room on the top floor, where the whole countryside gathers on occasions, as they did one hundred years ago. There is still the old water-mill by the river, where the wood is still brought to be sawed.

Edwin Robinson was only two or three years old, however, when his parents moved to the more considerable town of Gardiner, his father having become a director of the local bank.

In exchanging Head Tide for Gardiner, the Robinson family merely left an old-world village for an old-world town. I know of no place in America so English in atmosphere as Gardiner. Standing on the broad, blue Kennebec, the little town nestles proudly beside that strange anomaly in an American city — the Manor House. For Gardiner has, so far as custom is concerned, possessed a squire for over two hundred years. And this gentleman's house is as truly the "Great House," as that in any hamlet in England. A fine Tudor mansion of grey stone with rounded bow windows, it stands on a little hill above the river, and even the railroad tracks which modern commercialism has inconsiderately laid along the nearer bank, cannot take away from it its air of dominating dignity.

It is not only in appearance that Gardiner house harks back to English tradition. It is a house not only in material fact, but in genealogical, for there have been Gardiners of Gardiner ever since the first

fox-hunting squire transferred himself and his dogs
to the New World. From eldest son to eldest son,
keeping up a sentimental entail in lieu of the legal
one our country has eschewed, the house and grounds
have descended. Old customs, too, have not been
allowed to languish. Every Christmas, the country-
side repairs to the "Great House" for the annual
ball, and the polished floors still reflect the shine of
wax candles.

At the time the Robinson family went to live in
Gardiner, a momentary cloud hung over the fortunes
of the "Great House." The open-handed hospital-
ity of a hundred years was showing its effect, and the
Gardiner family possessed their house, some of their
land, and but little else. The owner was doing all
that thrift and skill could do to repair the mistakes
of his ancestors, but in order to accomplish this he
was engaged in business in Boston. The house was
vacant for months at a time, much of it was out of
repair, outlying acres had been sold. Still the owner
clung to his ancestral hall, to raise it, as he has done,
like a phœnix from the ashes. But the raising was
not yet. In Mr. Robinson's childhood, it stood as a
pathetic monument of the folly of attempting to
graft the old order of `things upon the new.

What the boy thought of this old stone mansion,
standing magnificent, still, and silent, beside the
growing little town, whether he ever speculated upon
its past, its present, we do not know. I have dwelt

upon it here as a symbol. A symbol of the world
into which he was born. Gardiner is the "Tilbury
Town" of so many of his poems, and his volume
"Captain Craig" is dedicated "To the Memory of
John Hays Gardiner," one of his first and most
sincere admirers.

Mr. Robinson has given us very few glimpses of
his childhood in his work, although a number of his
scenes seem to have Tilbury Town for a background.
But one, "Isaac and Archibald," published in the
volume, "Captain Craig," may very well be auto-
biographical. Whether it records an actual event,
or is merely a composite photograph of certain
remembered childish occasions, it is worth quoting
here for the picture it gives of the serious, contem-
plative little boy gazing with wide eyes at a strange,
contradictory world. A world which contains at
once such realities as apples and tired legs, and such
vague incomprehensibilities as old age and the
reactions of a Summer sun. This is New England,
but New England seen through a temperament, as
the French idiom puts it. It is all here, the sharp,
clear strokes of description, the psychological significance, the brooding melancholy which will not be
shaken off, the questioning which finds no answer.

The poem begins with the simplicity of statement
of an old ballad :

Isaac and Archibald were two old men.

This is noteworthy, for Mr. Robinson is one of the few modern poets who can manage the baldness of ballad technique without dropping into triviality. He seldom writes a whole poem in this manner, but uses it with telling effect on occasion.   But to return to the poem.

Archibald lives at a farm some distance from the village, and Isaac conceives the idea that Archibald's mind is failing, and that he probably is letting the farm run down.   The fact that it is Archibald's farm, and none of Isaac's business, in no wise deflects Isaac from his purpose.

> .   .   .   .   It was high time
> Those oats were cut, said Isaac; and he feared
> That Archibald — well, he could never feel
> Quite sure of Archibald.   Accordingly
> The good old man invited me — that is,
> Permitted me — to go along with him;
> And I, with a small boy's adhesiveness
> To competent old age, got up and went.

The two start for the farm on foot:

> With all the warmth and wonder of the land
> Around us, and the wayside flash of leaves.

But soon the boy begins to find such fast walking difficult, and in this passage Mr. Robinson shows a tenderness and humour rare in his work:

> .   .   somewhere at the end of the first mile
> I found that I was figuring to find

How long those ancient legs of his would keep
The pace that he had set for them.   The sun
Was hot, and I was ready to sweat blood;
But Isaac, for aught I could make of him,
Was cool to his hat-band.   So I said then
With a dry gasp of affable despair,
Something about the scorching days we have
In August without knowing it sometimes;
But Isaac said the day was like a dream,
And praised the Lord, and talked about the breeze.

After a while, however, the boy persuades his companion to sit down for a little, and the psychological theme, the main theme of the poem, begins on the old man's conversation:

"My good young friend," he said, "you cannot feel
What I have seen so long.   You have the eyes —
Oh, yes — but you have not the other things:
The sight within that never will deceive,
You do not know — you have no right to know;
The twilight warning of experience,
The singular idea of loneliness, —
These are not yours.   But they have long been mine,
And they have shown me now for seven years
That Archibald is changing."

He goes on to say how life is slipping from them both, but how Archibald is much farther on the downward path than he.   Always one feels the pathetic attempt to bolster up himself, to prove himself very much alive, by showing the failings of Archibald:

> ".   .   when the best friend of your life goes down,
> When you first know in him the slacking
> That comes, and coming always tells the end, —
> Now in a common word that would have passed
> Uncaught from any other lips than his,
> Now in some trivial act of every day,
> Done as he might have done it all along
> But for a twinging little difference
> That bites you like a squirrel's teeth."

Then the hints come which reveal what he is dreading for himself:

> ".   .   .   .   Look at me, my boy,
> And when the time shall come for you to see
> That I must follow after him, try then
> To think of me, to bring me back again,
> Just as I was to-day.   Think of the place
> Where we are sitting now, and think of me —
> Think of old Isaac as you knew him then,
> When you set out with him in August once
> To see old Archibald."

The poet sums up the old man's words:

> .   .   .   .   The words come back
> Almost as Isaac must have uttered them,
> And there comes with them a dry memory
> Of something in my throat that would not move.

The adjective "dry" is excellently chosen.
But the boy is puzzled and can find nothing to say:

.   .   .   .   .   My mouth was full
Of words, and they would have been comforting
To Isaac, spite of my twelve years, I think;
But there was not in me the willingness
To speak them out.   Therefore I watched the ground;
And I was wondering what made the Lord
Create a thing so nervous as an ant,
When Isaac, with commendable unrest,
Ordained that we should take the road again —
For it was yet three miles to Archibald's,
And one to the first pump.

They continue along the road until Archibald's
house comes in sight:

Little and white and high on a smooth round hill
It stood, with hackmatacks and apple-trees
Before it, and a big barn-roof beyond.

Isaac stops and gazes for a long time at a newly-
mown field.   Rather sorry to see it, perhaps; for is
he not here to tell Archibald that it is time to cut
his oats.   He says nothing, however, but the boy
understands:

.   .   .   .   .   .   I was young,
But there were a few things that I could see,
And this was one of them. — "Well, well!" said he;
And "Archibald will be surprised, I think,"
Said I.   But all my childhood subtlety
Was lost on Isaac, for he strode along
Like something out of Homer — powerful
And awful on the wayside, so I thought.

That touch, "out of Homer," strikes the hidden significance of the poem. To the boy, this adventure is epic. These are the doings of heroes, giant-men, and for a moment he is privileged to hear their thoughts, which are all the more wonderful to him because he cannot understand them. This throwing up of the commonplace actors of the real scene into the clouds of legend; juxtaposing two old men fast drawing toward senility and each fearing to be the first to pass, and jealous of every remaining proof of vigour in the other, with the god-like figures stalking through the boy's brain, makes the irony, the weird truth of the poem.

Archibald comes to greet them :

> .   .   .   .   with one hand on his back
> And the other clutching his huge-headed cane.

and they discuss the terrible heat, which leads to a suggestion of cider, and brings in one of the most beautiful descriptive passages of the poem :

> .   .   .   .   .   .   Down we went,
> Out of the fiery sunshine to the gloom,
> Grateful and half sepulchral, where we found
> The barrels, like eight potent sentinels,
> Close ranged along the wall. From one of them
> A bright pine spile stuck out alluringly,
> And on the black flat stone, just under it,
> Glimmered a late-spilled proof that Archibald
> Had spoken from unfeigned experience.

There was a fluted antique water-glass
Close by, and in it, prisoned, or at rest,
There was a cricket, of the brown soft sort
That feeds on darkness. Isaac turned him out,
And touched him with his thumb to make him jump,
And then composedly pulled out the plug
With such a practiced hand that scarce a drop
Did even touch his fingers. Then he drank
And smacked his lips with a slow patronage
And looked along the line of barrels there
With a pride that may have been forgetfulness:
"I never twist a spigot nowadays,"
He said, and raised the glass up to the light,
"But I thank God for orchards."

The cider-drinking over, Isaac suggests that Archibald and the boy wait in the shade while he takes a little walk — goes to the fields, in fact, although he does not say so. So Archibald and the boy sit in the orchard and the old man tells him a story which drifts away into talk, talk about the subject uppermost in his mind:

"   .   .   .   .   .   Archibald
And Isaac are old men. Remember, boy,
That we are old. Whatever we have gained,
Or lost, or thrown away, we are old men.

    .   .   .   .

The shadow calls us and it frightens us —"

Then gradually it comes out that Isaac is failing:

" .   .   .   Yes, I have seen it come
These eight years, and these ten years, and I know
Now that it cannot be for very long
That Isaac will be Isaac.   You have seen —
Young as you are, you must have seen the strange
Uncomfortable habit of the man?
He'll take my nerves and tie them in a knot
Sometimes, and that's not Isaac.   I know that —
And I know what it is: I get it here
A little, in my knees, and Isaac — here."
The old man shook his head regretfully
And laid his knuckles three times on his forehead.

Then the poem goes on in the boy's reminiscence:

Never shall I forget, long as I live,
The quaint thin crack in Archibald's old voice,
The lonely twinkle in his little eyes,
Or the way it made me feel to be with him.
I know I lay and looked for a long time
Down through the orchard and across the road,
Across the river and the sun-scorched hills
That ceased in a blue forest, where the world
Ceased with it.   Now and then my fancy caught
A flying glimpse of a good life beyond —
Something of ships and sunlight, streets and singing,
Troy falling, and the ages coming back,
And ages coming forward: Archibald
And Isaac were good fellows in old clothes
And Agamemnon was a friend of mine;
Ulysses coming home again to shoot

With bows and feathered arrows made another,
And all was as it should be.   I was young.

A quaint, homely touch gives it all :

So I lay dreaming of what things I would,
Calm and incorrigibly satisfied
With apples and romance and ignorance,
And the floating smoke from Archibald's clay pipe.

.   .   .   .

.   .   .   .   and I felt
Within the mightiness of the white sun
That smote the land around us and wrought out
A fragrance from the trees.

Again the grandiose vision impinges on fact :

The present and the future and the past,
Isaac and Archibald, the burning bush,
The Trojans and the walls of Jericho,
Were beautifully fused.

But reality breaks down the glory :

.   .   .   .   .   all went well
Till Archibald began to fret for Isaac
And said it was a master day for sunstroke.

Isaac returns, somewhat upset because there is
nothing with which he can legitimately find fault.
Still he must have the last word.   This last word and
its reception by Archibald are charmingly given :

> .   .   .   .   "But, Archibald,"
> He added, with a sweet severity
> That made me think of peach-skins and goose-flesh,
> "I'm half afraid you cut those oats of yours
> A day or two before they were well set."
> "They were set well enough," said Archibald, —
> And I remarked the process of his nose
> Before the words came out.

Then the two old men settle down to a game of cards, and the boy keeps tally and dreams his dreams :

> So I remember, even to this day,
> Just how they sounded, how they placed themselves,
> And how the game went on while I made marks
> And crossed them out, and meanwhile made some Trojans.
> Likewise I made Ulysses, after Isaac,
> And a little after Flaxman.   Archibald
> Was wounded when he found himself left out,
> But he had no heroics, and I said so:
> I told him that his white beard was too long
> And too straight down to be like things in Homer.
> "Quite so," said Isaac. — "Low," said Archibald;
> And he threw down a deuce with a deep grin
> That showed his yellow teeth and made me happy.
> So they played on till a bell rang from the door,
> And Archibald said, "Supper."

That night, the boy dreams of his old men in the guise of two old angels, sitting with palpitating wings in a silver light, and as he approaches them :

.   .   .   .   .   .   a dry voice
Cried thinly, with unpatronizing triumph,
"I've got you, Isaac; high, low, jack, and the game."

The poem ends with this stanza :

Isaac and Archibald have gone their way
To the silence of the loved and well-forgotten.
I knew them, and I may have laughed at them;
But there's a laughing that has honor in it,
And I have no regret for light words now.
Rather I think sometimes they may have made
Their sport of me; — but they would not do that,
They were too old for that.   They were old men,
And I may laugh at them because I knew them.

The last line is typical of Mr. Robinson. "And
I may laugh at them because I knew them." Does
the poet really laugh? Assuredly not, laughter is
the one emotion which he has not at command.
Does it mean a sneer? Less still. The poet does
not sneer. The life he sees about him is too solemn
and too sad. The line is cryptic, because it really
means just a question, pitying, fearful, cast into space
to go knocking about among the stars.

Notice the description of a bright, hot Summer
day, sketched in with sure, nervous strokes :

.   .   .   .   .   .   The world
Was wide, and there was gladness everywhere.

.   .   .   .

We walked together down the River Road

With all the warmth and wonder of the land
Around us, and the wayside flash of leaves, —

.   .   .   .

Under the scorching sun . . . a smooth-cut field
Faint yellow in the distance.

There are many such passages throughout the
poem. But in spite of the "gladness," the sun, the
warmth, the effect is not hot and gay, not redolent
of the unquestioning delight of boyhood, but a little
dark and chilly with mist, the mist of questioning,
where old faith has been swept away and no new
confidence has restored the balance. A disinherited
Puritan cannot suddenly turn Pagan and bask
contentedly under a blue sky. And the "new
Paganism" which raises science to the emotional
level of a religion, is achieved with difficulty by one
only lately freed from the shackles of a hampering
superstition.

That Mr. Robinson is conscious of the chief cause
of his melancholy, I think extremely doubtful. His
temper is too unscientific to lead him to a minute self-
examination, with the test-tube of atavism for a
guide. There is evidence of a greater peace of mind
in his later work, as we shall see, but even there,
"peace" is hardly the word, it is rather that his
recent poems are less mordant. He has raised for
himself a banner, and it bears upon it a single word:
"Courage."

But I am outstripping biography, and I must

return to a thoughtful little schoolboy in a Maine town, learning his lessons, playing his games, and storing up questions to be asked later, over and over again, when they have taken shape to his more mature mind.

In due course, Mr. Robinson entered the Gardiner High School, and from there went on to Harvard College, in 1891. He did not graduate, however, as his father's ill-health forced him to leave in 1893. Meanwhile, the family fortunes had waned, and the young man found himself at the beginning of life with very little to look to but his own efforts.

The Puritan temper is no stickler at obstacles, and Mr. Robinson bravely shouldered his destiny. Writing was the one thing he was fitted for, the one thing he wanted to do. Already, in 1896, a small volume of his verses had been privately printed. I cannot speak of this volume, I have not been able to obtain a copy, but his first published book, "The Children of the Night," appeared in 1897. Gardiner seemed a small horizon for one whose working material was to be life, and Mr. Robinson set out bravely into the world, although without resources, and the world he entered into was the City of New York.

We may take "The Children of the Night," therefore, as containing his early work, that done before the New York period. And, as such, this is the moment to study it.

It must be admitted that this is one of the most completely gloomy books in the whole range of poetry.   The note is struck in this quatrain :

> We cannot crown ourselves with everything,
>   Nor can we coax the Fates with us to quarrel:
> No matter what we are, or what we sing,
>   Time finds a withered leaf in every laurel.

But no one, even picking it up at a time when the poet's name was quite unknown, could have failed to have been struck by its sincerity and strength. There is no hint here of the artificial melancholy which has become so much the fashion among youthful aspirants to poetry.   The poet is fighting his sorrow, and that it masters him is due to no lack of personal virility.   Mr. Robinson himself is a strong man, his weakness is his inheritance, that outworn Puritan inheritance, no longer a tonic, but a poison, sapping the springs of life at their source.   His existence is one long battle between individual bravery and paralyzing atavism.   So the sentiments he voices are cynical, but the manner of them is sure and strong.

The first poem in the book shows the breaking down of the old belief, and the endeavour to feed his life without it.

THE CHILDREN OF THE NIGHT

For those that never know the light,
   The darkness is a sullen thing;
And they, the Children of the Night,
   Seem lost in Fortune's winnowing.

But some are strong and some are weak, —
   And there's the story.   House and home
Are shut from countless hearts that seek
   World-refuge that will never come.

And if there be no other life,
   And if there be no other chance
To weigh their sorrow and their strife
   Than in the scales of circumstance,

'Twere better, ere the sun go down
   Upon the first day we embark,
In life's imbittered sea to drown,
   Than sail forever in the dark.

But if there be a soul on earth
   So blinded with its own misuse
Of man's revealed, incessant worth,
   Or worn with anguish, that it views

No light but for a mortal eye,
   No rest but of a mortal sleep,
No God but in a prophet's lie,
   No faith for "honest doubt" to keep;

If there be nothing, good or bad,
　　But chaos for a soul to trust, —
God counts it for a soul gone mad,
　　And if God be God, He is just.

And if God be God, He is Love;
　　And though the Dawn be still so dim,
It shows us we have played enough
　　With creeds that make a fiend of Him.

There is one creed, and only one,
　　That glorifies God's excellence;
So cherish, that His will be done,
　　The common creed of common sense.

It is the crimson, not the gray,
　　That charms the twilight of all time;
It is the promise of the day
　　That makes the starry sky sublime;

It is the faith within the fear
　　That holds us to the life we curse; —
So let us in ourselves revere
　　The Self which is the Universe!

Let us, the Children of the Night,
　　Put off the cloak that hides the scar!
Let us be Children of the Light,
　　And tell the ages what we are!

As a poem, that is far less important than others in the volume, but as a psychological note, it is invaluable.

The true vigour of the book, however, the dominant chord, is chiefly to be found in the objective sketches of personalities which it contains.

Mr. Robinson preceded Mr. Masters in short pictures of men's lives. The unconscious cynicism I have spoken of is in them, but sometimes (unlike Mr. Masters) something more.

JOHN EVERELDOWN

"Where are you going to-night, to-night, —
　Where are you going, John Evereldown?
There's never the sign of a star in sight,
　Nor a lamp that's nearer than Tilbury Town.
Why do you stare as a dead man might?
Where are you pointing away from the light?
And where are you going to-night, to-night, —
　Where are you going, John Evereldown?"

"Right through the forest, where none can see,
　There's where I'm going, to Tilbury Town.
The men are asleep, — or awake, may be, —
　But the women are calling John Evereldown.
Ever and ever they call for me.
And while they call can a man be free?
So right through the forest, where none can see,
　There's where I'm going, to Tilbury Town."

"But why are you going so late, so late, —
    Why are you going, John Evereldown?
Though the road be smooth and the path be straight
    There are two long leagues to Tilbury Town.
Come in by the fire, old man, and wait!
Why do you chatter out there by the gate?
And why are you going so late, so late, —
    Why are you going, John Evereldown?"

"I follow the women wherever they call, —
    That's why I'm going to Tilbury Town.
God knows if I pray to be done with it all,
    But God is no friend to John Evereldown.
So the clouds may come and the rain may fall,
The shadows may creep and the dead men crawl, —
But I follow the women wherever they call,
    And that's why I'm going to Tilbury Town."

Again, in this poem, Mr. Robinson has recourse to
the ballad technique. The repetition of the last
word in the first line gives it at once. The simplicity
of the ballad manner covering an acute psychological
analysis is one of Mr. Robinson's favourite turns,
and it certainly heightens the force of the criticism,
growing as it does out of quaintness. It gives a
grotesque quality to the work, and sharpens the
edge of tragedy.

Another vignette, more subtle, more ironical, is
"Richard Cory."

RICHARD CORY

Whenever Richard Cory went down town,
We people on the pavement looked at him;
He was a gentleman from sole to crown,
Clean favoured, and imperially slim.

And he was always quietly arrayed,
And he was always human when he talked;
But still he fluttered pulses when he said,
"Good-morning," and he glittered when he walked.

And he was rich, — yes, richer than a king, —
And admirably schooled in every grace:
In fine, we thought that he was everything
To make us wish that we were in his place.

So on we worked, and waited for the light,
And went without the meat, and cursed the bread;
And Richard Cory, one calm summer night,
Went home and put a bullet through his head.

In reading Mr. Robinson, it is always necessary to note the almost unapproachable technique with which his poems are wrought. He employs the most complete reticence, he permits himself no lapses from straightforward speech to force a glittering effect. But the effect is never commonplace, never even unpoetic. It is indeed art concealing art. So admirable is his technique, that not only do we get the essence of poetry in these astringent poems, we get drama. In four words, "one calm summer night," is set a background for the tragedy which brings the bullet shot crashing across our ear-drums with the shock of an earthquake. They appear simple, these poems; and they are really so immensely difficult. Mr. Robinson has carefully studied that primary condition of all poetry : brevity; and his best effects are those gained with the utmost economy of means.

A moment ago, I referred to the grotesque note in these poems, and grotesque they often are. Weird — dour — a harsh, ghostly reverberation struck by a line. In "John Evereldown" is this picture :

> So the clouds may come and the rain may fall,
> The shadows may creep and the dead men crawl.

That has the slimy horror of coffin-worms about it. This, from "The Pity of Leaves," is also ghostly, but more subtly, spiritually, so :

> The brown, thin leaves on the stones outside
> Skipped with a freezing whisper. Now and then
> They stopped, and stayed there — just to let him know
> How dead they were.

In one poem, he writes :

> Trellises lie like bones in a ruin that once was a garden.

In "Stafford's Cabin," "something happened here before my memory began;" what, no one knows. But

> We found it in the morning with an iron bar behind,
> And there were chains around it.

So slight, yet so sharp, are these touches, it never seems as though the poet were conscious of them. He knows how to inject them into the context, by accident, as it were. This creating an atmosphere with a back-hand stroke is one of the most personal and peculiar traits of Mr. Robinson's style. Such passages blow across his pages like mists from the grey valley of the Styx.

I have spoken of Mr. Robinson's "unconscious cynicism." It is unconscious because he never dwells upon it as such, never delights in it, nor wraps it comfortably about him. It is hardly more than the reverse of the shield of pain, and in his later work, it gives place to a great, pitying tenderness. Even in this first book, there is the hint of the "something more":

CLIFF KLINGENHAGEN

Cliff Klingenhagen had me in to dine
With him one day; and after soup and meat,
And all the other things there were to eat,
Cliff took two glasses and filled one with wine

And one with wormwood.   Then, without a sign
For me to choose at all, he took the draught
Of bitterness himself, and lightly quaffed
It off, and said the other one was mine.

And when I asked him what the deuce he meant
By doing that, he only looked at me
And grinned, and said it was a way of his.
And though I know the fellow, I have spent
Long time a-wondering when I shall be
As happy as Cliff Klingenhagen is.

"Success through failure," that is the motto on
the other side of his banner of "Courage."   It is
true that he carries the doctrine almost too far.   So
far that it nearly lapses into Nirvana.   But one
must never forget that to him it is a symbol of a
protest against brutal, unfeeling materialism.

The stark sincerity and simplicity of this book must
have had the effect of a galvanic shock upon the small
company of readers who stumbled upon it.   But the
times were not yet ripe for such poetry, and it was
to be years yet before Mr. Robinson received his due.

Meanwhile he struggled along in New York, a poet
writing twenty years too soon.   Poetry is not a pay-
ing pursuit at any time, and Mr. Robinson did many
things to keep the life going which was to make the
poetry.   History has a number of stories which tell
of genius struggling against poverty and lack of
recognition in the midst of a busy, callous city.   Mr.

Robinson's early life is the same twice-told tale, but though he seemed to fail, he abundantly succeeded. For he was writing all the time, and we who have the poems can measure the outcome.

So five years passed before the next volume of poems was issued, "Captain Craig," published in 1902. The re-issue, bearing the date 1915, has on the title-page the legend, "Revised Edition, with Additional Poems," but we shall deal with this revised edition here, as the main content of the book is undoubtedly of the earlier date.

It is quite evident, in examining this book, that the five years of silence had not been without fruit. Already, there is a surer touch and a deeper-probing psychology. The excessive subjectivity of "The Children of the Night" is making way for an interest in the world outside of the poet. Although the first book contained many sketches of character, we feel that the interpretation of these characters is very much tinged by the author's personality. To the end, Mr. Robinson never succeeds in completely omitting the writer from the thing written, even in intentionally objective and dramatic pieces, but each volume of poems is an advance in this respect.

Here, again, I must deflect misunderstanding by hastening to add that of course no work of art can be (or should be) purely objective. An author's personality determines even his choice of subject, to say nothing of its manner of presentation, but there is a great difference between the reflections and shadows cast by a personality, and that personality thrust, a solid body, in front of a window. A man reveals himself by every sentence he utters in conversation; but he does more than reveal himself, he obscures everything else, when his conversation revolves about the pronoun "I."

In Mr. Robinson's case, it would seem that a self-centred and analytical boy is gradually giving place to a mature and kindly man of the world. The French critic, Remy de Gourmont, in his famous book of criticism, "Le Livre des Masques," often epitomizes an author's whole work in a fancied scene. This method applies peculiarly well to the Mr. Robinson of the later books. Let us suppose a man, mellowed, resigned, but a little seared withal, a kindly monk fled from the world after a large experience, sitting in his monastery, telling tales of old events, not judging, not extenuating, disillusioned, and calm because he has stamped so long upon the fires within him that now, for the most part, they burn quietly, obedient to control. He talks kindly, bringing up out of his past much that is interesting, some things that are terrifying. But he turns it all aside with a quiet smile. It is so long ago. There was really much to be said on the other side. It is over for him; these are only memories, you understand.

Such might be the picture these last books call up.

The most important poem in "Captain Craig" is not, to my mind, the title poem, but "Isaac and Archibald," which I quoted a few moments ago. "Captain Craig" is a dreary, philosophical ramble, occupying eighty-four pages, which, in spite of the excellent manipulation of its blank verse, reveals a fault which the earlier volume is conspicuously without, namely, verbosity. The one fault which has grown upon Mr. Robinson with the years is a tendency to long-windedness. There is an interminable amount of talking in "Captain Craig," and one must admit that the talking is both involved and dull.

The poem is built upon that favourite theory of the poet's : the success of failure. But here it is pushed too far, to the verge of the ridiculous, in fact. Captain Craig is an old wanderer, peddlar, beggar, what you please, drifted into Tilbury Town, and kept alive, and (alas !) talking, by the charity of four young men, who seem to find a solace in his conversation which the specimens of it given make it difficult to understand. When one of the group goes upon a journey, Captain Craig writes to him in this wise :

> "Since last I wrote — and I fear the weeks have gone
> Too long for me to leave my gratitude
> Unuttered for its own acknowledgement —
> I have won, without the magic of Amphion,
> Without the songs of Orpheus or Apollo,
> The frank regard — and with it, if you like,
> The fledged respect — of three quick-footed friends.

('Nothing is there more marvelous than man,'
Said Sophocles; and I say after him:
'He traps and captures, all-inventive one,
  The light birds and the creatures of the wold,
  And in his nets the fishes of the sea.')
Once they were pictures, painted on the air,
Faint with eternal color, colorless, —
But now they are not pictures, they are fowls.

"At first they stood aloof and cocked their small,
  Smooth, prudent heads at me and made as if,
  With a cryptic idiotic melancholy,
  To look authoritative and sagacious;
  But when I tossed a piece of apple to them,
  They scattered back with a discord of short squawks
  And then came forward with a craftiness
  That made me think of Eden.   Atropos
  Came first, and having grabbed the morsel up,
  Ran flapping far away and out of sight,
  With Clotho and Lachesis hard after her;
  But finally the three fared all alike,
  And the next day I persuaded them with corn.
  In a week they came and had it from my fingers
  And looked up at me while I pinched their bills
  And made them sneeze.   Count Pretzel's Carmichael
  Had said they were not ordinary Birds
  At all, — and they are not; they are the Fates,
  Foredoomed of their own insufficiency
  To be assimilated. — Do not think,
  Because in my contented isolation
  It suits me at this time to be jocose,

That I am nailing reason to the cross,
Or that I set the bauble and the bells
Above the crucible; for I do nought,
Say nought, but with an ancient levity
That is the forbear of all earnestness."

There is not one letter, there are three, and they occupy thirty-one pages of the poem. The traveller returns to find Captain Craig dying, but the same kind of conversation continues from his death-bed until the moment of his demise. The purport of all this speech seems to be that the garrulous old man has a kinship with the spheres which is denied to more efficient folk, but his vague, windy utterances hardly bear out this contention. One line, however, is true, truer than there is any reason to suppose that Captain Craig meant it to be. Speaking to the youths at his bedside, the old man says: "The truth is yours, God's universe is yours. . . ." For certainly the universe belongs to those who are willing to live in it and be amenable to its laws, rather than to those who are content to withdraw themselves aside and merely speculate upon its genesis and meaning.

Other authors have painted derelicts who have gained wisdom through much contemplation, real wisdom which we acknowledge to be sound, but in "Captain Craig" Mr. Robinson's craft has played him false. His technique is here, beautiful as always, but his content is neither convincing, dramatic, nor interesting.

"Captain Craig," as a volume, contains other excellent poems beside "Isaac and Archibald." "Aunt Imogen" is an interesting and tender study of the unmarried woman; it is the tragedy of the maiden aunt, so typical, unhappily, of New England. "The Book of Annandale" is a less accurate sketch of second marriage, approached first from the man's point of view and then from the woman's. A few lyrics, some sonnets, and a number of adaptations from the Greek, make up the book. Of the latter, this quotation will serve to show the poet's suggestive, ironically humorous touch:

A MIGHTY RUNNER

(Nicharchus)

The day when Charmus ran with five
In Arcady, as I'm alive,
He came in seventh. — "Five and one
Make seven, you say? It can't be done." —
Well, if you think it needs a note,
A friend in a fur overcoat
Ran with him, crying all the while,
"You'll beat 'em, Charmus, by a mile!"
And so he came in seventh.
Therefore, good Zoilus, you see
The thing is plain as plain can be;
And with four more for company,
He would have been eleventh.

During this part of Mr. Robinson's career, Colonel Theodore Roosevelt, then President of the United States, became interested in his work, and, in 1905, offered him a position in the New York Custom House. Mr. Robinson, with characteristic modesty, speaks of himself as "the least efficient public servant who ever drew his pay from the United States Treasury Department," an estimate which we should receive with a grain of salt, as he held the position for five years, relinquishing it in 1910, the same year which saw the publication of his third book, "The Town Down the River."

This volume contains, beside the title poem (a misty lyric of future and change, with a slight optimistic note which is absent in his earlier work), three studies of public characters: Lincoln, Napoleon, and Theodore Roosevelt. Of these, the Lincoln is the most successful. The truth is that Mr. Robinson is too individual a man, too wrapt up in his own reactions, to be a good mouthpiece for other individual men not of his creating. His Napoleon poem bears the title, "An Island," and is a monologue placed in the mouth of the dying Emperor. But the man who speaks is not in the least like Napoleon, these are not Napoleon's thought-processes. This is no character study; perhaps it was not an attempt at one. Call it a poem upon an imaginative theme, and it has some fine passages; for instance:

> He tells me that great kings look very small
> When they are put to bed.

Or:

> Flags that are vanished, flags that are soiled and furled,
> Say what will be the word when I am gone:
> What learned little acrid archive men
> Will burrow to find me out and burrow again.

"Little acrid archive men" is magnificent irony. But this querulous, puling invalid is not the dying Napoleon, as any student of the last days at Saint Helena can readily testify.

The poem on Mr. Roosevelt is called "The Revealer," and sounds strangely in this Year of our Lord, 1917.

In dealing with Lincoln, Mr. Robinson had the body of a great tradition to help him. It may be objected that Napoleon is as much a tradition as Lincoln, but the answer is simply — not to the average American. Possibly Mr. Robinson has not made an exhaustive study of Napoleon; in the case of Lincoln, no exhaustive study was necessary, he imbibed understanding with the air of his native town. The poem is fine, not so fine as Mr. Fletcher's on the same theme, but strong, reticent, and noble.

THE MASTER

(Lincoln)

A flying word from here and there
Had sown the name at which we sneered,
But soon the name was everywhere,
To be reviled and then revered:
A presence to be loved and feared,
We cannot hide it, or deny
That we, the gentlemen who jeered,
May be forgotten by and by.

He came when days were perilous
And hearts of men were sore beguiled;
And having made his note of us,
He pondered and was reconciled.
Was ever master yet so mild
As he, and so untamable?
We doubted, even when he smiled,
Not knowing what he knew so well.

He knew that undeceiving fate
Would shame us whom he served unsought;
He knew that he must wince and wait —
The jest of those for whom he fought;
He knew devoutly what he thought
Of us and of our ridicule;
He knew that we must all be taught
Like little children in a school.

We gave a glamour to the task
That he encountered and saw through,
But little of us did he ask,
And little did we ever do.
And what appears if we review
The season when we railed and chaffed?
It is the face of one who knew
That we were learning while we laughed.

The face that in our vision feels
Again the venom that we flung,
Transfigured to the world reveals
The vigilance to which we clung.
Shrewd, hallowed, harassed, and among
The mysteries that are untold,
The face we see was never young
Nor could it ever have been old.

For he, to whom we had applied
Our shopman's test of age and worth,
Was elemental when he died,
As he was ancient at his birth:
The saddest among kings of earth,
Bowed with a galling crown, this man
Met rancor with a cryptic mirth,
Laconic — and Olympian.

The love, the grandeur, and the fame
Are bounded by the world alone;

The calm, the smouldering, and the flame
Of awful patience were his own:
With him they are forever flown
Past all our fond self-shadowings,
Wherewith we cumber the Unknown
As with inept, Icarian wings.

For we were not as other men:
'Twas ours to soar and his to see.
But we are coming down again,
And we shall come down pleasantly;
Nor shall we longer disagree
On what it is to be sublime,
But flourish in our perigee
And have one Titan at a time.

One of the most characteristic sections of the book is a group of poems entitled "Calverley's," and here again we have the short character vignettes which gave so much distinction to "The Children of the Night." Calverley's is a tavern, and the host and its principal frequenters are drawn with Mr. Robinson's sympathetic, clear understanding. There are two other sketches, however, which I think surpass them. This, of a billiard expert:

DOCTOR OF BILLIARDS

Of all among the fallen from on high,
We count you last and leave you to regain
Your born dominion of a life made vain

By three spheres of insidious ivory.
You dwindle to the lesser tragedy —
Content, you say.   We call, but you remain.
Nothing alive gone wrong could be so plain,
Or quite so blasted with absurdity.
You click away the kingdom that is yours,
And you click off your crown for cap and bells;
You smile, who are still master of the feast,
And for your smile we credit you the least;
But when your false, unhallowed laugh occurs,
We seem to think there may be something else.

and this masterpiece of brevity and horror:

HOW ANNANDALE WENT OUT

They called it Annandale — and I was there
To flourish, to find words, and to attend:
Liar, physician, hypocrite, and friend,
I watched him; and the sight was not so fair
As one or two that I have seen elsewhere:
An apparatus not for me to mend —
A wreck, with hell between him and the end,
Remained of Annandale; and I was there.
I knew the ruin as I knew the man;
So put the two together, if you can,
Remembering the worst you know of me.
Now view yourself as I was, on the spot —
With a slight kind of engine.   Do you see?
Like this . . .   You wouldn't hang me?   I thought not.

There is one curious mannerism in Mr. Robinson's work, and one which is the absolute opposite of the ballad quality of which he is at times so fond. This mannerism consists in the obscuring of a thing under an epithet, more or less artificial and difficult of comprehension. In "Doctor of Billiards" he describes the billiard balls as "three spheres of insidious ivory." In "Miniver Cheevy," he refers to armour in this wise:

> Miniver cursed the commonplace
>   And eyed a khaki suit with loathing;
> He missed the mediæval grace
>   Of iron clothing.

In another poem, he mentions one of the characteristics of a gentleman as:

> His index of adagios.

The most extravagant case of this sort, however, is in "How Annandale Went Out," where he speaks of the hypodermic syringe as "a slight kind of engine."

In less skilful hands, such a mannerism would be unbearable, but Mr. Robinson often manages to convey with it a subtle symbolism, to underlay the fact of his poem with a cogent meaning, tragic, ironic, cynical, what he pleases. Doubtless the method contains hidden germs of danger; it may easily degenerate into artificiality. But, so far,

Mr. Robinson has not allowed it to degenerate, and employed as he employs it, it is valuable.

Fine though much of this book is, it seems more a maintaining of a position than a definite advance. The leap forward was not to come until six years later, with "The Man Against the Sky."

In the interval, Mr. Robinson turned his attention to plays, the first of which, "Van Zorn," appearing in 1914, and the second, "The Porcupine," in 1915.

It is always a dreary task to record the lapses of genius, and it is as lapses from his usual high achievement that Mr. Robinson's plays must be considered. In another man, they would merit praise for their sincerity and effort, but they fall much below the level of accomplishment of the poet's other work, and, coming from his pen, they must be considered as failures.

To be sure, "Van Zorn" is quite unlike any other play, and in these days of facile playwriting, that alone is a distinction. But a play certainly should be dramatic above all other things, and dramatic "Van Zorn" is not. The play depends rather upon hints of a drama carried on in the actor's minds than upon anything the audience actually sees or hears. The dialogue is pleasant, easy, colloquial, rather than brilliant; it stays on the same agreeable level, neither mounting nor sinking. So far as it and the action are concerned, the play is one of half tones. The swift vigour of the author's character poems is completely lacking. Those brief, virile dramas scattered throughout his books have lent no cutting edge to this long play. It is diluted, thinned to a mere essence, and strangely enough, realism has also fled, for neither plot nor characters bear the stamp of life.

One reason for this vagueness of the actual actors lies in the fact that behind all they do and say is the real drama, and the hero of it is Fate. It is Fate who shakes the lives of the characters into place and will not be denied; and it is this suggestion of brooding Fate which gives the play its peculiar atmosphere. Van Zorn is chosen as the interpreter of this Fate. He is at once its tool, and its avenging sword. He is constantly referred to as "a sort of Flying Dutchman," though why the poet has chosen the Flying Dutchman rather than any other fateful character it is hard to determine. In fine, Van Zorn is a very inconclusive personality. The uncanny element is not brought out with sufficient skill, he is shadowy as a man and vague as an instrument. The most successful person in the play is the painter, Farnham, who is at least of real flesh and blood. It is a pity that Mr. Robinson felt obliged to add a touch of what theatrical managers call "comic relief," in the person of Otto Mink. Mr. Robinson is not happy when he attempts light humour. The remarks of this character are often laboured, and impede the action of the play.

The second play, "The Porcupine," has even less to recommend it. The slightly supernatural light which dimmed the crudities of "Van Zorn" and lent it a suggestion of unseen possibilities, is absent here. "The Porcupine" reads like the work of a youth, unversed in the technique of the world and also of the theatre. The plot is confused and extraordinarily unlikely. It concerns the return of a wanderer to his step-brother's house in apparent poverty and real affluence. This gentleman has heard rumours to the effect that his step-brother is making love to a neighbour's wife, and he has come home to set matters straight. This he does by bribing the lady to leave her husband and the country-side forever, fondly hoping that her departure will lead to a union of the injured husband and his (the benefactor's) sister, who was jilted by this same man years before. The credulous wanderer is congratulating himself upon his success, even with the task before him of reconciling his step-brother and his step-brother's wife (the Porcupine), when the latter informs him that her child is really his also. The optimist, nothing daunted, announces that now he, she, and their child will live together in complete happiness, apparently oblivious to the condition of his step-brother, bereft of wife and mistress on the same day, when the wife, with a clearer sense of values, puts an end to an impossible situation by poisoning herself.

The play is a bookish production, compounded of reactions from Russian and German dramatists, but it lacks the stark reality which brings those authors to success. The strangest thing about it is its immaturity, and one asks whether it is, after all, merely an old work resurrected.

Whatever Mr. Robinson's accomplishment in his preceding books, there can be no doubt of the high position he holds in American poetry when we examine "The Man Against the Sky," published in 1916. It would seem as though his previous books were merely working up to this achievement, so far beyond them is this volume. A little book of one hundred and forty-nine pages, and yet, in reading it, one experiences a sensation akin to that of the man who opens a jar of compressed air. It is a profound wonder that so much can have been forced into so small a space. For "The Man Against the Sky" is dynamic with experience and knowledge of life.

In the twenty years which have elapsed since the publication of "The Children of the Night," we have seen Mr. Robinson's entire production to consist of four volumes of verse and two plays. Each volume is slim and reticent, and yet small as is the bulk of the work to make up the quota of the best years of a man's life, in it the poet has achieved the result of putting before us a personality of original thought, of original expression, and quietly and unobtrusively making that personality a force in present-day literature.

If we take the poetic currents in evidence in America to-day, we shall find certain distinct streams which, although commingling, keep on the whole very much to themselves. The strange thing about Mr. Robinson's work is that it seems to belong to none of these streams. And yet no one reading these poems would feel justified in calling him not modern. The truth is that they are modern because they are universal. The scenes, the conversations, are modern; were the poet writing in the fifteenth century, these accessories would differ, but the content would be as modern in one age as another, because the essential quality of humanity does not change; men clothe their philosophy in different terms, the philosophies even may vary, but human nature does not vary, and Mr. Robinson deals with something which may fitly be called raw human nature — not crude human nature, but human nature simple, direct, and as it is.

Those last three words contain the gist of the matter. In them lies Mr. Robinson's gift to the "new poetry": Simple, direct, and as it is. Mr. Robinson's modernity is unconcerned with forms, he has been tempted by no metrical experiments. It is in keeping with his serious outlook upon life that he is content to forge his stern poems out of existing material. Writing at a time when mellifluous verse

was the fashion, he made no compromise with popular
taste. He was a pioneer of hard, clear sincerity.
He dislikes inversions as much as do the Imagists,
and to him is due one of the earliest returns to the
sequence of the spoken phrase.

I have said that reticence is the keynote of Mr.
Robinson's work. His poems are astringent. Yet,
if the poet permits himself very few lyric outbursts,
one,

> As upward through her dream he fares
> Half clouded with a crimson fall
> Of roses thrown on marble stairs

proves that this astringency is of design.

"The Man Against the Sky" (a symbolic title of
great beauty) is curiously named from the last
poem in the book. Why it is the last is evident,
for it is a serious argument against a materialistic
explanation of the universe, and bears with it a sense
of finality which forbids its being followed by any
other poems. The picture of the man silhouetted
against a bright, sunsetting sky, is very fine :

> Between me and the sunset, like a dome
> Against the glory of a world on fire,
> Now burned a sudden hill,
> Bleak, round, and high, by flame-lit height made higher,
> With nothing on it for the flame to kill
> Save one who moved and was alone up there
> To loom before the chaos and the glare
> As if he were the last god going home
> Unto his last desire.

These lines strike the tone of the whole poem:
High Seriousness.   No other poet in America to-day
has this power of high seriousness in so marked a
degree as Mr. Robinson.   We have only to compare
this poem with "The Children of the Night" to find
how far Mr. Robinson has travelled, in twenty years,
toward the peace which he is seeking.   The bitterness of change is passing; in its stead, glimmers the
dim hope of a new order.

"The Man Against the Sky" is a remarkable
poem, but as a work of art, it is hardly so original
or so interesting as the other long poem in the volume,
"Ben Jonson Entertains a Man from Stratford."
At last Mr. Robinson has flung off himself.   Here is
another man speaking, absolutely another man, not
a projection of one or another portion of the poet's
ego.   This work is as successful in its portrayal of a
character, two characters, as "An Island" was
unsuccessful.   I can recall no imaginative work on
Shakespeare half so real and alive as this.   And the
two characters of Shakespeare and Ben Jonson in
juxtaposition are sharply contrasted.   A plague on
the Baconians, this poem should silence them forever!   I verily believe that this is Shakespeare to
the life, if it is not it ought to be.

This must be

> .   .   .   our man Shakespeare, who alone of us
> Will put an ass's head in Fairyland
> As he would add a shilling to more shillings,
> All most harmoniously.

It is so excellent, this poem, that one reads it over and over again, with growing interest each time. The lines run off as easily as conversation, proving Mr. Robinson a rare technician. The words never stand out of the poem to show how well chosen they are, but the whole is as vigorous as everyday talk. The last line:

> "O Lord, that House in Stratford!"

keeps the note of vigour to the end, finishes the poem on a crashing major chord, as it were, and makes the pathos of it much more pathetic because quite unsentimental.

But these are only two poems in a remarkable book. The volume opens with "Flammonde," and here the change from the poet's early work is very evident. There is a mellowness of soul, a gentle commiseration for the follies of the world, which has banished the acrid denunciation of such poems as "John Evereldown" or "Richard Cory."

FLAMMONDE

The man Flammonde, from God knows where,
With firm address and foreign air,
With news of nations in his talk
And something royal in his walk,
With glint of iron in his eyes,
But never doubt, nor yet surprise,

Appeared, and stayed, and held his head
As one by kings accredited.

Erect, with his alert repose
About him, and about his clothes,
He pictured all tradition hears
Of what we owe to fifty years.
His cleansing heritage of taste
Paraded neither want nor waste;
And what he needed for his fee
To live, he borrowed graciously.

He never told us what he was,
Or what mischance, or other cause,
Had banished him from better days
To play the Prince of Castaways.
Meanwhile he played surpassing well
A part, for most, unplayable;
In fine, one pauses, half afraid
To say for certain that he played.

For that, one may as well forego
Conviction as to yes or no;
Nor can I say just how intense
Would then have been the difference
To several, who, having striven
In vain to get what he was given,
Would see the stranger taken on
By friends not easy to be won.

Moreover, many a malcontent
He soothed and found munificent;

His courtesy beguiled and foiled
Suspicion that his years were soiled;
His mien distinguished any crowd,
His credit strengthened when he bowed;
And women, young and old, were fond
Of looking at the man Flammonde.

There was a woman in our town
On whom the fashion was to frown;
But while our talk renewed the tinge
Of a long-faded scarlet fringe,
The man Flammonde saw none of that,
And what he saw we wondered at —
That none of us, in her distress,
Could hide or find our littleness.

There was a boy that all agreed
Had shut within him the rare seed
Of learning. We could understand,
But none of us could lift a hand.
The man Flammonde appraised the youth,
And told a few of us the truth;
And thereby, for a little gold,
A flowered future was unrolled.

There were two citizens who fought
For years and years, and over nought;
They made life awkward for their friends,
And shortened their own dividends.
The man Flammonde said what was wrong
Should be made right; nor was it long

Before they were again in line,
And had each other in to dine.

And these I mention are but four
Of many out of many more.
So much for them.   But what of him —
So firm in every look and limb?
What small satanic sort of kink
Was in his brain?   What broken link
Withheld him from the destinies
That came so near to being his?

What was he, when we came to sift
His meaning, and to note the drift
Of incommunicable ways
That make us ponder while we praise?
Why was it that his charm revealed
Somehow the surface of a shield?
What was it that we never caught?
What was he, and what was he not?

How much it was of him we met
We cannot ever know; nor yet
Shall all he gave us quite atone
For what was his, and his alone;
Nor need we now, since he knew best,
Nourish an ethical unrest:
Rarely at once will nature give
The power to be Flammonde and live.

We cannot know how much we learn
From those who never will return,

Until a flash of unforeseen
Remembrance falls on what has been.
We've each a darkening hill to climb;
And this is why, from time to time
In Tilbury Town, we look beyond
Horizons for the man Flammonde.

Perhaps no poem which Mr. Robinson has written serves so well as this to illustrate certain qualities of the poet's style. Here we have one of the simple, direct stanza forms in which he delights. There is no very haunting lilt in this rhythm; there are no tricks, no advised and conscious expertness of rhyme schemes; no pleasure in new inventions; no uneven lines falling into an original pattern. It is all straight, severe, and quiet. It is also admirable. The poet never compromises with his metre; he allows himself no false accents nor over-long lines. In fact, the charm of the form is just here: in the apparent ease with which this fitting of words and metre is accomplished. They seem to be absolutely one and inevitable. His instrument is a three-stringed lute; but with what precision he plays upon it! There are no faults of intonation, although the song is limited within the compass of a few notes.

"Flammonde" reveals characteristics of style besides those of rhythm. Nowhere else can we find better illustrated the poet's extraordinary powers of condensation made possible by a rarely imagina-

tive use of epithet.   For instance, this description
of the man :

> He pictured all tradition hears
> Of what we owe to fifty years.

and again :

> His courtesy beguiled and foiled
> Suspicion that his years were soiled.

The most subtle of all these instances in the poem is
contained in the lines :

> There was a woman in our town
> On whom the fashion was to frown;
> But while our talk renewed the tinge
> Of a long-faded scarlet fringe,
> The man Flammonde saw none of that.

"A long-faded scarlet fringe" is not only imaginative, it has something of Flammonde's own forgiving
tenderness.

Tenderness is one of the finer qualities of Mr.
Robinson's later poetry.   The swift, caustic etching
of his early poems has mellowed into a gentle,
extenuating understanding.   Youth condemns; maturity condones.   And where maturity has lost
nothing of the vitality of youth, the result is great
poetry.

Throughout this chapter, I have spoken several
times of Mr. Robinson's obscure, sometimes posi-

tively cryptic, method of expressing an idea. In "Captain Craig," this method degenerated into a confusion so intense that the reader wearied in tracking the poet's meaning. In fact, it may very fairly be said to have ruined the poem.

Mr. Robinson never entirely shakes off this mannerism, but in "Flammonde," it is held in leash, with the result that instead of confusion, we get a sense of haunting mystery:

> What was he, when we came to sift
> His meaning and to note the drift
> Of incommunicable ways
> That makes us ponder while we praise?

The whole stanza, of which these lines are a part, is full of this strange, intangible feeling of mystery.

For a touch of modernity — science colouring the conceptions of the day, yet falling imaginatively and musically into the poem — take this passage:

> Nor need we now, since he knew best,
> Nourish an ethical unrest.

Mr. Robinson is always a poet; but he is also, and completely, a man of his own time. It is because this is so, that he has been able to give a new and different voice to that eternal thing which is poetry.

There are many poems in this volume which I should like to quote: "The Clinging Vine" for drama; "Stafford's Cabin" for suggestion. But I must content myself with only one. This "Fragment," not of a poem, but of a man's life, his whole, shattered, unfinished life, is one of Mr. Robinson's finest poems. Here is much in little, and, among other things, one of the most vivid, the most beautiful, descriptions to be found in his work.

FRAGMENT

Faint white pillars that seem to fade
As you look from here are the first one sees
Of his house where it hides and dies in a shade
Of beeches and oaks and hickory trees.
Now many a man, given woods like these,
And a house like that, and the Briony gold,
Would have said, "There are still some gods to please,
And houses are built without hands, we're told."

There are the pillars and all gone gray.
Briony's hair went white.   You may see
Where the garden was if you come this way.
That sun-dial scared him, he said to me;
"Sooner or later they strike," said he,
And he never got that from the books he read.
Others are flourishing, worse than he,
But he knew too much for the life he led.

And who knows all knows everything
That a patient ghost at last retrieves;

There's more to be known of his harvesting
When Time the thresher unbinds the sheaves;
And there's more to be heard than a wind that grieves
For Briony now in this ageless oak,
Driving the first of its withered leaves
Over the stones where the fountain broke.

Still the volume is sad. Joy the poet seems to fear, distrusting it, again and again portraying it as mere phantasmagoria; in its place as the consoler of mankind he would put courage. Courage and resignation, and the saving qualities of both, of what else are built the poems "Flammonde," "The Gift of God," "Old King Cole," "Eros Turannos," and many others. But how insufficient this nourishment for life, is evidenced by the profound melancholy which pervades the whole book.

The most recent poem which Mr. Robinson has written, "Merlin," was published by The Macmillan Company in March, 1917. This is, as its name implies, a re-telling of the Arthurian legend, and one cannot help a slight feeling of disappointment that this re-telling is neither so new nor so different as one might have expected. For some reason, the author seems here to have abandoned his peculiar and personal style. Instead of a vivid, modern reading of an old theme, instead of the brilliant psychological analysis applied to history and legend which made "Ben Jonson Entertains a Man from Stratford" so memorable, we find in this book only a rather feeble and emasculated picture, tricked out with charming lyrical figures, it is true, but lifeless and unconvincing.   Merlin is no great wizard, swept into Vivian's toils by a fascination which no man, not even he, can resist; he is a vain, weak old man, playing at a pastoral. Even when conflicting emotions are supposed to tear him, they do not tear, in spite of the author's assurances :

> ".   .   .   .   .   When we parted,
> I told her I should see the King again,
> And, having seen him, might go back again
> To see her face once more.   But I shall see
> No more the lady Vivian.   Let her love
> What man she may, no other love than mine
> Shall be an index of her memories.
> I fear no man who may come after me,
> And I see none.   I see her, still in green,
> Beside the fountain.   I shall not go back.
> We pay for going back; and all we get
> Is one more needless ounce of weary wisdom
> To bring away with us.   If I come not,
> The lady Vivian will remember me,
> And say: 'I knew him when his heart was young,
> Though I have lost him now.   Time called him home,
> And that was as it was; for much is lost
> Between Broceliande and Camelot.' "

This is the language of weakness, not of resolution. To be sure, Merlin is a broken man; but nothing in the poem carries a conviction that he was ever very much otherwise.

It is a long, meandering tale of some thirteen hundred blank verse lines. But the fault is not in its length, it is in the manner in which the poet has composed his story. Now the poet who would be a story-teller must concern himself with something beside poetry, beside psychology; he must learn the manipulation of plot. It is just in this matter of plot that Mr. Robinson's work reveals its less able side. When a tale is to be told in a single scene, Mr. Robinson is sure, swift, and adequate. String it out to a series of episodes, and it becomes, not only diluted, but involved to the point where it loses that sharp stroke of drama which makes the glory of his shorter pieces.

"Merlin" is not so long-winded or obscure as "Captain Craig"; but neither is it so brilliant a character study as "Ben Jonson Entertains a Man from Stratford," nor so well-presented a tragedy as "The Clinging Vine." In reading it, we feel that Mr. Robinson was hampered by the weight of tradition hanging about his subject. He could not quite get to its kernel, absorb it as his own, and, forgetting the necessity of doing something remarkable with it, make it remarkable because remoulded in the fires of his own brain. It is good work, creditable work, but it is not great work, and the poet's peculiar excellencies are often lacking. There is too much of the fustian of the antiquary ; too little of the creative vision of the poet. This is just the opposite of "Ben Jonson," which, true always to the place and the time, is nevertheless instinct with life. In "Ben Jonson," we pass a couple of men in the street, and overhear a little of their conversation ; there is no feeling of anachronism, we might be there, or they here, so little is the age obtruded. What there is, is quite natural, and falls into its proper, subordinate place. In "Merlin," we turn over the pages of a beautiful picture-book, a portfolio of old, rare prints. They have nothing to do with us, nor we with them. They are charming, but remote, and — they are only pictures.

Mr. Robinson is constantly desiring a larger canvas than his fugitive poems permit. He has tried plays, now he essays a narrative poem. Yet, for some reason, he seems never to have realized the different technique necessary for these more sustained efforts. He still remains the poet of the fleeting instant.

"Merlin" teases by a constant change of scene, now forward, now backward ; now action, now reminiscence. Recollection, knitting up the past with the present, is one of the most difficult things to manage in all narrative writing, whether it be poem, novel, or play. "Merlin" opens with the return of the magician to Camelot, sent for by King Arthur, who feels his throne rocking, menaced as it is by the plotting of his natural son on the one hand, and, on the other, by the intrigues of Lancelot and Queen Guinevere. Merlin comes, but his power is gone, he has nothing to suggest, no vigour to impart. He tells the King what the King knows already:

" Now, Arthur, since you are a child of mine —
A foster-child, and that's a kind of child —
Be not from hearsay or despair too eager
To dash your meat with bitter seasoning,
So none that are more famished than yourself
Shall have what you refuse.   For you are King,
And if you starve yourself, you starve the state;
And then by sundry looks and silences
Of those you loved, and by the lax regard
Of those you knew for fawning enemies,
You may learn soon that you are King no more,
But a slack, blasted, and sad-fronted man,
Made sadder with a crown.   No other friend
Than I could say this to you, and say more;
And if you bid me say no more, so be it."

This contains no help for Arthur, and he breaks out:

" .   .   .   .   Why tell a king —
A poor, foiled, flouted, miserable king —
That if he lets rats eat his fingers off
He'll have no fingers to fight battles with?
I know as much as that, for I am still
A king — who thought himself a little less
Than God; a king who built him palaces

On sand and mud, and hears them crumbling now,
And sees them tottering, as he knew they must.
You are the man who made me to be King —
Therefore, say anything."

But Merlin has very little to say; of Modred he urges, "Trust him not;" he tells the King, however, that Lancelot "will have you first;" and ends, "Let that be all, for I can say no more." Cold comfort, indeed! And the King goes to bed to toss with nightmares through the long night. There is no more beautiful passage in the poem than these lines which end the third section:

No tide that ever crashed on Lyonnesse
Drove echoes inland that were lonelier
For widowed ears among the fisher-folk,
Than for the King were memories tonight
Of old illusions that were dead forever.

Merlin returns to Brittany and Vivian, but this is hardly touched upon; instead, the poem harks back to Merlin's first coming, ten years before, and continues as reminiscence for fifty pages. Then we come back to the present and Merlin's return.

Some of the best parts of the whole volume lie in these fifty pages. Still, this long mood of recollection delays the action, stays the movement so completely that it is never quite recovered, and the feeling of unreality, of dream, persists to the end.

Can the poem be said really to end? So little rounded is it, that it almost seems as though it might have stopped before or after the last line without affecting the result. True, Merlin finally parts from Vivian. But it is all misty and unreal — there may be other meetings, other partings, changes so constant as to make a never-ending progression. It is possible that the poet may have meant just this, but I doubt it, as there seems no reason for such a meaning. The poem is a piece snipped off a heavily brocaded tapestry, but the scissors might have cut either to the right or to the left of the line they did take without much injuring the whole. For the pattern is too large for any such clipping; wherever it was severed, we should get only an unrelated square.

A work of art should round its pattern somehow. "Merlin" fails to satisfy because the ends ravel away without any such rounding.

This is not to say that, because the complete conception is outlined with insufficient firmness, there are not beautiful parts in this long poem. Some passages are the finest of their kind that Mr. Robinson has written. For once, he seems to have allowed his lyricism free play, and the result makes the reader hope that he will never again feel it necessary to curb it. The whole account of Merlin's first coming to Broceliande is charming. Let us take a few lines here and there:

Over the waves and into Brittany
Went Merlin, to Broceliande.   Gay birds
Were singing high to greet him all along
A broad and sanded woodland avenue
That led him on forever, so he thought,
Until at last there was an end of it;
And at the end there was a gate of iron,
Wrought heavily and invidiously barred.
He pulled a cord that rang somewhere a bell
Of many echoes, and sat down to rest,
Outside the keeper's house, upon a bench
Of carven stone that might for centuries
Have waited there in silence to receive him.
The birds were singing still; leaves flashed and swung
Before him in the sunlight; a soft breeze
Made intermittent whisperings around him
Of love and fate and danger, and faint waves
Of many sweetly-stinging fragile odors
Broke lightly as they touched him; cherry-boughs
Above him snowed white petals down upon him,
And under their slow falling Merlin smiled
Contentedly.

I can recall few such images as "leaves flashed
and swung," or "many sweetly-stinging fragile odors
broke lightly as they touched him," in the earlier
books.

Merlin and his guide proceed

Down shaded ways, through open ways with hedgerows.
And into shade again more deep than ever,

But edged anon with rays of broken sunshine
In which a fountain, raining crystal music,
Made faery magic of it through green leafage,
Till Merlin's eyes were dim with preparation
For sight now of the lady Vivian.

The description of the magician's eyes as "dim with preparation" is one of those sudden stampings of emotion into fact which make Mr. Robinson's work so poetically, so actually, true. We see the same thing when Merlin says:

" If I were young, God knows if I were safe
Concerning you in green, like a slim cedar,
As you are now, to say my life was mine:
Were you to say to me that I should end it,
Longevity for me were jeopardized.
Have you your green on always and all over?"

There is another beautiful, lyrical touch when Vivian leads Merlin to the house:

Along a dusky way between tall cones
Of tight green cedars.

But then, the poem is full of them. I shall cite only two others. This:

The sun went down, and the dark after it
Starred Merlin's new abode with many a sconced
And many a moving candle.

and this, when Merlin joins Vivian at supper:

The lady Vivian in a fragile sheath
Of crimson, dimmed and veiled ineffably
By the flame-shaken gloom wherein she sat,
And twinkled if she moved, heard Merlin coming,
And smiled as if to make herself believe
Her joy was all a triumph; yet her blood
Confessed a tingling of more wonderment
Than all her five and twenty worldly years
Of waiting for this triumph could remember;
And when she knew and felt the slower tread
Of his unseen advance among the shadows
To the small haven of uncertain light
That held her in it as a torch-lit shoal
Might hold a smooth red fish, her listening skin
Responded with a creeping underneath it,
And a creeping that was incident alike
To darkness, love, and mice.

So they sup, to the music of

   .   .   half-heard, dream-weaving interludes
Of distant flutes and viols, made yet more distant
By faint nostalgic hautboys blown from nowhere.

Certainly, a poem which contains such beauties as
these must be forgiven whatever lapses of construction it exhibits as a whole. It is just these portions
which prove Mr. Robinson to be still advancing. If
the book, in its entirety, is not so successful as
"The Man Against the Sky," there are directions

in which he has distanced the achievement of that volume.

Probably the key-note of the story is much the same as in the title poem of the earlier book. We seem to have it here, in the words of Dagonet, the fool, commenting upon what Merlin has told him:

> ".   .   .   .   You say the torch
> Of woman and the light that Galahad found
> Are some day to illuminate the world?
> I'll meditate on that."

The same note as in "The Man Against the Sky," but less vaguely conceived, with more of tangibility, and also, sadly enough, more of question. From "The Children of the Night" to these last pages of "Merlin," the preoccupation continues. The preoccupation of a man flung ruthlessly out of one age into another, and seeking — seeking — for some sure ground on which to stand. The Grail, and Woman! So he searches, hoping, half-convinced, and suffers; and the magician who has prophesied can only sigh and add:

> "Not wholly dead, but old.   Merlin is old."

So Merlin and the fool

> .   .   .   .   arose
> And, saying nothing, found a groping way
> Down through the gloom together.   Fiercer now,

> The wind was like a flying animal
> That beat the two of them incessantly
> With icy wings, and bit them as they went.
> The rock above them was an empty place
> Where neither seer nor fool should view again
> The stricken city.   Colder blew the wind
> Across the world, and on it heavier lay
> The shadow and the burden of the night;
> And there was darkness over Camelot.

Again the sense of tragedy, of courage, of hope and pain.

It is idle to ask if the greatest poetry can be built upon such negative lines.   Certainly, no one will ever go to Mr. Robinson's books to make a gay mood more gay, to fill himself with the zest and sparkle of life.   These things Mr. Robinson has not to give.   His poems do not invigorate; they mellow and subdue.   But in our material day, the spirituality of Mr. Robinson's work is tonic and uplifting.

The cryptic expression of much of his poetry can hardly be considered other than a flaw, as it often is in Browning, and why the failure in atmospheric sense which permits such names as "Flammonde" and "Bokardo" to connote New England types, is a question difficult to answer.   Mr. Robinson is a painstaking poet, a poet of many revisions.   He prunes every tendency to luxuriance from his style. He aims at the starkness of absolute truth, and granted that what he sees be the truth, he usually attains it.

This poetry is "cribbed, cabin'd and confined" to a remarkable degree, but it is undeniably, magnificently noble.

Robert Frost

ROBERT FROST

ROBERT FROST

IT is the fashion to-day to speak as though New England mattered very little in the life and thought of these United States of America. New England is small geographically, but concentrated psychically, and thought is one of the things in which concentration counts for more than bulk. Poetry is the most concentrated form of literature; it is the most emotionalized and powerful way in which thought can be presented, and it is an interesting commentary on the easy scorn with which many non-New Englanders regard New England, that two of the six poets of whom I have to speak in this book should be of the very bone and sinew of New England.

In Mr. Robinson, we saw a highly developed, highly sensitized and intellectual, product of the old plain-living and high-thinking generations, throwing off the shackles of a superstition and an environment grown too narrow. We saw the poet realizing his century and its changed point of view through a long process of self-analysis. We saw him becoming the first spokesman of the New Order in this country through his following of truth in his observation of the world and of himself. Mr. Robinson represents New England, Mr. Robert Frost is New England. Mr. Robinson is one of the most intellectual poets writing in America to-day; Mr. Frost is one of the most intuitive. But it must never be forgotten that both these men are poets. So when I say, "intellectual," I would not be construed as meaning "devoid of passion," for Mr. Robinson is a passionate poet, even though the passion be carefully restrained; and when I say, "intuitive," I do not intend the inference that Mr. Frost is deficient in thought, for every line he writes is most carefully considered. I would point out, simply, the different manner in which these two men approach life and their own work. Mr. Robinson speculates about the world, wonders about it, almost agonizes over some of its phases; Mr. Frost, plastic and passive, permits the world to make upon him what imprint it will. Mr. Robinson is concerned that his work tally with the thing observed; Mr. Frost is anxious to trace accurately the markings burnt into the sensitive plate of his mind. Both poets are conscious of the actual work, as every artist must be, but Mr. Robinson is conscious of the substance out of which the work grows, while, with Mr. Frost, this process goes on in the subconscious stratum of his brain. Again, with Mr. Robinson,

New England is a thing remembered, compounded of childhood memories and race atavism; with Mr. Frost, New England is daily environment. Mr. Robinson's characteristics are a composite of the New England of three centuries; while Mr. Frost typifies the New England of to-day in its entirety — a remark which should perhaps be qualified by adding the words, "in the country districts." Mr. Robinson is more universal; Mr. Frost is more particular.

The strand which Mr. Frost exemplifies in the woven cord of modern poetry is — poetic realism. I might also add that his is the only true bucolic poetry being written in America to-day, and these are no mock bucolics, they are true pastorals of the hill country in which he spends his life.

All compounded as he seems to be of the granite and gentians of our Northern mountains, Mr. Frost is only of New England stock on his father's side. His mother was born in Edinburgh, of lowland Scotch descent. A curious fancy, however, might trace here a kinship shared with his native hills, for geologists tell us that the New Hampshire hills and the Scotch Highlands are cousin-german to each other; I have heard, even, that a species of land-locked trout found in Scotland is caught nowhere else but in New Hampshire ponds.

The poet's father, William Prescott Frost, was born in Kingston, New Hampshire, the ninth gen-

eration of his family on New England soil. Becoming a schoolmaster, this gentleman met his
wife, Belle Moody, when both were teaching in a
small Pennsylvania town, and there they were
married, shortly afterwards emigrating to San
Francisco where Mr. William Frost became editor
of a local newspaper. Their son, Robert Frost,
was born in San Francisco on March 26, 1875.

For some unexplained reason, considering his
descent, Mr. William Frost was an ardent Democrat. Throughout the Civil War, he was a copper-
head, and so strong were his feelings on the subject
that at one time he entertained an idea of running
away and joining the Confederate Army. He
thought better of it, however, and later salved his
sympathies by naming his son "Robert Lee."

Mr. Frost, senior, found the editorship of a
democratic paper in a growing, rather filibustering,
community such as was the San Francisco of those
days, thoroughly congenial. The city was only
just evolving from the "'Frisco" of the gold fever,
and life there was picturesque and adventurous.
Robert Frost well remembers the first Cleveland
election, when his father was manager of the Democratic City Committee. The boy was taken out
of school to run errands and make himself generally
useful, and he has often told of his father's excite-
ment and delight when the Democratic party won
— its first victory since the war.

It is not a little singular that these early years in San Francisco should have made so little impression upon the poet. He, who has proved himself extraordinarily receptive to environment, seems to possess that receptivity only in regard to one environment. We shall see the same phenomenon at work during his three years' sojourn in England, at a time when he would appear to have been at the very height of his powers. It is true, however, that, in his published work, there is no poem which has San Francisco as a background, nor which seems to owe its inception to this time of the author's life.

Robert Frost lived in San Francisco for the first ten years of his life, scampering up and down its hills, running in and out of newspaper offices, jostling against the somewhat rough and very determined men of the place and period, going to school in a desultory fashion. With most poets, one would add, "storing up impressions," but this seems to have been just what Robert Frost did not do. Remembrances of those days he must have, but not the vivid ones which lead to expression. This is a strange psychological fact. If one believed in supernatural intervention, one would say that Mr. Frost was dedicated from his cradle to be the poet of latter-day New England, and of that alone.

Mr. William Frost died when his son was ten years old, and the little boy and his mother found themselves alone, with no relations nearer than the distant East.   Mrs. Frost's parents were dead, but her husband's father offered a home to her and her child in Lawrence, Massachusetts, where he held the position of overseer in one of the mills.

From this time, begins Robert Frost's real life. From this time, the impressions grow and multiply. There are few moments in Mr. Frost's life in New England that do not have their bearing on his career as a poet.   Yet, again, it is the things native to the soil which count.   Living in a mill town in which the inhabitants were becoming extraordinarily mixed as to race, still it is only the New England types which stamp themselves into his consciousness.   Lawrence was even then expanding into a fair-sized city, but it was the farmhouses on its outskirts, the villages strewn along the winding roads, that captivated his imagination.   At one time, he worked in a mill, and yet there is not a single mill throughout his poems, while every wild flower picked in his rambles was photographed on his heart with the accuracy born of passion.   In making him keenly alive to certain impressions and quite dead to others, Nature knew her business superlatively well; she was moulding a poet to her purposes, and how excellently she has done it we shall soon see.

Mrs. Frost, the poet's mother, was a great reader, and the boy preferred to have her read aloud to him to reading himself.   He says that he never read a book through before he was fourteen.   His favorite volume was "Tom Brown's School Days," and this he never finished because he could not bear to feel that it was ended.

It is hard to tell at just what moment the artistic impulse first makes itself felt in a future author. Is it working when the impressions are being gathered? I should say — yes, undoubtedly. But, whatever he saw and collated, Robert Frost did not begin to write poetry until he was fifteen. Then occurred that series of love affairs with the great masters which every future poet must go through. His first love was Poe. Then came Shakespeare, Christina Rossetti, Edward Rowland Sill, Bryant, and a host of others. Still, in spite of these coquettings by the way, Mr. Frost has never been a literary poet. His inspiration does not come from books. No imaginative reconstruction of the past has ever intrigued him. He derives his inspiration from direct contact with the world — the little world of hill and upland, of farmhouse and country town.

The boy was put to school in Lawrence, a proceeding which, like most healthy boys, he found not at all to his taste. He loafed along as best he could, doing as little as possible, but still pushing up from grade to grade perforce, and always attending classes assiduously in the great academy of "Out of Doors."

The work of most poets contains at least one direct reference to their childhood. But, in Mr.

Frost's case, there appears to be no poem which can be taken as referring certainly to this period of his life. Rather, the whole bulk of his work would seem to be a very part of his growth.   Still, in his last volume, "Mountain Interval," is a poem, "Birches," which, besides being one of Mr. Frost's most beautiful things, seems to contain more than a hint of the boy he was.

BIRCHES

When I see birches bend to left and right
Across the lines of straighter darker trees,
I like to think some boy's been swinging them.
But swinging doesn't bend them down to stay.
Ice-storms do that.   Often you must have seen them
Loaded with ice a sunny winter morning
After a rain.   They click upon themselves
As the breeze rises, and turn many-colored
As the stir cracks and crazes their enamel.
Soon the sun's warmth makes them shed crystal shells
Shattering and avalanching on the snow-crust —
Such heaps of broken glass to sweep away
You'd think the inner dome of heaven had fallen.
They are dragged to the withered bracken by the load,
And they seem not to break; though once they are bowed
So low for long, they never right themselves:
You may see their trunks arching in the woods
Years afterwards, trailing their leaves on the ground
Like girls on hands and knees that throw their hair
Before them over their heads to dry in the sun.
But I was going to say when Truth broke in

With all her matter-of-fact about the ice-storm
(Now am I free to be poetical?)
I should prefer to have some boy bend them
As he went out and in to fetch the cows —
Some boy too far from town to learn baseball,
Whose only play was what he found himself,
Summer or winter, and could play alone.
One by one he subdued his father's trees
By riding them down over and over again
Until he took the stiffness out of them,
And not one but hung limp, not one was left
For him to conquer.   He learned all there was
To learn about not launching out too soon
And so not carrying the tree away
Clear to the ground.   He always kept his poise
To the top branches, climbing carefully
With the same pains you use to fill a cup
Up to the brim, and even above the brim.
Then he flung outward, feet first, with a swish,
Kicking his way down through the air to the ground.
So was I once myself a swinger of birches.
And so I dream of going back to be.
It's when I'm weary of considerations,
And life is too much like a pathless wood
Where your face burns and tickles with the cobwebs
Broken across it, and one eye is weeping
From a twig's having lashed across it open.
I'd like to get away from earth awhile
And then come back to it and begin over.
May no fate wilfully misunderstand me
And half grant what I wish and snatch me away

Not to return.   Earth's the right place for love:
I don't know where it's likely to go better.
I'd like to go by climbing a birch tree,
And climb black branches up a snow-white trunk
Toward heaven, till the tree could bear no more,
But dipped its top and set me down again.
That would be good both going and coming back.
One could do worse than be a swinger of birches.

We know at least that he was once himself "a swinger of birches."   We know, too, that much of his play

.   .   .   .   was what he found himself,
Summer or winter, and could play alone.

And we know, by the description of the ice-covered birch-trees, how eagerly he offered his mind to the impress of such pictures.

In due time, Robert Frost left the Grammar School and entered the High School, and here for the first time his studies began to appeal to him. Probably his teachers were more intelligent and farther advanced than those in the Grammar School, possibly, also, he began to find out that study is only a means, not an end.   Whatever the cause, the four years in the High School were successful and pleasant.   One of his fellow pupils at the High School was Miss Elinor Miriam White, the lady he afterwards married.   Miss White was a good scholar and a serious young woman, and Mr. Frost owes an immeasurable debt to the steadfast purpose of his wife.

It was in 1892, while still a pupil at the High School, that Mr. Frost began sending poems to magazines. And his first poem to be accepted was taken by "The Independent" for the very usual sum of fifteen dollars, which, however, seemed a munificent figure to the young man.

In 1893, Mr. Frost graduated from the High School, and the following Autumn he entered Dartmouth College. College, however, did not agree with his state of mind, the inertia of the Grammar School overcame him again. He could not learn from his teachers; he could get no mental pabulum from the prescribed courses. Miss White was no longer at his side to spur him on. She had gone to Saint Lawrence University, where, more resolved than the young poet, she followed the entire course and graduated.

Far from graduating, Robert Frost only stayed at Dartmouth a few months, then he left, "ran away" would perhaps state the fact more accurately, and returned to his grandfather's house in Lawrence.

It needs very little imagination to picture the consternation with which he was received. Indeed, his grandfather's disgust was so great that for a time he left the young man to shift for himself. This he did by becoming, among other things, bobbin boy in a mill. Now, the position of bobbin boy is not an exalted one, indeed it is practically at the bottom of the long grade of mill workers.   For a young man of eighteen, a High School graduate and an aspirant for a College degree, to take such a position is certainly unusual.   But it offered, it meant bread and butter, and he took it.   Mr. Frost often says that he has no pride.   A most misleading statement. Rather is it that his pride in the profession to which he has dedicated himself is so great that it dulls all other prides, such as the foolish one of social strata, for instance.   Again and again throughout his career, we shall see Mr. Frost the sport, I had very nearly said, of winds of chance.   With his eyes firmly fixed upon his chosen goal of poetry, he moves along unconscious of the particular ground on which his feet are treading.   It almost seems as though he turned to the right or the left as the wind blew, yet whether right or left, the path leads him always forward.

For four years, the poet pursued various avocations in which his heart was not, and wrote poems in which his heart most emphatically was, sending them out once a year to "The Century," "Scribner's," "The Atlantic," or "Harper's," all four the chief publications for poetry at that time.   Gradually, "The Youth's Companion" was added to the list, and these, and "The Independent," were the only papers to which he sought entrance for twenty years.   For twenty years this persevering endeavour continued, and for twenty years the poet remained, to all intents and purposes, unknown.

While Mr. Frost was living this outwardly rather vagrant life, he was persisting in another cause as well as that of poetry. He was trying to persuade Miss Elinor White to abandon her college course and marry him. But the young lady was firm of purpose, and it was not until after her graduation that the marriage took place, in October, 1895.

Possibly it was her influence which led him to return again to the idea of an ordered course of study. At any rate, in 1897, he moved his little family to Cambridge and entered Harvard, especially to study Latin. He stayed at Harvard for two years, but it was uphill work. He was too old for college curriculums, for one thing, for another, a married undergraduate is naturally set apart from his fellows and cannot, by the nature of things, get all that a university has to offer. Again he gave way before the blowing wind of distaste, and returned to Lawrence with his wife and child.

Then followed another period of attempts. He tramped, taught school, made shoes, edited a weekly paper called "The Sentinel," and seemed to his family to be moving toward nothing at all. For they did not count the spasmodic appearances of his poems as anything, after the usual manner of mothers, and grandfathers, and uncles.

Finally his grandfather, almost in despair, took pity on him, as he supposed, and, in 1900, bought him a farm in Derry, New Hampshire.

A great many of the poems in his published books would seem to date from the Derry period, if not in actual writing, certainly in substance. Such poems as "Mowing," "Mending Wall," "After Apple-picking," "Putting in the Seed," and a number of others, are written by one who has been in the places described, and doing the things here done. This is not the work of a mere observer, but of a man who has lived what he writes about:

MOWING

There was never a sound beside the wood but one,
And that was my long scythe whispering to the ground.
What was it it whispered? I knew not well myself;
Perhaps it was something about the heat of the sun,
Something, perhaps, about the lack of sound —
And that was why it whispered and did not speak.
It was no dream of the gift of idle hours,
Or easy gold at the hand of fay or elf:
Anything more than the truth would have seemed too weak
To the earnest love that laid the swale in rows,
Not without feeble-pointed spikes of flowers
(Pale orchises), and scared a bright green snake.
The fact is the sweetest dream that labor knows.
My long scythe whispered and left the hay to make.

Is it likely that anyone who has not followed a scythe would realize that it "whispered," or would so vividly picture the bright green snake darting off through the stubble?

Here is another poem which could not have been written without actual experience:

MENDING WALL

Something there is that doesn't love a wall,
That sends the frozen-ground swell under it,
And spills the upper boulders in the sun;
And makes gaps even two can pass abreast.
The work of hunters is another thing:
I have come after them and made repair
Where they have left not one stone on stone,
But they would have the rabbit out of hiding,
To please the yelping dogs.   The gaps I mean,
No one has seen them made or heard them made,
But at spring mending-time we find them there.
I let my neighbour know beyond the hill;
And on a day we meet to walk the line
And set the wall between us once again.
We keep the wall between us as we go.
To each the boulders that have fallen to each.
And some are loaves and some so nearly balls
We have to use a spell to make them balance:
"Stay where you are until our backs are turned!"
We wear our fingers rough with handling them.
Oh, just another kind of out-door game,
One on a side.   It comes to little more:
There where it is we do not need the wall:
He is all pine and I am apple orchard.
My apple trees will never get across
And eat the cones under his pines, I tell him.

> He only says, "Good fences make good neighbours."
> Spring is the mischief in me, and I wonder
> If I could put a notion in his head:
> "*Why* do they make good neighbours?   Isn't it
> Where there are cows?   But here there are no cows.
> Before I built a wall I'd ask to know
> What I was walling in or walling out,
> And to whom I was like to give offence.
> Something there is that doesn't love a wall,
> That wants it down."   I could say "Elves" to him,
> But it's not elves exactly, and I'd rather
> He said it for himself.   I see him there
> Bringing a stone grasped firmly by the top
> In each hand, like an old-stone savage armed.
> He moves in darkness as it seems to me,
> Not of woods only and the shade of trees.
> He will not go behind his father's saying,
> And he likes having thought of it so well
> He says again, "Good fences make good neighbours."

Do most laymen know that a wall should be built by two men working from either side at the same time?   Could anyone not a farmer say:

> He is all pine and I am apple orchard.
> My apple trees will never get across
> And eat the cones under his pines, I tell him.

It is by such touches as these that Mr. Frost's poems are great; real pastorals, not artificial bucolics, racy with current speech, tanged of the soil.

I shall consider them more at length when we come
to the publication of the volumes of which they form
a part. For the time itself was brightened by no
publications, except those yearly batches of poems
sent to the magazines, of which some were accepted
and many were not. Mr. Frost was still a sort of
ne'er-do-weel in the eyes of the older generation,
laboriously starving on one of the stone-infested
farms of Southern New Hampshire.

Derry is in Rockingham County, the South-
easternmost extremity of New Hampshire, and not
so very far North of Lawrence. Kingston, his
father's birthplace, is also in Rockingham County
and not many miles to the North of Derry; in
buying his grandson a farm in Derry, therefore, Mr.
William Frost was merely in a measure returning
upon his own life. But returns are dangerous things.
The whole farming industry of New England had
been knocked on the head by the opening up of the
West. The enterprising youths of these country
districts had gone to make their fortunes on the
stretching meadows of Western plains. To start
life in San Francisco and work back to a farm in
Derry, New Hampshire, would have been retrogres-
sion indeed for anyone with a less special destiny
than Mr. Frost. Here was a young man, twenty-
five years old, whose horizon since he was ten had
been bounded by Hanover on the North and Boston
on the South, only a few hundred miles either way.

Here was this same young man working from morning till night to tear a living out of the thin soil. Yet, however despairing the outlook seemed, this was the very concatenation of circumstance and surrounding that the poet needed. A few hundred miles was to contain all his poetic world, but these few hundred miles were to be deepened indefinitely by the delving of his own spade.

Robert Frost was digging poetry with every shovelful, but he was not digging a sustenance for his growing family. Derry boasts that most New England institution, an academy. In this case, the Pinkerton Academy; and Mr. Frost was taken into it as a teacher, going on from there to the Normal School in Plymouth, New Hampshire, in 1911.

Plymouth is a small town of some fifteen hundred inhabitants, standing among the swelling foot-hills of the White Mountains. Perhaps his residence there widened the poet's horizon by another twenty or thirty miles, still the few hundred held good, and a great desire to get away, to see somewhere else — England — took possession of him.

We can very well believe that, all unconscious, Mr. Frost felt the need of rest. Rest from those mental impressions which constantly crowded upon him in his chosen environment. What he probably said to himself was that he wanted change and a new outlook; what he really desired was peace, and no outlook at all, or rather only that detached outlook we get when we observe something with which we are in no way concerned. The opportunity came by the sale of his farm in Derry, and in September, 1912, Mr. Frost and his family set sail for England.

England just before the war was an exceedingly stimulating place for poets. The present interest in poetry had not yet started in America, although circumstances were moving toward it. It is a significant fact that "Poetry," Miss Monroe's "Magazine of Verse," appeared for the first time in October, 1912, just one month after Mr. Frost went away. He left a country apparently deaf to his work, he came back to find — but I anticipate.

London was full of poets, and, what is better, the beliefs, and protests, and hates of poets. They made a lively buzzing which meant that the art was in a vigorous condition. There was "The Poetry Review," edited by Stephen Phillips, and devoted to the more conservative practitioners of the art; there was "Poetry and Drama," sprung off from the older periodical in revolt, and opening its columns to a more radical group; and lastly there was Ezra Pound and a little band of insurgents gathered about him, who denounced both groups with a charming impartiality.

Mr. Harold Munro had just started his Poetry Book Shop, where readings by poets of their own work were held periodically; and here, there, and everywhere, if you happened to be a poet, was talk of forms and directions, technique and substance, the thousand and one things which, if taken in small doses, do so much to keep the poet's craft sound and sane.   The wise man does not spend his days in any *cénacle*, no matter how alluring, he can only spare a few days and nights of his life to talking about his art lest the thing itself should take unto itself wings and fly away from this clogging mist of discussion.

The better poets knew this, and although there was a constant coming and going, the persons changed but the meetings went on.   "By ones, by twos, by threes," to paraphrase "The Ingoldsby Legends," poets met, and talked, and parted, and met again. To anyone less firmly set on his own artistic feet than Mr. Frost, the situation was intoxicating, but it is characteristic of the man that he lost neither his head nor his originality.   He changed no whit in poetry, speech, or appearance. He talked and listened, and went home and did the same thing right over again only better, I am forced to believe, since his second book is much finer than his first. This first, "A Boy's Will," was published by David Nutt, London, in 1913.

"A Boy's Will" is a slender little volume of sixty-three pages.   In the Table of Contents, each poem has a sort of explanation under it.   For instance:

> INTO MY OWN
> The youth is persuaded that he will be
> rather more than less himself for having
> forsworn the world.

GHOST HOUSE
He is happy in society of his own choosing.

WIND AND WINDOW FLOWER
Out of the winter things he fashions a
story of modern love.

A DREAM PANG
He is shown by a dream how really well
it is with him.

MOWING
He takes up life simply with the small
tasks.

These are only a few of the titles, but they will
serve to show how much more subjective the book
is than Mr. Frost's other volumes.

The poet has not quite attained his own particular
speech in most of these poems, the ability to bring
up a whole picture or emotion in a simple word
is not yet fully his. This poem is most charming,
particularly the last line, but it might have been
written by some other poet than Robert Frost:

ROSE POGONIAS

A saturated meadow,
   Sun-shaped and jewel-small,
A circle scarcely wider

Than the trees around were tall;
Where winds were quite excluded,
    And the air was stifling sweet
With the breath of many flowers, —
    A temple of the heat.

There we bowed us in the burning,
    As the sun's right worship is,
To pick where none could miss them
    A thousand orchises;
For though the grass was scattered,
    Yet every second spear
Seemed tipped with wings of color,
    That tinged the atmosphere.

We raised a simple prayer
    Before we left the spot,
That in the general mowing
    That place might be forgot;
Or if not all so favoured,
    Obtain such grace of hours,
That none should mow the grass there
    While so confused with flowers.

This next one, however, has some of his later
flavour, and with it a delightful lyric quality:

TO THE THAWING WIND

Come with rain, O loud Southwester!
Bring the singer, bring the nester;
Give the buried flower a dream;

Make the settled snow-bank steam;
Find the brown beneath the white;
But what'er you do to-night,
Bathe my window, make it flow,
Melt it as the ices go;
Melt the glass and leave the sticks
Like a hermit's crucifix;
Burst into my narrow stall;
Swing the picture on the wall;
Run the rattling pages o'er;
Scatter poems on the floor;
Turn the poet out of door.

The book has lovely things in it, characteristic things. For instance, of a mower:

I looked for him behind an isle of trees;
I listened for his whetstone on the breeze.

And, of an October morning:

Retard the sun with gentle mist;
Enchant the land with amethyst.
Slow, slow!
For the grapes' sake, if they were all,
Whose leaves already are burnt with frost,
Whose clustered fruit must else be lost —
For the grapes' sake along the wall.

Yet the clean-cut vigour of his later work is absent.
"A Boy's Will" was pleasantly received by the London papers. "The Academy" said of it: "We

have read every line with that amazement and delight which are too seldom evoked by books of modern verse." What was more remarkable was that the various warring groups of young poets were for once agreed. They all recognized the beauty of this poetry, in one way or another. The book was, in fact, without being in any sense great, an excellent start.

Meanwhile, the poet and his family were living in the little suburban town of Beaconsfield in Buckinghamshire. Hitherto, the money for the farm had been the active support of the family, now, unfortunately, this fund was becoming exhausted. Something had to be done. Mr. Frost had been a farmer, he understood the business and it offered the only practical means of subsisting while he continued to write poetry. He took the lease of a small farm on the outskirts of the village of Leddington, near Ledbury, in Herefordshire, and went there to live in the early Spring of 1914.

This farming venture was not a professional one. Mr. Frost did not concern himself with raising produce for the market, he was content to raise enough to feed his family, and so reduce the household expenses and put off the final disappearance of his small capital.

Country life in England is not the isolated and lonely thing it is in America. For one reason, nowhere is very far from London, and the poet could run up to town from time to time and enjoy his poetical talks without putting too great a strain upon either his time or his finances. Even at home he had his discussions, for two of the younger poets were his neighbours: Lascelles Abercrombie, the writer of sonorous blank verse, and Wilfrid Wilson Gibson, poet of harsh drama and rough tragedy, whose work is so well known to Americans. But if Ezra Pound's preciosity had no effect upon Mr. Frost, neither did Mr. Abercrombie's classicism, nor Mr. Gibson's stern brutality. He went his own way, grew his vegetables, and wrote "North of Boston."

"North of Boston" appeared, again from the press of David Nutt, in the Spring of 1914.

It speaks volumes for the still somnolent state of American publishers, that such an intensely American volume should have been issued first in England. Things had begun to change here as far as the magazines were concerned, but the publishers remained skeptical. I am happy to say that all that is different now.

I had passed the Summer of 1914 in England, and there I had heard much talk of "North of Boston." I well remember purchasing the little green volume at The Poetry Book Shop, and spending an evening reading it with ever increasing delight. On my return home, I suggested its publication to no less than two publishing houses, but the suggestion met with no response, and with its subsequent issue by

Messrs. Henry Holt and Company I regret to say that I had nothing to do.

With the publication of "North of Boston," Mr. Frost's reputation was suddenly made. There was hardly a dissenting voice as to its merits. A paper usually so hostile to American verse as "The Times" wrote: "Poetry burns up out of it, as when a faint wind breathes upon smouldering embers." A beautiful and accurate characterization, for, through the homely, quiet words rises a faint pungency, the very aroma of poesy floating thinly up into the air.

"North of Boston" is a "book of people," as Mr. Frost has said in his dedication. It is a volume of stories; long, interesting stories of those New Hampshire folk dwelling between the two poles of Mr. Frost's "few hundred miles." There is no whisper of English influence in this poetry, it is the very nostalgia of his New England hills. The speech is New England, except in one particular which I shall mention later, although the poet eschews dialect. His eyes may see the soft rounded English country, with its stiles and tufted trees, but the lines etched upon his heart are the articulate outlines of rock and hemlock, the angular sharpness of stone walls and white clapboarded houses against a hard blue sky.

A little poem in italics serves as motto to the volume, and may very well serve as motto to all

Mr. Frost's work. For here in a few words is an upland pasture with the farmer at work in it, and here is that tenderness, that love of place and people which marks all that this poet does:

THE PASTURE

I'm going out to clean the pasture spring;
I'll only stop to rake the leaves away
(And wait to watch the water clear, I may):
I sha'n't be gone long. — You come too.

I'm going out to fetch the little calf
That's standing by the mother. It's so young,
It totters when she licks it with her tongue.
I sha'n't be gone long. — You come too.

"North of Boston" is a very sad book. All the sadder, perhaps, because the poet is at no pains to make it so. He is holding no brief for or against the state of things he portrays, he is too much a part of it himself to exhibit it as an illustration of anything. He writes of it because it is his, his to love and present. Yet, in spite of its author's sympathetic touch, the book reveals a disease which is eating into the vitals of our New England life, at least in its rural communities.

What is there in the hard, vigorous climate of these states which plants the seeds of degeneration? Is the violence and ugliness of their religious belief

the cause of these twisted and tortured lives? Have
the sane, full-blooded men all been drafted away to
the cities, or the West, leaving behind only feeble
remainders of a once fine stock? The question again
demands an answer after the reading of Mr. Frost's
book.

Other countries can rear a sturdy peasantry which
maintains itself for generations, heavy and slow,
perhaps, but strong and self-replenishing; and this
for a length of time beside which our New England
civilization is as nothing. We are often told that
the telephone has done much to decrease insanity
in the farming districts, and doubtless it is true.
New England Winters are long and isolating. But
what about Russian Winters, Polish, Swedish, Nor-
wegian? After all, the telephone is a very modern
invention, and these countries have been producing
a hardy peasantry for hundreds of years. It is said
that the country people of these nations are
less highly organized, less well educated, than are
New Englanders, and so better able to stand the
loneliness of long Winters. But this does not explain the great numbers of people, sprung from old
New England stock, but not themselves living in
remote country places, who go insane.

It is a question for the psychiatrist to answer, and
it would be interesting to ask it with "North of
Boston" as a text-book to go by. Mr. Frost has
reproduced both people and scenery with a vividness

which is extraordinary. Here are the huge hills, undraped by any sympathetic legend, felt as things hard and unyielding, almost sinister, not exactly feared, but regarded as in some sort influences nevertheless. Here are great stretches of blueberry pasture lying in the sun; and again, Autumn orchards cracking with fruit which it is almost too much trouble to gather. Heavy thunder-storms drench the lonely roads and spatter on the walls of farmhouses rotting in abandonment; and the modern New England town, with narrow frame houses, visited by drummers alone, is painted in all its ugliness. For Mr. Frost's is not the kindly New England of Whittier, nor the humorous and sensible one of Lowell; it is a latter-day New England, where a civilization is decaying to give place to another and very different one.

Mr. Frost does not deal with the changed population, with the Canadians and Finns who are taking up the deserted farms. His people are leftovers of the old stock, morbid, pursued by phantoms, slowly sinking to insanity. In "The Black Cottage," we have the pathos of the abandoned house, after the death of the stern, narrow-minded woman who had lived in it. In "A Servant to Servants," we have a woman already insane once and drifting there again, with the consciousness that her drab, monotonous life is bringing it upon her. "Home Burial" gives the morbidness of death in these remote places — a woman unable to take up her life again after her only child has died. The charming idyll, "After Apple-picking," is dusted over with something uncanny, and "The Fear" is a horrible revelation of those undercurrents which go on as much in the country as in the city, and with anxiety eating away whatever satisfaction the following of desire might have brought. There is very much the same theme in "The Housekeeper," while "The Generations of Men" shows that foolish pride in a useless race which is so strange a characteristic of these people. It is all here — the book is an epitome of a decaying New England.

Mr. Frost writes almost as a man under a spell. As though he were the mouthpiece of something beyond himself, only conscious of the necessity of stating what is in him. There is throughout the entire book an undercurrent of his own lines:

> .   .   .   .   .   I am overtired
> Of the great harvest I myself desired.

Still he must gather it; it is what he is here to do. The whole of the poem from which that quotation is taken, "After Apple-picking," is mystical with this sense of an unsought burden imposed.

AFTER APPLE–PICKING

> My long two-pointed ladder's sticking through a tree
> Toward heaven still,

And there's a barrel that I didn't fill
Beside it, and there may be two or three
Apples I didn't pick upon some bough.
But I am done with apple-picking now.
Essence of winter sleep is on the night,
The scent of apples : I am drowsing off.
I cannot rub the strangeness from my sight
I got from looking through a pane of glass
I skimmed this morning from the drinking trough
And held against the world of hoary grass.
It melted, and I let it fall and break.
But I was well
Upon my way to sleep before it fell,
And I could tell
What form my dreaming was about to take.
Magnified apples appear and disappear,
Stem end and blossom end,
And every fleck of russet showing clear.
My instep arch not only keeps the ache,
It keeps the pressure of a ladder-round.
I feel the ladder sway as the boughs bend.
And I keep hearing from the cellar bin
The rumbling sound
Of load on load of apples coming in.
For I have had too much
Of apple-picking : I am overtired
Of the great harvest I myself desired.
There were ten thousand thousand fruit to touch,
Cherish in hand, lift down, and not let fall.
For all
That struck the earth,

> No matter if not bruised or spiked with stubble,
> Went surely to the cider-apple heap
> As of no worth.
> One can see what will trouble
> This sleep of mine, whatever sleep it is.
> Were he not gone,
> The woodchuck could say whether it's like his
> Long sleep, as I describe its coming on,
> Or just some human sleep.

Is it not true that he cannot tell "what form his dreaming is about to take"? I have said that Mr. Frost is an intuitive poet. This poem shows his sense of intuition becoming almost conscious.

Truly the mysticism in "After Apple-picking" "burns up out of the poem," for, on the surface, it is one of the most beautifully clear that Mr. Frost has done. The two-pointed ladder sticking through the trees is exceedingly clean and bright as a picture, indeed the whole of the description is excellent. Here, too, we have those touches so simple, so true, so original, which give Mr. Frost's work such a rare distinction. For instance :

> My instep arch not only keeps the ache,
> It keeps the pressure of a ladder-round.

Such passages are scattered through all the poems in "North of Boston." Sometimes they are purely beautiful, as in this, from "The Death of the Hired Man":

" I'll sit and see if that small sailing cloud
Will hit or miss the moon."
                    It hit the moon.
Then there were three there, making a dim row,
The moon, the little silver cloud, and she.

Sometimes they are beautiful because of their absolute fidelity to fact, as in the lines about the ladder I have just quoted, or these from "The Woodpile":

It was a cord of maple, cut and split
And piled — and measured, four by four by eight.
And not another like it could I see.
No runner tracks in this year's snow looped near it.
And it was older sure than this year's cutting,
Or even last year's or the year's before.
The wood was grey and the bark warping off it
And the pile somewhat sunken.   Clematis
Had wound strings round and round it like a bundle.

"North of Boston" is a book of stories in verse. And Mr. Frost's genius shows itself not only in the verse, but in the stories as such.   In verse or in prose, they would be unusual.   They are so natural, so obvious, that, in reading them, one says, "I wonder why I never thought of making a story like that?" But, in spite of the numbers of stories on New England life, nobody has thought of making such stories before.   In some cases, the theme is exceedingly slight, yet the characters are so sharply drawn that they hold the reader's interest in spite of the extreme

vagueness of the plot.   Is it that, or is it that Mr.
Frost possesses the gift of style, as the English critic,
Mr. Edward Garnett, has pointed out?   For, in the
final count, it is always this fact of style which makes
the glory of a work of art and keeps it alive.   Works
of art live or die by the manner of their telling
rather than by their content, however strange such
an idea may be to the contemporary reader.   Times
change, and what appears significant to one generation is insignificant to another, but beauty of expression remains and is immortal.

The story of "The Death of the Hired Man" is
very simple and very slight.   A poor, half-crazed
old labourer comes back to the farm where he has
occasionally worked.   The farmer's wife is in the
house, she permits the man to come into the kitchen
and rest.   Then she goes out to meet her returning
husband and beg him to be kind to the old man, and
give him something to do, and while her husband
goes in to speak to him, she sits on the doorstep and
watches the little cloud sailing toward the moon.
But, as written by Mr. Frost, this story is full
of tenderness, and the foreboding of a silent close.
It begins:

> Mary sat musing on the lamp-flame at the table
> Waiting for Warren.   When she heard his step,
> She ran on tip-toe down the darkened passage
> To meet him in the doorway with the news
> And put him on his guard.   "Silas is back."

She pushed him outward with her through the door
And shut it after her. "Be kind," she said.
She took the market things from Warren's arms
And set them on the porch, then drew him down
To sit beside her on the wooden steps.

They talk, the wife persuading, the husband a
trifle unwilling. At length,

> Part of a moon was falling down the west,
> Dragging the whole sky with it to the hills.
> Its light poured softly in her lap. She saw
> And spread her apron to it. She put out her hand
> Among the harp-like morning-glory strings,
> Taut with the dew from garden bed to eaves,
> As if she played unheard the tenderness
> That wrought on him beside her in the night.
> "Warren," she said, "he has come home to die:
> You needn't be afraid he'll leave you this time."

"Home," he mocked gently.

> "Yes, what else but home?
> It all depends on what you mean by home.
> Of course he's nothing to us, any more
> Than was the hound that came a stranger to us
> Out of the woods, worn out upon the trail.
> Home is the place where, when you have to go there,
> They have to take you in."

> "I should have called it
> Something you somehow haven't to deserve."

> Warren leaned out and took a step or two,
> Picked up a little stick, and brought it back
> And broke it in his hand and tossed it by.
> "Silas has better claim on us you think
> Than on his brother? Thirteen little miles
> As the road winds would bring him to his door.
> Silas has walked that far no doubt to-day.
> Why didn't he go there? His brother's rich,
> A somebody — director in the bank."

Finally, her husband (Warren) goes into the house, and she is left musing on the moon and the cloud until

> Warren returned — too soon, it seemed to her,
> Slipped to her side, caught up her hand and waited.

"Warren," she questioned.

> "Dead," was all he answered.

That is all, and yet, somehow, it is an adequate and profoundly moving story.

"The Mountain" is an eery bit of *genre* painting. The mountain, huge, dominating, remote in its austerity, is the poem:

> The mountain held the town as in a shadow
> I saw so much before I slept there once;
> I noticed that I missed stars in the west,
> Where its black body cut into the sky.
> Near me it seemed: I felt it like a wall
> Behind which I was sheltered from a wind.

And yet between the town and it I found,
When I walked forth at dawn to see new things,
Were fields, a river, and beyond, more fields.
The river at the time was fallen away,
And made a widespread brawl on cobble-stones;
But the signs showed what it had done in spring;
Good grass-land gullied out, and in the grass
Ridges of sand, and driftwood stripped of bark.
I crossed the river and swung round the mountain.

Then comes the countryman, driving an ox-team, who has "heard tell" of a brook "on the top, tip-top" which is

".   .   .   . always cold in summer, warm in winter.
One of the great sights going is to see
It steam in winter like an ox's breath,
Until the bushes all along its banks
Are inch-deep with the frosty spines and bristles —
You know the kind."

But "I never saw it." All his life he has lived at its base, but never cared to see what was above:

".   .   .   . I've always meant to go
And look myself, but you know how it is:
It doesn't seem so much to climb a mountain
You've worked around the foot of all your life.
What would I do? Go in my overalls,
With a big stick, the same as when the cows
Haven't come down to the bars at milking time?
Or with a shotgun for a stray black bear?
'Twouldn't seem real to climb for climbing it."

Then :

> He drew the oxen toward him with light touches
> Of his slim goad on nose and offside flank,
> Gave them their marching orders and was moving.

It is an amazing thing, because it is nothing and yet everything — the whole terrible inertia which has settled upon these people dwelling among the unyielding hills.

The most remarkable stories in the book are "Home Burial," "A Servant to Servants," and "The Fear," and they are also the most terrible. They are the ones which most reveal disease, the disease which starts with a sort of coma of the brain, as in the countryman of "The Mountain," and ends with complete insanity.

"Home Burial" is a ghastly indictment of the small family, only too common, alas! throughout New England. The child dies, and the loneliness, the emptiness, the horror, unsettle the mother's mind. The father has at least the healthiness of work amid the constantly changing seasons to sustain him, but the mother has only her dull round of household tasks.

HOME BURIAL

> He saw her from the bottom of the stairs
> Before she saw him.   She was starting down,
> Looking back over her shoulder at some fear.

She took a doubtful step and then undid it
To raise herself and look again.   He spoke
Advancing toward her: "What is it you see
From up there always — for I want to know."
She turned and sank upon her skirts at that,
And her face changed from terrified to dull.
He said to gain time: "What is it you see,"
Mounting until she cowered under him.
"I will find out now — you must tell me, dear."

But the wife will not tell him:

She let him look, sure that he wouldn't see,
Blind creature; and a while he didn't see.
. . . .
But at last he murmured, "Oh," and again, "Oh."

What he saw was his child's grave.   He goes on:

"The wonder is I didn't see it at once.
I never noticed it from here before.
I must be wonted to it — that's the reason.
. . . .
There are three stones of slate and one of marble,
Broad-shouldered little slabs there in the sunlight
On the sidehill.   We haven't to mind *those*.
But I understand; it is not the stones,
But the child's mound —"

"Don't, don't, don't, don't," she cried.

That cry of the woman is terrible in its stark truth.
It hurts the reader, it is as unbearable as the real

cry would have been, one wants to stop one's ears
and shut it out.   Printed words can go no farther
than this.   She says only one word, and it is not the
mere repetition which gives it its tragic force, it is
the context, the way in which the passage is worked
up to this devastating cry.   Afterwards:

> She withdrew shrinking from beneath his arm
> That rested on the banister, and slid downstairs;
> And turned on him with such a daunting look,
> He said twice over before he knew himself:
> "Can't a man speak of his own child he's lost?"

Then she bursts out:

> "Not you!   Oh, where's my hat?   Oh, I don't need it!
> I must get out of here.   I must get air.
> I don't know rightly whether any man can."

He talks to her, tries to soothe her, but everything
he says chafes the rawness of her grief:

> "Don't — don't go.
> Don't carry it to someone else this time.
> Tell me about it if it's something human.
> Let me into your grief.   I'm not so much
> Unlike other folks as your standing there
> Apart would make me out.   Give me my chance.
> I do think, though, you overdo it a little.
> What was it brought you up to think it the thing
> To take your mother-loss of a first child
> So inconsolably — in the face of love.
> You'd think his memory might be satisfied —"

"There you go sneering now!"

> "I'm not, I'm not!
> You make me angry.   I'll come down to you.
> God, what a woman!   And it's come to this,
> A man can't speak of his own child that's dead."

But she has lost all sense of values; she sees only
with the blurred vision of the partially unbal-
anced :

> "You can't because you don't know how.
> If you had any feelings, you that dug
> With your own hand — how could you? — his little grave;
> I saw you from that very window there,
> Making the gravel leap and leap in air,
> Leap up, like that, like that, and land so lightly
> And roll back down the mound beside the hole.
> I thought, Who is that man?   I didn't know you.
> And I crept down the stairs and up the stairs
> To look again, and still your spade kept lifting.
> Then you came in.   I heard your rumbling voice
> Out in the kitchen, and I don't know why,
> But I went near to see with my own eyes.
> You could sit there with the stains on your shoes
> Of the fresh earth from your own baby's grave
> And talk about your everyday concerns.
> You had stood the spade up against the wall
> Outside there in the entry, for I saw it."

He has no idea how to cope with her unreason :

> "I shall laugh the worst laugh I ever laughed.
> I'm cursed.   God, if I don't believe I'm cursed."

The woman does not spare him.   She talks on and on in a torrent of words:

> "I can repeat the very words you were saying.
> 'Three foggy mornings and one rainy day
> Will rot the best birch fence a man can build.'
> Think of it, talk like that at such a time!
> What had how long it takes a birch to rot
> To do with what was in the darkened parlour."

He holds himself in.   Gently he urges her:

> "There, you have said it all and you feel better.
> You won't go now.   You're crying.   Close the door.
> The heart's gone out of it: why keep it up.
> Amy!   There's someone coming down the road!"

But he is dealing with a force he does not understand — the insidious, creeping force of mental disease.   He cannot stop her, reason is powerless:

> .   .   .   She was opening the door wider.
> "Where do you mean to go?   First tell me that.
> I'll follow and bring you back by force.   I *will*! —"

Catholic countries, with their insistence upon consecrated ground in which to lay the dead, give no chance for horror like this.   In England, a state church makes such a situation practically

impossible. Happily it is unusual, even in New
England, but what a travesty of happiness our
vaunted freedom has led us into! The old pioneers
came here to be free, strong, God-fearing, and up-
right; and, behold, they are decayed and demoralized.
They flaunted Nature, and she has had her revenge.

"Home Burial" shows monotony and a mistaken
attitude toward life bringing on insanity. In "The
Fear," moral degeneration is leading to the same end.
A woman, who has left her husband to live with
another man, thinks she sees something in the bushes
as she and he are driving home one night:

> "I saw it just as plain as a white plate,"
>   She said, "as the light on the dashboard ran
>   Along the bushes at the roadside — a man's face.
>   You *must* have seen it too."
>
>   "I didn't see it.
>   Are you sure —"
>
>   "Yes, I'm sure!"
>
>   "— it was a face?"
>
> "Joel, I'll have to look.   I can't go in,
>   I can't, and leave a thing like that unsettled."

She takes the lantern and goes down the road,
refusing to let Joel go with her. There she comes
face to face with her first husband:

> She stood her ground against the noisy steps
> That came on, but her body rocked a little.
>
> "You see," the voice said.
>
> "Oh."   She looked and looked.
>
> "You don't see — I've a child here by the hand."
>
> "What's a child doing at this time of night —?"
>
> "Out walking.   Every child should have the memory
> Of at least one long-after-bedtime walk.
> What, son?"
>
> "Then I should think you'd try to find
> Somewhere to walk —"
>
> "The highway as it happens —
> We're stopping for the fortnight down at Dean's."
>
> "But if that's all — Joel — you realize —
> You won't think anything.   You understand?
> You understand that we have to be careful.
> This is a very, very lonely place.
> Joel!"   She spoke as if she couldn't turn.
> The swinging lantern lengthened to the ground,
> It touched, it struck it, clattered and went out.

Does he kill her, or does she merely think that he
is going to do so?   Which one is crazed, he or she?
Either way, Nature has taken her toll.

The most powerful of all these stories, and one of
the truest, is "A Servant to Servants." A farmer's
wife is talking to a camper:

"I didn't make you know how glad I was
To have you come and camp here on our land.
I promised myself to get down some day
And see the way you lived, but I don't know!
With a houseful of hungry men to feed
I guess you'd find. . . . It seems to me
I can't express my feelings any more
Than I can raise my voice or want to lift
My hand (oh, I can lift it when I have to).
Did ever you feel so? I hope you never.
It's got so I don't even know for sure
Whether I *am* glad, sorry, or anything.
There's nothing but a voice-like left inside
That seems to tell me how I ought to feel,
And would feel if I wasn't all gone wrong.
You take the lake. I look and look at it.
I see it's a fair, pretty sheet of water.
I stand and make myself repeat out loud
The advantages it has, so long and narrow,
Like a deep piece of some old running river
Cut short off at both ends. It lies five miles
Straight away through the mountain notch
From the sink window where I wash the plates,
And all our storms come up toward the house,
Drawing the slow waves whiter and whiter and whiter.
It took my mind off doughnuts and soda biscuit
To step outdoors and take the water dazzle
A sunny morning."

She has been insane once, and feels it coming on her again :

> "It's rest I want — there, I have said it out —
> From cooking meals for hungry hired men
> And washing dishes after them — from doing
> Things over and over that just won't stay done."

She tells a dreadful story of her father's mad brother kept in a cage in the barn-loft, shouting obscene words all night long :

> "He'd pull his bars apart like bow and bow-string,
> And let them go and make them twang until
> His hands had worn them smooth as any ox-bow."

Then, wearily, after the story is told, with all its undercurrent of bearing on herself :

> "Bless you, of course you're keeping me from work,
> But the thing of it is, I need to *be* kept.
> There's work enough to do — there's always that;
> But behind's behind.   The worst that you can do
> Is set me back a little more behind.
> I shan't catch up in this world, anyway.
> I'd *rather* you'd not go unless you must."

Alas, if "Home Burial" is unusual, even in New England, overworked women are not.   And the madman kept in the barn was a miserably common fact a generation ago.

These are stark stories, but they are not all so terrible as the three we have been considering.

I believe Mr. Frost intends "A Hundred Collars" to be humorous; I find it nothing except a little dull. Doubtless the timid doctor, the hotel clerk, and the tipsy, provincial reporter, with collars, size eighteen, are well drawn. So is the ugly town

> .   .   .   a place of shrieks and wandering lamps
> And cars that shock and rattle — and *one* hotel.

The poem is a laborious attempt at humour. Mr. Frost is a kindly and genial poet, but he is never either whimsical or quaint. For this reason, I find his people untrue to type in one important particular. In none of them do we find that pungency of thought or expression which is so ingrained in the New England temper. Characters and situations impress him, speech does not. It is probably for this reason that he uses no dialect in these poems. New England turns of speech would lose much of their raciness without the peculiar pronunciation which accompanies them.

Mr. Frost gives us no such delicious bits of humour as James Russell Lowell's:

> We're curus critters: Now ain't jes' the minute
> That ever fits us easy while we're in it.

or Alice Brown's: "I tried to do all I could for them that was in need. But I never lived my life with 'em, even when I was tendin' upon 'em and gettin' kind of achey trottin' up an' down stairs."

Speech like that is of the essence of New England. Picturesque words, quaintly turned to half conceal, half reveal, a solemn truth. For the New Englander's comedy borders upon tragedy; and his tragedy is expressed with a whimsicality from which the tears are never far away. Vivid, paradoxical, constantly interesting, such is New England talk, and yet Mr. Frost has ignored it absolutely. He feels the people, but he has no ear for their peculiar tongue.

It speaks marvellously for the vividness of the poet's work in other ways that it is still personal and particular with this element of local speech left out. What would J. M. Synge's plays be without the Irish idiom he employs? But in this matter, Synge's was the easier task, for Irish can be written acceptably without changing ordinary spelling, and Yankee dialect cannot. It is commonly said that an author adds many decades to his literary life, and widens his appeal at the time of writing, if he does not use dialect. I would amend that dictum by suggesting that it depends upon the author. Scott's novels are very little read, it is true, but that is less because so many of them are in dialect, as that they are all so largely mere fustian, a sort of material which is apt to become moth-eaten with time. Burns's dialect poems, on the other hand, are still much read and cherished. As it is, Mr. Frost has succeeded admirably in portraying the New England that he sees.

What he does not portray is simply what he does
not see.

He sees much, however, both into the hearts of
persons, and into the qualities of scenes. How
deftly he draws a background. Take this picture:

> We chanced in passing by that afternoon
> To catch it in a sort of mental picture
> Among tar-banded ancient cherry trees,
> Set well back from the road in rank lodged grass,
> The little cottage we are speaking of.
> A front with just a door between two windows,
> Fresh painted by the shower a velvet-black.

or this, of blueberries:

> It must be on charcoal they fatten their fruit,
> I taste in them sometimes the flavour of soot.
> And after all really they're ebony skinned:
> The blue's but a mist from the breath of the wind.
> A tarnish that goes at a touch of the hand,
> And less than the tan with which pickers are tanned.

"The Fear" begins with these lines, and we get not
only the picture, but the accompanying noises:

> A lantern light from deeper in the barn
> Shone on a man and woman in the door
> And threw their lurching shadows on a house
> Near by, all dark in every glossy window.
> A horse's hoofs pawed once the hollow floor,
> And the back of the gig they stood beside
> Moved in a little.

The creak and shift of the wheels is quite plain, although it is not indicated.

The secret of Mr. Frost's success in such passages as these, lies in his accurate observation, coupled with a perfect simplicity of phrase; the latter, an inheritance from a race brought up on the English Bible. He tells what he has seen *exactly* as he has seen it. He is never seduced into subtleties of expression which would be painfully out of place. His words are simple, straightforward, direct, manly, and there is an elemental quality in all he does which would surely be lost if he chose to pursue niceties of expression. For Mr. Frost has chosen his medium with an unerring sense of fitness. As there is no strange and explosive imaginative force playing over his subjects, so there is no exotic music pulsing through his verse.

The poems are written for the most part in blank verse, a blank verse which does not hesitate to leave out a syllable or put one in, whenever it feels like it. To the classicist, such liberties would be unendurable. But the method has its advantages. It suggests the hardness and roughness of New England granite. It is halting and maimed like the life it portrays, unyielding in substance, and broken in effect.

That Mr. Frost has justified the liberties which he has taken with an ancient and dignified metre is evident from the fact that it has hardly aroused a protest, even from the classicists. So scholarly a critic as Mr. Edward Garnett, praises Mr. Frost's style, and praises it, amusingly enough, for its very liberties. He says: "so extraordinarily close to normal everyday speech is it that I anticipate some academic person may test its metre with a metronome, and declare that the verse is often awkward in its scansion. No doubt. But so also is the blank verse of many a master hard to scan, if the academic foot-rule be not applied with a nice comprehension of where to give and when to take." I say "amusingly enough," because it is always amusing when a classicist has to shift his canons to include and justify a beauty he cannot help feeling. But what would the purists of an earlier day have thought of this blank verse? What would the reviewer who reviled Keats's iambic pentameter in the "Quarterly," have made of Mr. Frost's?

Here are a few lines taken at random from "North of Boston":

> Mary sat musing on the lamp-flame at the table.

The reader will observe that the accent falls shockingly (shockingly to that elder taste, I mean) on the second syllable of "Mary," on "on," and on "at." Here is another:

> I crossed the river and swung round the mountain.

To make this a passable iambic pentameter line, the "and" has to be stamped into place, but no one would ever really read it in that way ; the only possible way to read it is to make the line tetrameter with two iambs, followed by two anapests, the line finishing with a feminine ending :

I crossed / the riv / er and swung / round the moun / tain.

What of these two lines :

> She withdrew shrinking from beneath his arm
> That rested on the banister and slid downstairs.

The first line can be made to scan by accenting the "with" of "withdrew," but the second again is obliged to hop along on a couple of anapests to say all it has to say by the end of the line. Perhaps the worst of all is :

> Call her Nausicaa, the unafraid

in which the feet are obviously trochees not iambs, try it as iambs and listen to the result. But, in pulling these lines to pieces, I am not representing my own view. I agree with Mr. Garnett that these lapses from strict blank verse vary the lines delightfully, and give a rich and tonic effect.

In August, 1914, came the war, and on no body of people did the war have a more devastating effect than upon the poets. In the belligerent countries especially, all interest in verse other than war verse vanished for the time. England was no longer the soothing and inspiring place for literary workers that it had been. Besides, England had done its work, so far as Robert Frost was concerned. He had come to it unknown, a quasi-failure; he left it, in March, 1915, with his feet well set upon the ladder of fame.

I had preceded Mr. Frost to this country by six months, and during that time I had spoken much of "North of Boston." When Mr. Croly, of "The New Republic," asked me to write a paper, and to choose my own subject, I chose "North of Boston," then in the press of Messrs. Henry Holt and Company, but not yet issued, as that subject.

By a pleasant coincidence, Mr. Frost, whom at that time I had not met, although we had heard much of each other, ran across this review at a book-stall, as he was walking up town from the steamer after landing in New York. He has since told me that it seemed to him when he saw it that America was holding out a friendly hand to welcome him home. America's welcome was more than friendly, it was loyal and enthusiastic. The American edition of "North of Boston" ran through several printings in rapid succession.

But no success could change Mr. Frost. What did he do on returning to America? Went promptly back to his hills with the quick certainty of a homing pigeon. He might be able to live on the proceeds of his books, but he had always been a farmer, farming seemed the natural and sane order in which his life should run, so he bought a farm in Franconia, New Hampshire, and moved into it during the summer of 1915.

The next year was spent, partly in writing, a great deal in lecturing, and a very little in actual farming. And now that Mr. Frost has joined the teaching staff of Amherst College, we can see the future of the farm as an emblem rather than as a fact. He might take it as a shield, and crest it with pine-trees, for if it did not yield him a career in one way it has in another.

Now we have come to Mr. Frost's latest book, published in the Autumn of 1916, "Mountain Interval." (Mr. Frost has a rare felicity in choosing titles.) One would like to write at great length about this book. But, after all, what is there new to say? Mr. Frost is not an author of experiments and surprises. He writes as he has written, but his touch grows surer and more personal with each volume.

"Mountain Interval" is a less homogeneous book than "North of Boston." There are in it narratives, lyrics, mild bits of irony. A jumble of jottings, pages from his portfolio; excellent in kind, but each quite unrelated to the others. The lyric quality of "A Boy's Will" is here, but far more developed in expression in such poems as "Pea Brush," "An Encounter," and "The Telephone." There are three long narratives, "In the Home

Stretch," "The Hill Wife," and "Snow," but although these are technically good specimens of the
poet's manner, the subjects have neither the depth,
nor the poignancy, of those in "North of Boston."
Of the three shorter narratives, "Out, Out —"
"The Gum Gatherer," and "The Vanishing Red,"
only one, "Out, Out —" can be said to be up to
Mr. Frost's usual standard.   But this one, a horrible
story of a boy losing his hand in a steam saw, is
among the best things of its kind that he has done.
The war has registered itself slightly in two poems,
"Range-finding," and "The Bonfire." And they
are interesting as being the only published work of
Mr. Frost's in which any foreign element has dis-
turbed the restricted New Hampshire atmosphere.

On the whole, it must be admitted that in spite of
much that is beautiful, this volume will add nothing
to the poet's already fine achievement.   But neither
will it detract; it is more than adequate, it is excellent, but except in the case of the short lyrics, it is
not an advance.

Yet the book contains two poems which are among
Mr. Frost's best.   "Birches," which I quoted some
time ago, and this poem :

AN OLD MAN'S WINTER NIGHT

All out of doors looked darkly in at him
Through the thin frost, almost in separate stars,
That gathers on the pane in empty rooms.

What kept his eyes from giving back the gaze
Was the lamp tilted near them in his hand.
What kept him from remembering what it was
That brought him to that creaking room was age.
He stood with barrels round him — at a loss.
And having scared the cellar under him
In clomping there, he scared it once again
In clomping off ; — and scared the outer night,
Which has its sounds, familiar, like the roar
Of trees and crack of branches, common things,
But nothing so like beating on a box.
A light he was to no one but himself
Where now he sat, concerned with he knew what,
A quiet light, and then not even that.
He consigned to the moon, such as she was,
So late-arising, to the broken moon
As better than the sun in any case
For such a charge, his snow upon the roof,
His icicles along the wall to keep ;
And slept.   The log that shifted with a jolt
Once in the stove, disturbed him and he shifted,
And eased his heavy breathing, but still slept.
One aged man — one man — can't fill a house,
A farm, a countryside, or if he can,
It's thus he does it of a winter night.

Nowhere in Mr. Frost's work is there a finer thing
than that, in spite of the false accent in the eighteenth line.   There is sound, and sight, and suggestion, and all painting surely and reticently the tragedy
of lonely old age.   The poem is superb ; with what

it says and what it does not say. Mr. Frost is gaining in subtlety, but sometimes this subtlety ends in
the blind alley of obscurity. He is never cryptic, in
the way that Mr. Robinson is cryptic, but he sometimes ends a poem abruptly with a smile, as though
he said, "You see the end, so I won't read you the
last page." And sometimes we do not see the end,
as in "The Fear," it may be one of two ends, or,
perchance, there really is no end at all, only a perpetual continuation.

In looking back over the three volumes which
make up Mr. Frost's poetical output at present, we
ask ourselves, what place does he hold among his
contemporaries? I should say that he has gained a
success in his chosen field which can be equalled by
no other poet in our series. But his canvas is
exceedingly small, and no matter how wonderfully he
paints upon it, he cannot attain to the position held
by men with a wider range of vision. As Jane
Austen is perfect in her way, still we cannot rank
her with Shakespeare; nor can Theocritus ever be
considered as great as Homer. Mr. Frost's work is
undoubtedly more finished in its kind than the
work of any other living American poet, but this very
finish precludes growth. In some other poets we
feel potentialities, in Mr. Frost we find achievement.

Mr. Robinson represents realism; with a much
broader imagination than Mr. Frost, this force is
nevertheless held in check by an innate pessimism

which makes the real seem important and the visions of imagination almost frivolous. Mr. Frost is realism touched to fire by idealization, but in the final count, and in spite of its great beauty, it remains realism. We have no such rare imaginative bursts from him as Mr. Masefield gives us time and again in "The Dauber"; for instance, the description of the flying fishes.

Mr. Frost writes down *exactly* what he sees. But, being a true poet, he sees it vividly and with a charm which translates itself into a beautiful simplicity of expression. He is an eminently sympathetic poet. He wins first by his gentle understanding, and his strong and unsentimental power of emotion; later, we are conquered by his force, and moved to admiration by his almost unapproachable technique. Still, his imagination is bounded by his life, he is confined within the limits of his experience (or at least what might have been his experience) and bent all one way like the wind-blown trees of New England hillsides. After all, art is rooted in the soil, and only the very greatest men can be both cosmopolitan and great. Mr. Frost is as New England as Burns is Scotch, Synge Irish, or Mistral Provençal, and it is perhaps not too much to say that he is the equal of these poets, and will so rank to future generations.

Edgar Lee Masters

EDGAR LEE MASTERS
AND
CARL SANDBURG

EDGAR LEE MASTERS

AND

CARL SANDBURG

MR. MASTERS is the author of a number of books, but one has made his fame; and it seems probable that only one will outlive the destructive work of time. But this one is so remarkable that it may very well come to be considered among the great books of American literature. I refer, of course, to "The Spoon River Anthology." I think it is not too much to say that no book, in the memory of the present generation, has had such a general effect upon the reading community as has this. Every one who reads at all has read it. Its admirers are not confined to those who like poetry, people who have never cared for a poem before are enthusiastic over "Spoon River," while professed poetry lovers stand, some aghast and some delighted, but all interested and amazed. Even its enemies admit it to be extraordinary. It has been characterized as an American "Comédie Humaine," but I think Dostoevsky in *vers libre* would be more accurate. Mr. Masters' habit of thought is more akin to the Russian than to the French.   In fact, Mr. Masters is in some ways closer to the Swede, August Strindberg, than to any other modern writer.

Of course, analogies of this kind must not be pushed too far.   If Mr. Masters resembles Balzac in the fecundity he shows in inventing characters and lives to fit them, he is also like Strindberg in showing only a narrow stratum of society.   If he is like Balzac in confining his *mise en scène* in a small compass, he is again like Strindberg in being primarily interested in one important phase of life — that of sex.   Balzac was no poet, but he realized that man is impelled by many motives; in Strindberg, the actions of the characters are all dependent upon their sex impulses.   Mr. Masters is a poet, but he too sees life through the medium of sex.   Perhaps no author writing in America to-day shows more clearly the breaking down of an old tradition, the effect on the Anglo-Saxon mind of much contact with the minds of other peoples.

In Mr. Robinson and Mr. Frost, we saw the breaking down of tradition, but in both poets the traditional racial characteristics remained unaltered; in Mr. Masters, tradition is not only breaking, but broken, and the racial type is quite altered.

All racial changes begin by a disappearance, a slow fading of the fundamental beliefs upon which that particular civilization was reared, but the results of these beliefs still retain their hold upon the people brought up in them. The next step finds the beliefs so much a thing of the past that they have no power to mould character, and the result, for the moment, is a sort of mental chaos, in which cynicism becomes a dominant attitude, in many cases ending in downright despair. The third stage is that in which the change is so complete that it no longer requires to be considered as such at all. The old tradition has passed into the line of history, and departure from it is the rule not the exception. Men have reared new beliefs, are living upon other planes of thought, and that being for the moment settled, they are able to turn their attention to other things, for instance: Beauty.

In the first stage, beauty is a thing remembered and haunting; in the third stage, it is re-discovered and intoxicating; but in the second, it is crowded out by the stress of travail, by the pangs of a birth which has not yet occurred.

The truth is that America is in the making, and as poets are the articulate part of a community, we see this change very clearly in the work of the modern poets. If this is a true poetical "movement," as I believe it to be, it is so because of the basic changes going on in the poets themselves, and to a lesser degree in the large body of the people. What the American nation will eventually be, none of us living in this moment of flux can possibly foretell.

But there appear in the work of a few of our poets hints of a new beauty, a differing religious concept, which may herald the slow approach of the third stage. That third stage, that era of accomplishment which will endure until another "movement" shakes the world again and mankind takes another step on its eternal path.

I have said that Mr. Robinson and Mr. Frost represent various things in the "new movement" — Realism, Direct Speech, Simplicity, and the like. They represent also the first stage of the progression I have been analyzing. Mr. Masters, who also stands for other things as well, embodies the second stage. I have put him and Mr. Sandburg together principally for that reason, although they have other points of contact besides this one. We may regard the work of these two poets as being the most revolutionary that America has yet produced. And here I want to make the distinction between "revolutionary" and "evolutionary."

Evolution is growing into, revolution is violently and consciously opposing something in order to bring about something else. In my last chapter, I shall speak of two poets who may properly be said to be entering upon the last stage of this "movement," and whose work may very well be called evolutionary.

Of course, this dividing a movement into sections has nothing to do with the merit of the individual poets, but a consideration of it as a whole helps us to understand its reasons for being, and, through it, the work of the poets who make it.

Edgar Lee Masters was born at Garnet, Kansas, on August 23, 1869, where his father, who had been admitted to the bar shortly before that date, was practising law.

The Masters family is said to have come to Massachusetts from England in the seventeenth century, one branch going to Nova Scotia and one to Virginia. The poet is descended from the Virginia branch, his great-great-grandfather, Hillary Masters, being a soldier in the Continental Army during the Revolution, mustered in from Wythe County, Virginia.

At what period the family, or a part of it, moved from Virginia to Tennessee is not recorded. But Davis Masters, a grandson of the Revolutionary soldier, was born in the latter state, where he married a certain Lucinda Young, the grand-daughter of another Revolutionary soldier from North Carolina. These two migrated into Illinois during the 'twenties of the last century, and settled first in Morgan County, where their son, the poet's father, Hardin Wallace Masters, was born, and later in Menard County, living there to the advanced ages of ninety-two and ninety-six, respectively.

It will be seen that the poet comes of a sturdy stock and a pioneering one. A stock which has been moving ever Westward, to newer, cruder, freer lands. From Massachusetts to Virginia, from Virginia to Tennessee, from Tennessee to Illinois. For two centuries, the exodus continued. Never resting, never staying, a forceful folk, one not afraid of hard work, and yet, curiously enough, unable to strike its roots into any soil deep enough to have it hold them for long. One can see this race, developing those rugged qualities needed to cope with a nature still unsubdued; harsh, powerful, perpetually resisting conditions, always dominating them, but not quite enough to deaden the lure of new and farther places just beyond the horizon.

On his mother's side, Mr. Masters also inherits the tradition of force. For his mother is of the narrow, stern, bigotedly religious folk who still linger in New England, particularly in the rural districts. A fine people, with high moral qualities, as I have pointed out in my chapters on Mr. Robinson and Mr. Frost, but more strong than graceful, more firm than widely comprehending. Her father, the Reverend Deming S. Dexter, was a Methodist minister in the town of Marlborough, New Hampshire. He died in 1870. His wife, Jerusha, was a descendant of the long line of Putnams, whose name appears so often and so variously in the pages of New England history — gloriously, in the case of General Israel Putnam, of the Battle of Bunker Hill; with sinister import, when we speak of Anne Putnam, who, with her father and mother, was chiefly responsible for the outbreak of witchcraft at Salem.

Where Mr. Hardin Masters met his wife, I do not know, possibly she was one of that series of New England school-mistresses who gave their lives to educate the West. At any rate, the poet says that he never saw either of his maternal grand-parents.

Mr. Davis Masters, a true agricultural pioneer, looked somewhat askance at his son's passion for the law. He wished him to be a farmer. He, himself, had found prosperity in the rich farm lands of Illinois, and he wanted his son to follow in his footsteps. For a time he prevailed, and when the poet was a year old his parents left Garnet and returned to the homestead in Illinois.

Mr. Masters tells us that this old house is his earliest memory. Dim recollections of it rise in his mind from a time when he can scarcely be supposed to remember at all. He has a vision of a sofa upon which a woman is lying. An aunt of his was ill for seven years, and he was often taken to her in his grandmother's arms, but whether he really remembers this, or has visualized a later knowledge, it is impossible to say. Another recollection, and a much clearer one, is of sitting in his mother's lap in a fence corner and watching windrows of corn-stalks ablaze, as they were lit, one after another, by his father.

Some two years after his parents' return to Illinois, Mr. Davis Masters bought a farm for his son, hoping by so doing to remove him forever from politics and

the law.   But natural bents are often too strong for
paternal regulation.   Mr. Hardin Masters was
elected State Attorney, and he and his family
moved to Petersburg.   Here it was that Edgar Lee
Masters began to go to school.   His grandfather's
farm was only six miles from the town, and he
spent much time there, riding horses, fishing, working in the garden, and burrowing in old chests of
books stored away in the garret, a place which he
had christened "The Dark Ages."   The pioneers of
this country were anything but uneducated people.
They were not peasants in the countries from which
they came, but God-fearing, middle-class folk,
brought up on the English Bible and "Pilgrim's
Progress."   When we remember that one of the
first things they did in this new country was to
found a college, we can see what temper of men they
were.   As they moved Westward, their small and
carefully hoarded stock of books was packed with
the household goods for reading during the long
Winter evenings when there was nothing else to do.
The facile amusements and the cheap printing of the
present day are responsible for many things; among
others, the deterioration of literary taste.

There were many books in "The Dark Ages" —
Scott, Dickens, Tennyson, Moore — and the boy
read them all with the omnivorous appetite of
youth.   This early reading does more to form a
writer's style than anything else in the world.

No matter how individual he may become, contact with "the best that has been thought and said in the world" gives him a command of language that later study can never bestow.   Mr. Masters says that his grandfather spoke "with a patriarchal eloquence at once clear, vigorous, and charming," and that "both in speech and in writing he had formed himself upon the Bible."

When he was eleven years old, the boy was taken from the public schools and sent for a short time to a private German school.   He was not there long enough to acquire more than a slight reading acquaintance with the German language, and certainly not long enough to gain the Teutonic virtues of method and thoroughness.   With his particular characteristics, it is certain that the Teutonic was the last influence under which Mr. Masters should have come. He needed clarity, taste, and delicacy, and none of these are German traits.   In fact, these particular things have never been a part of Mr. Masters' schooling.   So little indeed, that he does not seem to recognize his lack of them.

Before long, his father moved to Lewiston, and the boy experienced his first radical change of atmosphere.   Lewiston was fifty miles from his grandfather's farm, and had it not been for periodic attacks of illness, the little boy would probably have been cut off entirely from farm life.   As it was, however, he made long visits there every Spring, and

so constantly renewed his acquaintance with fields
and woods, and the kindly activities of farm life.

When Mr. Masters was about fourteen years old,
there came to Lewiston as assistant to the Principal
of the High School a certain Mary Fisher. This
lady, who in later life wrote some books of local
fame, had come in contact, through a friend, with
the activities of that group of New England women of
which Louisa May Alcott was one. It was a rather
washed-out and faded intellectual atmosphere, but
to the young Western woman it seemed like the
very Elixir of Life, and turned her interests definitely
to literature. So ardent was she in the cause that
she succeeded in imbuing her pupils with the same
ardour. She was only in Lewiston a year, but during that year she planted the love of literature
definitely in the heart of Edgar Lee Masters. Before
that, he had been a careless student, now he began
to read in earnest. At first it was a desultory reading,
but three years later he suddenly braced himself for
effort and worked hard to finish his High School
course.

Like so many boys, he found the mechanical art of
printing attractive, and he had almost learnt the
printer's trade before he was fourteen. At seventeen,
he graduated from the High School and took up
printing for a time, writing also for the local papers,
corresponding for Chicago, Peoria, and St. Louis
papers, writing poetry, essays, and short stories;

for the reading was bearing fruit, that abortive fruit, withered before it is ripe, which wrecks so many clever youths.

It is hardly necessary here to recapitulate the truism that our educational systems in America do not educate. And this is particularly true of our High Schools. A smattering of many subjects is not education, and Edgar Masters' mind at this juncture was a lamentable jumble of smatterings. It was like a Christmas tree, hung with bits of tinsel in unrelated splotches. To a certain extent, this is true of the poet of to-day. His mind glitters, but it is without cohesion.

Mr. Hardin Masters regarded these literary activities with anything but a sympathetic eye. "This newspaper work," as he called it, would not do. On general principles he was right, for journalism is seldom the portal to literature. An embryonic author had better spend his days in selling buttons than in writing down to popular taste. How could Mr. Masters, senior, know that he was dealing with a genius, whose mental processes must not be interfered with. No such prophetic vision was vouchsafed to the clever lawyer so sure of his prominence in the little growing town. Following his own father's example, he wished to rule the destinies of his son. He was trying to snatch this son from literature and make a lawyer of him, as his father had tried to snatch him from the law and turn him into a

farmer.   But the Masters family is a race of individ-
ualists; they must be what the gods decide.   Mr.
Hardin Masters was partly successful, but the gods
have won the ultimate game, for they have simply
turned his desires to their own ends.

So Edgar Lee Masters started to read Blackstone
and other law books, without, however, giving up
his reading in other fields and his constant scribbling.
At nineteen, he took up the study of Latin, but did
not abandon his law; in fact, he was now well embarked on the dual career of letters and law which he
has pursued ever since.

Other artists have followed two professions, apparently without detriment to either.   Henry Fielding
was an eminent lawyer and judge; Chaucer was a
county magistrate; Shakespeare was a hack play-
wright and actor in a stock company; one Russian
composer, Borodine, was an eminent physician,
director of a hospital, and author of a monumental
work on chemistry; another, Rimsky-Korsakov, was
an officer in the Russian navy.   One could go on for
long multiplying these examples.   Doubtless, it is
always difficult to follow two vocations at the same
time.   It requires a doubly rounded talent, and a
profound habit of concentration.

Now concentration is one of the chief things which
American educational systems do not inculcate.
Mr. Masters' note-books of this period show that
he was an enthusiastic reader, but the soil had not

been properly tilled in which the seed was dropped. Facts! — the young man's mind was stored with facts. But the facts settled into no systematic order, they connoted only themselves and not their places in a general scheme. First one study attracted him, then another, but each was followed for its own sake, not for its bearing upon the whole.

It is hard for a young man to learn by himself, with no wise and mellow guidance to keep a chosen end constantly before him. Few people are born with so decided a bent that they must pursue it without excursions hither and yon. Other systems than our American one temper knowledge with counsel, with the experience of men who have gone before. But where was Edgar Lee Masters to find such counsel and such experience? His teachers were almost as crude as himself, men who had mastered their subjects and that was all. Legal advice and experience he could get, but a legal advice which gave no consideration to his literary aspirations. His early life is a record of wandering. First he would follow one road, then he would retrace his steps and go down another, only to cut across country back to the first, to leave that again farther on, jump over a stone wall, and regain the second. It was inevitable; and if the direction at times seemed lost, that was illusion. It was a steady progress, although a slow and meandering one.

When Mr. Masters was twenty-one, the literary impulse asserted itself too strongly to be denied, and his father consented to send him to Knox College for a year. Here he took up Greek, continued his Latin, and resumed the German abandoned so many years before. But how much of anything can one learn in a year? Probably the libraries did more for the poet than the class-rooms, for he read the Greek dramatists, Homer, Virgil, Goethe, and also dipped into philosophy and criticism.

Had Mr. Masters been an English lad, a French, a German, all these studies would probably have had constructive results. But in the West, at that date, they made themselves chiefly evident by a vague unrest. They set the poet apart from his fellows, and engendered a questioning, carping habit of mind. They set his feet on the road to adventure, and lured him along a path of unrelieved monotony.

At the end of one year, Mr. Masters returned to Lewiston, resumed his law studies, and was admitted to the bar. For a year he practised with his father, then circumstances impelled him to seek his fortune in Chicago. The chief of these was the terrible monotony I have mentioned. In his own words, "the pathos of the country depressed my imagination indescribably."

A poet feeds on beauty as a plant feeds on air. To see the beauty, to grasp the epic meaning, of our small Western cities requires maturity and a life spent in sympathetic observation. The poet must himself provide the touchstone which will fuse the crude elements into a plastic and symbolic whole. The author of "Spoon River" has done this more completely than any other living man. But it was years yet before such a thing could be. In the mean time, he thirsted for colour, for music, for joy, and could find them nowhere about him. Background means much to a poet, and here there was no background, suitable to the moment, that is.

I believe that this struggle, this constant warring of a spirit in pain, has left its lasting mark upon the poet. The ugliness, the bitterness, the materialism, with which he believed himself surrounded, have been burnt into his soul, so that now he gives them out perforce. There are hints of beauty in his poems, but they are almost smothered under other things. Here is strength, vigour, vividness; here, too, is coarseness, brutality, cynicism; here is compelling originality; but of the subtle forces of artistic balance, penetrating sensibility, beauty of form and syllable, suggestion, there is scarcely a trace.

What is strange about this, however, is that while circumstances were forcing him one way, it was in quite another that he would have progressed if he could. Speaking of what turned his thoughts to poetry, he has said : "It was music running through my brain, my first passion was Burns and afterwards Shelley."

He knew what he needed, longed for it, hungered for it, and because he did not get it at that time, his poetry will probably always be without it.

Is this a fault? In his verse, I hardly think so. I am inclined to doubt if his poetry would have the same stark reality were the form more mellifluous and suave. Whitman, too, was portraying a pioneer civilization, and he found a free, almost rough, rhythmical prose the best instrument to his purpose. One can hardly figure that a statuette of a back-woodsman cut in jade would have a happy effect. Possibly this is the reason that so many poets who have attempted to write of the West in the old forms have failed. I only say "perhaps," for in the hands of genius form is plastic; but it is also a sign of genius to know what form intrinsically fits the subject in hand. Mr. Masters has expressed this idea in a somewhat exaggerated manner in his "Petit, the Poet." The exaggeration lies in the fact that Petit is not a poet, but a poetaster; it is true criticism, nevertheless.

PETIT, THE POET

Seeds in a dry pod, tick, tick, tick,
Tick, tick, tick, like mites in a quarrel —
Faint iambics that the full breeze wakens —
But the pine tree makes a symphony thereof.
Triolets, villanelles, rondels, rondeaus,
Ballades by the score with the same old thought:
The snows and the roses of yesterday are vanished;

And what is love but a rose that fades?
Life all around me here in the village:
Tragedy, comedy, valor and truth,
Courage, constancy, heroism, failure —
All in the loom, and oh what patterns!
Woodlands, meadows, streams and rivers —
Blind to all of it all my life long.
Triolets, villanelles, rondels, rondeaus,
Seeds in a dry pod, tick, tick, tick,
Tick, tick, tick, what little iambics,
While Homer and Whitman roared in the pines?

At the time Mr. Masters went to Chicago he had already written about four hundred poems. These were, to quote their author once more, "the products of moods, psychic states, attempts to reproduce music, or interpret the moods produced by music. More poems came to me as sounds. Sometimes as vision, but mostly as sound. The idea was negligible. I was working under the influence of Poe, Shelley, Keats: sometimes as to nature poems, looking to Theocritus. I wrote many sonnets and many vague things in the music of Swinburne."

Four hundred poems before one is twenty-three is certainly a goodly count, but like all the products of immature fecundity they were abortive. The poet had not found himself, and it was to be more than twenty years before he did so. Meanwhile, this failure to be what he desired threw him into a sort of spiritual despair. He was in rebellion because he had not been able to control his career, to finish his college course, to pursue his literary studies without interruption.

He wanted to be a writer, but, after all, what was there in writing? He must live, and writing is not well paid until one has already made a success at it. He was a lawyer, he could practise law and still write. He could pursue two careers, constantly chafing at the one which supported him, constantly failing at the one upon which his heart was set. Meanwhile, the law upheld him and he prospered at it, which added the gall of irony to an already embittered situation.

In 1895, he wrote a blank verse play on Benedict Arnold, and, in 1898, he selected some sixty poems out of his four hundred and published them through the firm of Way and Williams in Chicago. Neither the poems nor the play attracted any attention. Truth to tell, they did not deserve it, and their complete failure served to throw Mr. Masters back on his law with an increased interest. He could be a good lawyer; he was a good lawyer; and for a time he put all his energies into that scale, working with unsparing industry.

About this time, the poet married, and shortly after entered the political arena. The campaign of 1896 stirred him deeply; the campaign of 1900 had a still greater effect, and, in 1911, he published a volume of political essays.

But the love of literature was not dead, merely overlaid. In 1902, he had printed another play in verse, "Maximilian," which, having no better success than "Benedict Arnold," decided him to try his hand at prose drama, and, with his usual fecundity, he promptly wrote eight prose plays, hoping by their production to make enough money to settle down and devote himself entirely to literature. But none of the eight succeeded in winning a hearing. Also, three little volumes of poems, published under pseudonyms in 1905, 1910, and 1912, respectively, met with no better reception. Certainly, whom the gods love, they first chastise.

It is cruel to have to admit that these set-backs were Mr. Masters' fault as well as his misfortune. They were the result of the unrelated, uncritical temper of his mind. He had not found himself, had not realized wherein lay his real power. Seeing a world before him in which no single thing had hardened to a certainty, a world of flux and recoil, a world of experiments and change, he gave to his environment, drifted, returned, floated hither and thither, his feet striking only the hard ground of politics and law as a support. For want of a better resting place they stuck there and gradually the poet's head lifted above the waters, gradually he came to himself, and so standing, set himself to solidify, to order, the chaos about him.

A poet's method of ordering a thing is to throw a

strong light upon it.   To fling it into relief, so that, being seen, it may be attacked and altered, or cherished and protected, as the case may be.   A revolutionary poet, a poet bent upon revaluing the civilization in which he finds himself, has no stronger weapon than this glare of vivid words.   Mr. Masters is a revolutionary poet, he has been caught in the sociological wave which has been sweeping over the world of late years.   Without any definite idea of how a better state of things is to be brought about, he nevertheless ardently desires one.   He has infinite sympathy for the cramped, monotonous lives of ugly little towns.   But he sees them through a bitter mist; misery can cramp souls as well as bodies, and if it sometimes has the opposite effect of ennobling them, this Mr. Masters is in too great a haste to see. His is not a vision to note *nuances*, he sees things broadly, flatly, but he sees them with extraordinary precision and clarity.

Constantly failing, constantly persisting, Mr. Masters' literary life is one long record of indomitable pluck.   And all the time, through early associations, through his law practice, through his political encounters, he was laying aside the material out of which his real work was to be fashioned.

While Mr. Masters continued to imitate the forms, and to a certain extent the thoughts, of the older poets, his writing was negligible, he seemed unable to express even a small part of what was in him.   But a release was in sight. Mr. Masters belongs among those poets who take their forms ready made, merely adapting them slightly to ease the thought they are to contain. This fact is no aspersion on a poet's genius. Shakespeare belonged to this class. Indeed, it is doubtful if poetical experimenters ever bring their experiments to the finest flowering. They widen possibilities, but the ultimate beauty of their aim lies in other hands.

In 1911, Miss Harriet Monroe, of Chicago, a cultivated woman, a poet and a writer on art, conceived the idea of starting a poetry magazine. Faith will move mountains, and Miss Monroe's undaunted enthusiasm promptly secured a list of guarantors, and a fund was raised to endow such a periodical for five years. The first number was issued in October, 1912, and so "Poetry, A Magazine of Verse," came into being. From the first, Miss Monroe's object was to give a hearing to young poets, to open the door to sincere experimenters. It was to be a forum in which youth could thrash out its ideas, and succeed or fail according to its deserts, unhampered by the damp blanket of obscurity.

The *vers libre* movement was then in its infancy; a number of poets were experimenting with this form, but very little that they did had yet been published. The older established magazines always look askance upon anything new, and the whole new movement with which we are dealing in this

book was seething for years beneath the surface
before such periodicals took cognizance of its being.
There is nothing unusual in such a state of things, but
it makes Miss Monroe's magazine all the more important. "Poetry" did not bring about the movement,
it happened on a lucky wave of time, that is all.
But it undoubtedly did bring the movement to recognition some years earlier than would otherwise have
been the case. Poets are not sporadic outbursts,
they are the results of obscure causes. The same
causes which produced the poets, produced Miss
Monroe and her magazine.

I shall go into this subject more at length in the
next essay on the Imagists. Here I only wish to
point out that "Poetry" published many *vers libre*
poems during the first years of its existence, and Mr.
Masters has often said that it was these poems which
opened for him the way to "Spoon River." In
fact, they gave him the clue to just what he needed —
freedom from the too patterned effects of rhyme
and metre, brevity, and conciseness. Such a form
seemed absolutely made for his purpose. Substance he had never lacked, fitting his substance to
these short, sharp lines gave him a perfect instrument.

What suggested the idea of the anthology, I do
not know, possibly he took it from the "Greek
Anthology"; I shall show later how analogous much
of "Spoon River" is to that famous volume. The

idea of epitaphs grew naturally out of the succinct brevity of the form, much in little, and in this very brevity Mr. Masters has found his happiest expression. Of course, a *vers libre* poem is not necessarily short, it may or may not be, as the author chooses. But the first poems in this form published by "Poetry" happened to be so, and that was fortunate for Mr. Masters. Had he attempted long poems in this medium in the beginning, I fear he would have wrecked "Spoon River" at the start. He has written many long *vers libre* poems since, but none of them has attained the rounded strength of the shorter, earlier pieces.

For many years, Mr. Masters had been sending work to "Reedy's Mirror," St. Louis. Now, in 1914, he sent a batch of these new attempts. The editor, Mr. William Marion Reedy, at once detected the rugged, vigorous note in them. For a whole year he published them, a few in each number, and with each number they attracted more and more attention.

At the end of the year, Mr. Masters collected them in a volume, entitled "The Spoon River Anthology," which was published by The Macmillan Company in April, 1915. The *furore* with which the book was received is unprecedented in the annals of American poetry. It went into edition after edition in a few months. Mr. Masters was hailed as the successor to Walt Whitman, as the creator of a purely

American verse. Fame had come at last, after all the years in which the poet had assiduously courted her.

Spoon River purports to be a small town in the Middle West. It is said that Hanover, Illinois, served as its prototype. The poems are supposed to be the epitaphs in the cemetery of this town. Or rather, it is as if its dead denizens arose, and each speaking the truth, perforce, revealed his own life exactly as it had been, and the real cause of his death. When I add that there are two hundred and fourteen of these people, we can see what a colossal study of character the book is. The mere inventing of two hundred and fourteen names is a staggering feat. How many names Balzac invented, or Scott, or Shakespeare, or Molière, I have not an idea, but the work of these men extended over a lifetime; Mr. Masters' two hundred and fourteen were all collected in one year.

The quality of the book already stands revealed in these names. They are uncompromising in their realism; hard, crude, completely local. Mr. Masters permits himself no subterfuges with fact. He throws no glamour over his creations. We hear of no Flammondes, no Bokardos, instead are Hannah Armstrong, Archibald Higbie, Bert Killion, Faith Matheny, Jennie M'Grew, Reuben Pantier, Albert Schirding, George Trimble, Oaks Tutt, Zenas Witt, and a host of others. What are these names?

Some are Anglo-Saxon, some are clearly German; one, "Russian Sonia," tells of an origin, if not distinctly national, at least distinctly cosmopolitan; another, "Yee Bow," is as obviously Chinese.

We do not find German, French, Chinese names in Mr. Frost's books. Here, therefore, at once, in the table of contents, we are confronted with the piquant realism of locality. The highest art is undeniably that which comprises the farthest flights of imagination, but next to that, the most satisfying is the one which holds within it the pungency of place, undiluted. John M. Synge combines the two to a remarkable extent, it is true, but without this local tang his imagination would not have been strong enough to have sustained him; and what would Burns have been without Scotland, or Theocritus without Sicily?

I dwelt upon this at some length when we were dealing with the New England of Mr. Frost. But the difference between Mr. Frost and Mr. Masters is not only that they write about different parts of the country, it is a profound divergence of points of view. Mr. Frost, as I said before, belongs to the first stage of the "new movement"; Mr. Masters to the second. Mr. Frost records with quiet sympathy; Mr. Masters is mordant and denunciatory. Mr. Frost is resigned, smilingly thinking resistance futile; Mr. Masters resists with every fibre of his being. Mr. Frost's work gives us the effect of a constant withdrawal; Mr. Masters' of a constant pushing forward.

"Spoon River" is a volume which should be read from the first page to the last. (Always excepting the final poem, "The Spooniad," a dreary effusion, which fits but slightly into the general scheme, and should never have been included.) No idea of its breadth and variety can be gained from fragmentary quotations. Each poem is a character, and as the characters multiply, the whole town is gradually built up before us. Other authors have given us characters, other authors have given us cross-sections of a community. But in most books we have a set of primary characters, and the others are forced more or less into the background by the exigencies of the case. We see the life from this or that angle, we do not get it entire.

In "Spoon River," there are no primary characters, no secondary characters. We have only a town and the people who inhabit it. The Chinese laundry-man is as important to himself as the State's Attorney is to himself. None are forced back to give others prominence, but all together make the town.

Here are four poems. Three are of a family, and the fourth of the school-teacher who taught the son. The teacher, Emily Sparks, is one of the few fine characters in the book, fine without being at the same time foolish.

BENJAMIN PANTIER

Together in this grave lie Benjamin Pantier, attorney at law,
And Nig, his dog, constant companion, solace and friend.
Down the gray road, friends, children, men and women,
Passing one by one out of life, left me till I was alone
With Nig for partner, bed-fellow, comrade in drink.
In the morning of life I knew aspiration and saw glory.
Then she, who survives me, snared my soul
With a snare which bled me to death,
Till I, once strong of will, lay broken, indifferent,
Living with Nig in a room back of a dingy office.
Under my jaw-bone is snuggled the bony nose of Nig —
Our story is lost in silence.   Go by, mad world!

MRS. BENJAMIN PANTIER

I know that he told that I snared his soul
With a snare which bled him to death.
And all the men loved him,
And most of the women pitied him.
But suppose you are really a lady, and have delicate tastes,
And loathe the smell of whiskey and onions.
And the rhythm of Wordsworth's "Ode" runs in your ears,
While he goes about from morning till night
Repeating bits of that common thing;
"Oh, why should the spirit of mortal be proud?"
And then, suppose;
You are a woman well endowed,
And the only man with whom the law and morality
Permit you to have the marital relation

Is the very man that fills you with disgust
Every time you think of it — while you think of it
Every time you see him?
That's why I drove him away from home
To live with his dog in a dingy room
Back of his office.

REUBEN PANTIER

Well, Emily Sparks, your prayers were not wasted,
Your love was not all in vain.
I owe whatever I was in life
To your hope that would not give me up,
To your love that saw me still as good.
Dear Emily Sparks, let me tell you the story.
I pass the effect of my father and mother;
The milliner's daughter made me trouble
And out I went in the world,
Where I passed through every peril known
Of wine and women and joy of life.
One night, in a room in the Rue de Rivoli,
I was drinking wine with a black-eyed cocotte,
And the tears swam into my eyes.
She thought they were amorous tears and smiled
For thought of her conquest over me.
But my soul was three thousand miles away,
In the days when you taught me in Spoon River.
And just because you no more could love me,
Nor pray for me, nor write me letters,
The eternal silence of you spoke instead.
And the black-eyed cocotte took the tears for hers,

As well as the deceiving kisses I gave her.
Somehow, from that hour, I had a new vision —
Dear Emily Sparks!

EMILY SPARKS

Where is my boy, my boy —
In what far part of the world?
The boy I loved the best of all in the school? —
I, the teacher, the old maid, the virgin heart,
Who made them all my children.
Did I know my boy aright,
Thinking of him as spirit aflame,
Active, ever aspiring?
Oh, boy, boy, for whom I prayed and prayed
In many a watchful hour at night,
Do you remember the letter I wrote you
Of the beautiful love of Christ?
And whether you ever took it or not,
My boy, wherever you are,
Work for your soul's sake,
That all the clay of you, all the dross of you,
May yield to the fire of you,
Till the fire is nothing but light! . . .
Nothing but light!

Nowhere in the book is the wearing of one character upon another better described than in those four poems.

Mr. Masters constantly shows up the irony of hypocrisy, as in

NICHOLAS BINDLE

Were you not ashamed, fellow citizens,
When my estate was probated and everyone knew
How small a fortune I left? —
You who hounded me in life,
To give, give, give to the churches, to the poor,
To the village! — me who had already given much.
And think you I did not know
That the pipe-organ, which I gave to the church,
Played its christening songs when Deacon Rhodes,
Who broke the bank and all but ruined me,
Worshipped for the first time after his acquittal?

But there is another kind of irony, more subtle, more penetrating. Mr. Masters seldom attains to it, only rarely does he perceive the force of suggestion, as a rule he is downright and static. But in "Sam Hookey," suggestion is beautifully handled. Little is said; all is implied:

SAM HOOKEY

I ran away from home with the circus,
Having fallen in love with Mademoiselle Estralada,
The lion tamer.
One time, having starved the lions
For more than a day,
I entered the cage and began to beat Brutus
And Leo and Gypsy.
Whereupon Brutus sprang upon me,

And killed me.
On entering these regions
I met a shadow who cursed me,
And said it served me right . . .
It was Robespierre!

It is true, as has been said, that Mr. Masters sees life from the standpoint of the novelist. The material which the novelist spreads out and amplifies is condensed to its essence in these vignettes of a few lines. In them, Mr. Masters gives us background, character, and the inevitable approach of inexorable Fate:

COONEY POTTER

I inherited forty acres from my Father
And, by working my wife, my two sons and two daughters
From dawn to dusk, I acquired
A thousand acres.   But not content,
Wishing to own two thousand acres,
I bustled through the years with axe and plow,
Toiling, denying myself, my wife, my sons, my daughters.
Squire Higbee wrongs me to say
That I died from smoking Red Eagle cigars.
Eating hot pie and gulping coffee
During the scorching hours of harvest time
Brought me here ere I had reached my sixtieth year.

This same approach of Fate in a higher sphere, a mental rather than a physical tragedy, appears in "George Gray":

GEORGE GRAY

I have studied many times
The marble which was chiseled for me —
A boat with a furled sail at rest in a harbor.
In truth it pictures not my destination
But my life.
For love was offered me and I shrank from its disillusionment;
Sorrow knocked at my door, but I was afraid;
Ambition called to me, but I dreaded the chances.
Yet all the while I hungered for meaning in my life.
And now I know that we must lift the sail
And catch the winds of destiny
Wherever they drive the boat.
To put meaning in one's life may end in madness,
But life without meaning is the torture
Of restlessness and vague desire —
It is a boat longing for the sea and yet afraid.

Mr. Masters has humour of a kind, a robust and rather brutal kind, it must be admitted, but still the quality is there. The humour of juxtaposition is well, if sardonically, handled in this little sketch.

A. D. BLOOD

If you in the village think that my work was a good one,
Who closed the saloons and stopped all playing at cards,
And haled old Daisy Fraser before Justice Arnett,
In many a crusade to purge the people of sin;
Why do you let the milliner's daughter Dora,

And the worthless son of Benjamin Pantier,
Nightly make my grave their unholy pillow?

Here is another juxtaposition spread over two poems:

ALBERT SCHIRDING

Jonas Keene thought his lot a hard one
Because his children were all failures.
But I know of a fate more trying than that:
It is to be a failure while your children are successes.
For I raised a brood of eagles
Who flew away at last, leaving me
A crow on the abandoned bough.
Then, with the ambition to prefix Honorable to my name,
And thus to win my children's admiration,
I ran for County Superintendent of Schools,
Spending my accumulations to win — and lost.
That fall my daughter received first prize in Paris
For her picture, entitled, "The Old Mill" —
(It was of the water mill before Henry Wilking put in steam)
The feeling that I was not worthy of her finished me.

JONAS KEENE

Why did Albert Schirding kill himself
Trying to be County Superintendent of Schools,
Blest as he was with the means of life
And wonderful children, bringing him honor
Ere he was sixty?
If even one of my boys could have run a news-stand,
Or one of my girls could have married a decent man,

I should not have walked in the rain
And jumped into bed with clothes all wet,
Refusing medical aid.

The following studies are tragedy looking out
through a horrible, grinning mask:

ELSA WERTMAN

I was a peasant girl from Germany,
Blue-eyed, rosy, happy and strong.
And the first place I worked was at Thomas Greene's.
On a summer's day when she was away
He stole into the kitchen and took me
Right in his arms and kissed me on my throat,
I turning my head.   Then neither of us
Seemed to know what happened.
And I cried for what would become of me
And I cried and cried as my secret began to show.
One day Mrs. Greene said she understood,
And would make no trouble for me,
And, being childless, would adopt it.
(He had given her a farm to be still.)
So she hid in the house and sent out rumors,
As if it were going to happen to her.
And all went well and the child was born—They were so kind to me.
Later I married Gus Wertman, and years passed.
But—at political rallies when sitters-by thought I was crying
At the eloquence of Hamilton Greene—
That was not it.
No! I wanted to say:
That's my son! That's my son!

HAMILTON GREENE

I was the only child of Frances Harris of Virginia
And Thomas Greene of Kentucky,
Of valiant and honorable blood both.
To them I owe all that I became,
Judge, member of Congress, leader in the State.
From my mother I inherited
Vivacity, fancy, language;
From my father will, judgment, logic,
All honor to them
For what service I was to the people!

Mr. Masters, with all his sociological tendencies, does not deify the working-man as Mr. Sandburg and many other sociological poets do.   He sees life in too rounded a compass for that.   There is much painful truth in this picture, and the last two lines may well become a proverb:

JOHN HANCOCK OTIS

As to democracy, fellow citizens,
Are you not prepared to admit
That I, who inherited riches and was to the manner born,
Was second to none in Spoon River
In my devotion to the Cause of Liberty?
While my contemporary, Anthony Findlay,
Born in a shanty and beginning life
As a water carrier to the section hands,
Then becoming a section hand when he was grown,

Afterwards foreman of the gang, until he rose
To the superintendency of the railroad,
Living in Chicago,
Was a veritable slave driver,
Grinding the faces of labor,
And a bitter enemy of democracy.
And I say to you, Spoon River,
And to you, O republic,
Beware of the man who rises to power
From one suspender.

These are strange tales. So brutal that one wonders, if life in our little Western cities is as bad as this, why everyone does not commit suicide. Crime follows crime, and most of them of an extreme violence and sordidness. Some are crimes of ambition, many of them are the terrible, meaningless crimes which monotony breeds, most of them are crimes of sex. Mr. Masters is more preoccupied with sex than any other English or American author has ever been, and in a different way. I likened him to Strindberg at the beginning of this chapter advisedly. Both see life through the medium of sex, and sex for the most part cruel, untamed, perverted, tragic. The English poet and novelist, Mr. D. H. Lawrence, is also greatly preoccupied with sex, but in his work there is a certain rapture, sex is treated as a burgeoning of the mental and physical life, he throws over it the transparent and glittering cloak of joy. But the pages of Mr. Masters and August Strindberg read like extracts from the Newgate Calendar. Everything that is coarse and revolting in the sexual life is here. "Spoon River" is one long chronicle of rapes, seductions, liaisons, and perversions. It is the great blot upon Mr. Masters' work. It is an obliquity of vision, a morbidness of mind, which distorts an otherwise remarkable picture.

The treatment of sex is one of the most insidious dangers in the career of an artist; a step one way, and we have the colourless, lifeless work of so much of the Victorian period; a step the other, and the poet is a nine days wonder, and is then rejected by a sane world and relegated to the nefarious collections of the erotically minded. How many excellent books of a past age are neglected because of this over-insistence upon sex! The plays of Congreve would be as well known as those of Sheridan were it not for this. It is slow suicide for an author to commit this blunder.

Life is the material of art. But raw life is not art; to become art, it must be fused and transmuted. Also, the professed realists are apt to forget that idealism, a perception of beauty, an aspiration after fineness and nobleness, are also real. Mankind would have perished long ago, self-killed from despair, if it had not been for these glimpses of the poetry of existence. To make all such aspirations end in disillusion and death is to have a twisted point of

view. It cannot be denied even by Mr. Masters'
most convinced admirers that, with all his vitality
and courage, with all his wealth of experience and
vividness of presentation, his point of view is often
tortured and needlessly sensual and cruel.

Undoubtedly this element added to the immediate
notoriety of "Spoon River." But the book would not
be worth commenting upon, and Mr. Masters would
in no sense rank as the poet he does, if its sensuality
were not counteracted by other and great qualities.

Within certain limits, Mr. Masters has an extraordinary range of vision. Granted the limits, his
is a crowded canvas, and one teeming with life.
He raises local politics to the realm of a world force.
The squabbles in the County Court House take on
an epic fire. Indeed, "Spoon River" might be
called an epic of everyday life. One feels that if Mr.
Masters had had the good fortune to be born in a
great period, one momentous in its effect, the period
of the Civil War, let us say, or Europe at the present
time, or the Napoleonic Era, he would have known
how to give it due significance.

Perhaps our entrance into the Great War may
prove just the experience the poet needs. This
would certainly be the case were America nearer to
the firing line. It seems as though no living man
would be more keenly sensitive to the shock and
change which the war must inevitably bring upon
us. But it will be for later critics to record his

reactions to this upheaval. Writing at the beginning of this period, we can only note what he has already done, and it is his misfortune that he has lived at a moment of pause, apparent pause, that is, when the meanings of change are hidden. And, in that moment, his part has been that of questioner — a revolutionary, as I said before, a man who urges his world on to change, but without any definite idea of what such change is to bring about. What he sees is that old shibboleths no longer hold, that an exclusive Anglo-Saxon civilization does not fit our multi-racial population. That our institutions and our social fabric frequently jar upon our sensibilities, that thought in America is in advance of custom, and that personality being at variance with official life results in a painful chafing. What he does not see is that while he and his school are chiefly conscious of the pain, forces are at work beneath the surface which are already bearing the fruit of a new order. That a more balanced and homogeneous life is even now in process of formation. His attitude of mind is the attitude of to-day, while other poets are already concerned with the ideas of to-morrow.

One might illustrate by supposing a boy to receive the gift of a jacket. At first it is wholly comfortable and easy and a joy to its possessor, he takes pleasure in its neat cut, and its delectable warmth. But before long the stuff shows signs of wear, it has ceased to be a sure protection from the cold, his growth has made it somewhat too small.   It catches him when he stretches out his arm, it constricts his chest when he tries to button it, he is constantly aware of it because of a continual cramping.   Once he has divested himself of it, however, he is free again, and as he goes about his business, he gives little or no thought to the cast-off garment lying in a corner.

We cling to the old jackets because we have not imagination enough to conceive that there may be new ones.   It is the poets, it always has been the poets, who supply the imagination, and so gradually bring about a new condition.

"Spoon River" undoubtedly errs on the side of a too great preoccupation with crime and disease. But it would be unfair to its author not to remark the occasional bursts of tenderness throughout the book.   One, "Emily Sparks," I have already quoted. But there is another which is to me the most beautiful and most tragic poem in the volume.   This is real tragedy, not the tragedy of sordid giving way to inclination, but the tragedy of circumstance nobly faced, the tragedy of success out of failure, of joy denied and yet abundantly received :

DOC HILL

I went up and down the streets
Here and there by day and night,
Through all hours of the night caring for the poor who were sick.
Do you know why?

My wife hated me, my son went to the dogs.
And I turned to the people and poured out my love to them.
Sweet it was to see the crowds about the lawns on the day of my
　　funeral,
And hear them murmur their love and sorrow.
But oh, dear God, my soul trembled: scarcely able
To hold to the railing of the new life
When I saw Em Stanton behind the oak tree
At the grave,
Hiding herself, and her grief!

Technically, the poems in "Spoon River" show Mr. Masters' work at its best; always excepting "The Spooniad," which is hardly worth considering from any point of view. The poems are in *vers libre*, a form which I shall consider more carefully in the next chapter, suffice it here to repeat the often repeated characterization of it as "a verse-form based upon cadence." Mr. Masters' rhythms are not very subtle, but they are simple, and carry in them a certain elementary seriousness and power. Sometimes they differ very slightly from the rhythms of prose, but they do differ. Here are some lines taken at random:

> They would have lynched me
> Had I not been secretly hurried away
> To the jail at Peoria.
> And yet I was going peacefully home,
> Carrying my jug, a little drunk,
> When Logan, the marshal, halted me.

Now suppose these lines had been written :

> They would have lynched me,
> If I had not been hurried off before anyone knew
> And lodged at once in the Peoria jail.
> And yet I was going home quite peacefully
> With my jug, possibly a little bit drunk,
> When I was held up by Logan, the marshal.

It can be seen, by comparing these two versions, what excellent rhythm Mr. Masters' lines have.

Lyricism is not the antagonist of realism. On the contrary, it is the enforcer and brightener of it. Mr. Frost points his realism with many lyric bursts. Mr. Masters, on the contrary, is no lyrist. Considering his early love for the music of English verse, it is strange to find how seldom he even attempts such effects. Nor do we find many passages which, in a few words, show us the beauty of nature. Neither the lyricism of sound nor vision are a part of Mr. Masters' equipment. What he excels in is direct and forceful statement, which in his best passages mounts to a certain grandeur.

I mentioned in the chapter on Edwin Arlington Robinson that it had been stated that Mr. Masters was indebted to Mr. Robinson for his idea of these short sketches of men's lives. As a matter of fact, I know it to be true that, at the time he wrote "Spoon River," Mr. Masters had not read a line of Mr. Robinson's poetry. It is only the most superficial observer who could ever have supposed one to be derived from the other. The whole scheme upon which the two poets work is utterly different. Mr. Robinson analyzes the psychology of his characters to the minutest fraction, he splits emotions and sub-splits them. His people are interesting to him because of their thought-processes, or as psychic reactions to environment. Indeed, the environment is frequently misty, except where it impinges upon personality. Mr. Masters reveals the character of his *dramatis personæ* chiefly through their actions. What they do is, of course, the outcome of what they think, but it is usually the doing which the poet has set down on paper. His people are elementary and crude, carved on broad, flat planes.

The Tilbury Town of Mr. Robinson's books belongs more to the realm of mental phenomena than to actual fact. It is a symbol of certain states of mind. We feel it, but we do not see it. Spoon River, on the other hand, is indubitably and geographically a place. We know it even better than we do its inhabitants. Just as a person is a whole to us although made up of parts — eyes, ears, hands, nose, hair, etc. — so Spoon River is a whole, although constructed out of the life-histories of two hundred and fourteen of its citizens. We can see the cemetery, the Court House, the various churches, the shops, the railroad station, almost with our physical eyes.

It is not only that Mr. Robinson and Mr. Masters

employ a different method of approach, an absolutely different technique; it is that fundamentally their ideas, not only of art, but of life, differ.   To one, fact is the vague essence through which the soul of man wanders; to the other, man is a part, usually a tortured part, of a huge, hard, unyielding substance, the unalterable actuality of the world he inhabits.

If Mr. Masters has a prototype, that prototype can best be found in some of the poems in the "Greek Anthology."   This one by Carphylides is in the very spirit of some of the "Spoon River" poems.   It, too, is an epitaph, or a voice from the tomb:

> O traveller, listen as you pass by;
> Blame not my monument.
> Even when dead I am
> Worthy of lamentations.
> I have left children's children
> And have enjoyed one wife
> Of equal age with myself.
> Three children have I held in my lap many times.
> Nor have I had occasion to lament
> The illness or death of one of them.
> But they have poured out their libation in my honour
> And met no harm
> And have sent me on my way
> To the land of the blessed
> To sleep sweet sleep.

Another, by Meleager, recalls much of Mr. Masters' irony:

A gale blowing from the East,
Rough and calamity-bringing,
And night and the billows,
While Orion and the stars were invisible,
Have done me a hurt:
And I, Kallaischros, have slipt out of life
While passing through the Lybian Sea
And tost about in the deep, have become food for the fishes.
But the tombstone here tells a lie.

That last line is extraordinarily like Mr. Masters. Indeed, humanity varies very little throughout the ages. It is just this which makes "Spoon River" so remarkable — its humanity. These are not artificial personages, these two hundred men and women, they are real flesh and blood, with beating hearts and throbbing brains, revealing themselves to us with all their foibles and weaknesses, and their occasional grandeur. If, heaped one upon another, this monument of mid-Western American life errs on the side of over-sordidness, over-bitterness, over-sensuality, taken each one for itself, we have a true picture. It is never the individual characters who are false to type; it is only in the aggregate that the balance is lost by a too great preponderance of one sort of person.

It has been insisted over and over again, since the publication of "Spoon River," that here was the great American poet, this verse was at last absolutely of America, that not since Whitman had anything so national appeared in print. The importance of "Spoon River" can hardly be overstated, and its dominant Americanism is without doubt a prime factor in that importance; but, because Mr. Masters' work is thoroughly local, is not to deny the same quality to work of quite a different kind. Was Poe less American than Whitman? — is a question which may very pertinently be asked here. Was Shakespeare less English because he wrote "Hamlet"? Was that arch-Englishman, Matthew Arnold, false to his birthright because he published "Empedocles on Etna"? How foolish this point of view is when so stated, is apparent at a glance. Nationality is so subtle a thing that it permeates all a man says and does. He cannot escape it, no matter what subjects stimulate his imagination. One would suppose that the myths of Ancient Greece were (if any things are) proof against the subtle transforming of national temper, and yet look how they change in the hands of Hawthorne.

Mr. Masters is a thoroughly American poet, but not because he deals exclusively with American subjects. Truth to tell, he does not, as we shall see when, in a moment, we consider his later books. No, Mr. Masters is American because he is of the bones, and blood, and spirit of America. His thought is American; his reactions are as national as our clear blue skies.

The poets of the New Movement are all intensely

national; they are not, as I have already pointed out, what the older generation were, followers of an English tradition. They love their country, and are proud of being her sons. But people differ in their way of showing affection. Some men never speak of it, although it is a constant influence; others shout it to the house-tops. When Mr. Masters is intensely moved, he becomes blatant. He keeps nothing to himself, out it comes on a swirl of passion. So this Americanism of his is a very obvious thing. It is a sort of *leit-motif* appearing again and again, and preferably on the trumpets. The symbol of this Americanism is the figure of Lincoln.

Washington and Lincoln are the two great symbols of American life. But to deal adequately with Washington needs a historical sense, a knowledge of the eighteenth century, which few of our poets yet possess. (The only man I know who has given this feeling for Washington at all, is a Frenchman, Henri de Régnier, and he has done it in prose.) It is therefore to Lincoln that our poets turn as an embodiment of the highest form of the typical American, the fine flower and culmination of our life as a separate nation.

We have seen how a poet in the first stages of this new movement dealt with Lincoln; in the next chapter, I shall show how a poet in the third stage deals with him. In Mr. Robinson's poem, he is part symbol, part man, slightly conventionalized, and a little remote and cold withal ; in Mr. Fletcher's poem, he is raised almost to the rank of pure symbol, as elusive and pervading as a brooding god ; with Mr. Masters, Lincoln is a man first of all, but a man who, in his actual life, typifies a national aspiration. He is conceived as boldly, as surely, as any other of Mr. Masters' characters, and although venerated and loved with unchanging ardour, it is always as a man, neither conventionalized by tradition, nor flung by a powerful imagination into the realm of legend.

There is one little touch of Lincoln in "Spoon River," a very beautiful touch, although only a collateral one. It is the epitaph of Ann Rutledge, the girl whom Lincoln loved, but who died before they could be married.

ANN RUTLEDGE

Out of me unworthy and unknown
The vibrations of deathless music ;
"With malice toward none, with charity for all."
Out of me the forgiveness of millions toward millions,
And the beneficent face of a nation
Shining with justice and truth.
I am Ann Rutledge who sleep beneath these weeds,
Beloved in life of Abraham Lincoln,
Wedded to him, not through union,
But through separation.
Bloom for ever, O Republic,
From the dust of my bosom !

Just one year after the publication of "The Spoon River Anthology," appeared another book from Mr. Masters' pen, a new volume of poems, "Songs and Satires."

It has been hinted that many of the poems in this volume are reprinted from those earlier books which have slipt into oblivion. One would prefer to hope so, for it seems inconceivable that the author of the stark, vigorous "Spoon River" poems could afterwards perpetrate such a banality as the following:

WHEN UNDER THE ICY EAVES

When under the icy eaves
  The swallow heralds the sun,
And the dove for its lost mate grieves
  And the young lambs play and run;
When the sea is a plane of glass,
  And the blustering winds are still,
And the strength of the thin snows pass
  In the mists o'er the tawny hill —
The spirit of life awakes
  In the fresh flags by the lakes.

That one stanza is an epitome of the magazine verse of the 'eighties, and not very good magazine verse at that. Here are all the old *clichés*: doves grieving for their lost mates, young lambs at play, swallows who *herald* the sun, winds that *bluster*, snows which *pass* over *tawny* hills, even the *spirit of life* awaking by a *lake* bordered with *flags*. It would be difficult for one stanza to be a more complete illustration of the old poetical jargon than that. It reads like a parody; yet it is not intended as a parody, but as a serious and beautiful lyric. It gives us more than an insight into the reasons for Mr. Masters' early failures.

It would be unfair to the volume, however, to give the impression that all the poems are as bad as this. There are a number of weak lyrics scattered through the book, however, which no admirer of Mr. Masters can do other than deplore. And there are narrative poems on such hackneyed subjects as "Helen of Troy" and "Launcelot and Elaine," in which the treatment does nothing to add freshness to the themes.

This stanza from "Helen of Troy" will illustrate what I mean:

> We would behold fresh skies
> Where summer never dies
> And amaranths spring;
> Lands where the halcyon hours
> Nest over scented bowers
> On folded wing.

Or this other, from the "Ballad of Launcelot and Elaine":

> Then uprose brave Sir Launcelot
> And there did mount his steed,
> And hastened to a pleasant town
> That stood in knightly need.

There are ghastly attempts at an old English diction in this poem. We have "trees of spicery," "morn's underne," "spake with a dreary steven."

That Mr. Masters should have written these poems among his early four hundred is not strange, what is strange is that he should have considered them worth resurrecting after he had written "Spoon River."

Mr. Masters is seldom original when he writes in regular forms. It seems as though some obscure instinct of relation set his mind echoing with old tunes, old words, old pictures. Sometimes the result is a parody of the verse of the past; sometimes it is only a copy, quite beautiful, were it only his own. For instance, in "St. Francis and Lady Clare":

> Candles of wax she lit before
> A pier glass standing from the floor;
> Up to the ceiling, off she tore
> With eager hands her jewels, then
> The silken vesture which she wore.
> Her little breasts so round to see
> Were budded like the peony.
> Her arms were white as ivory,
> And all her sunny hair lay free
> As marigold or celandine.

What makes the book such a jumble is that these ancient ditties are interspersed with perfectly modern poems like "The Cocked Hat," "'So We Grew Together,'" "All Life in a Life," and the underworld studies: "Arabel," and "Jim and Arabel's Sister."

But, in these modern poems, Mr. Masters has deserted the brevity of the "Spoon River" pieces, and his doing so has lost him much and won him nothing. When he allows himself a free hand, he does not know when to stop. In "'So We Grew Together,'" he takes nine pages where in "Spoon River" one would have sufficed. "Arabel" is six pages in length, "The Cocked Hat" is seven, and none of these poems gains anything, either in vigour or analysis, by the change.

"The Loop" is a descriptive sketch of the heart of Chicago. But there is no quick flash of vision here, no unforgettable picture imposed upon the mind in a few words. Instead, the poem enumerates long catalogues of objects, one after the other. They have neither form, colour, nor relation. They are not presented poetically, pictorially, not even musically (as the older verse counted music), for the poem is marred by such false rhymes as "current" and "torrent." They are just lists, as dreary as an advertisement from a department store.

THE LOOP

From State street bridge a snow-white glimpse of sea
Beyond the river walled in by red buildings,
O'ertopped by masts that take the sunset's gildings,
Roped to the wharf till spring shall set them free.
Great floes make known how swift the river's current.
Out of the north sky blows a cutting wind.

Smoke from the stacks and engines in a torrent
Whirls downward, by the eddying breezes thinned.
Enskyed are sign boards advertising soap,
Tobacco, coal, transcontinental trains.
A tug is whistling, straining at a rope,
Fixed to a dredge with derricks, scoops and cranes.
Down in the loop the blue-gray air enshrouds,
As with a cyclops' cape, the man-made hills
And towers of granite where the city crowds.
Above the din a copper's whistle shrills.
There is a smell of coffee and of spices.
We near the market place of trade's devices.
Blue smoke from out a roasting room is pouring.
A rooster crows, geese cackle, men are bawling.
Whips crack, trucks creak, it is the place of storing,
And drawing out and loading up and hauling
Fruit, vegetables and fowls and steaks and hams,
Oysters and lobsters, fish and crabs and clams.
And near at hand are restaurants and bars,
Hotels with rooms at fifty cents a day,
Beer tunnels, pool rooms, places where cigars
And cigarettes their window signs display;
Mixed in with letterings of printed tags,
Twine, boxes, cartels, sacks and leather bags,
Wigs, telescopes, eyeglasses, ladies' tresses,
Or those who manicure or fashion dresses,
Or sell us putters, tennis balls or brassies,
Make shoes, pull teeth, or fit the eye with glasses.

That is only the first section. The poem is seven
pages long!

There is one poem in the book which shows Mr. Masters assuming a new rôle, or rather an old rôle in a new manner. "In Michigan" has a lyric quality very unusual to the poet's work. Most of his lyrics are couched in regular metres, and, for some strange reason, Mr. Masters does not seem able to think his own thoughts in conventional verse. Not only his expressions, his very ideas, run merrily back into the old moulds. On the other hand, Mr. Masters' free verse poems are singularly devoid of the lyricism of either sound or vision. So much so, indeed, that certain critics have declared him to be a novelist rather than a poet. "In Michigan" proves this verdict to be but partially true, for only a poet could write such a passage as this:

> I stole through echoless ways,
> Where no twigs broke and where I heard
> My heart beat like a watch under a pillow.
> And the whippoorwills were singing.
> And the sound of the surf below me
> Was the sound of silver-poplar leaves
> In a wind that makes no pause. . . .
> I hurried down the steep ravine,
> And a bat flew up at my feet from the brush
> And crossed the moon.
> To my left was the lighthouse,
> And black and deep purples far away,
> And all was still.
> Till I stood breathless by the tent

And heard your whispered welcome,
And felt your kiss.

Lovers lay at mid-night
On roofs of Memphis and Athens
And looked at tropical stars
As large as golden beetles.
Nothing is new, save this,
And this is always new.
And there in your tent
With the balm of the mid-night breeze
Sweeping over us,
We looked at one great star
Through a flap of your many-colored tent,
And the eternal quality of rapture
And mystery and vision flowed through us.

If "The Loop" is without poetical images, "In Michigan" shows that the poet is really sensitive to beauty, and at times possesses the power to catch that beauty in a phrase:

.   .   .   a quiet land
A lotus place of farms and meadows

gives the sleepy, lost quality of the landscape excellently well. Beautiful, too, is

.   .   .   on the hill
From where we could see Old Mission
Amid blues and blacks, across scores of miles of the Bay,
Waving like watered silk under the moon!

He speaks of the "misty eyelids" of "drowsy lamps," of a moon sinking "like a red bomb," of a land-spit running out into the lake until

> .   .   .   it seemed to dive under,
> Or waste away in a sudden depth of water.

But even in this free-verse lyric, echoes of the older poets haunt him, and not to his advantage:

> .   .   a star that shows like a match which lights
> To a blue intenseness amid the glow of a hearth

challenges a comparison, which proves Browning's

> blue spurt of a lighted match

to be infinitely finer.

The haste with which Mr. Masters has followed up the success of "Spoon River" has undoubtedly been his undoing. Temporary, let us hope, but for the time, a fact. Eight months after the publication of "Songs and Satires," his third book, "The Great Valley," made its appearance.

The Great Valley is of course that flat stretch of continent between the Alleghany Mountains and the Rockies. It is a paraphrase for what we commonly call the Middle West. In other words, these are again poems of a locality. The book is a sort of extended "Spoon River." The place is no more a little provincial town, but Chicago and the country adjacent. The horizon of place and character is wider than "Spoon River," the poems are longer and more detailed; but, as in the long poems in "Songs and Satires," the stretching out of his stories has not worked to the poet's advantage. Had "Spoon River" never been written, "The Great Valley" would have been a remarkable book. Unfortunately, it is still surpassed by the earlier volume. One of the most interesting traits of "Spoon River" was its homogeneity; the volume was a whole, as closely related within itself as is a novel, or a volume of essays grouped about a central theme. I have called "Songs and Satires" a jumble, Mr. Masters' taste again fails him in "The Great Valley." What have such classical subjects as "Marsyas," "The Furies," "Apollo at Pheræ," to do with the shouting Americanism of the rest of the book?

The truth is that in the back of the poet's heart, he still longs for that atmosphere of poesy which we have seen as the unappeased desire of his adolescence. These poems represent the nostalgia of beauty. It eludes him still. He is the poet of the real, the absolute. He cannot break his bonds. Co-ordination is an integral part of beauty; in art, we call this co-ordination — taste, and of this particular kind of taste Mr. Masters has not a particle. The classic poems are thrown pell-mell among the others so carelessly that one wonders if Mr. Masters really arranged the book at all. One of the most unpleasant of the author's modern sex-tragedies is printed immediately after "Apollo at Pheræ."

There is one new note in the volume, a sort of tinkling sneer. As though a funeral march were to be played on the *glockenspiel*. This kitchen lyric is excellent in technique, but whether the sort of thing is worthy of a man who could produce some of the "Spoon River" poems is another question.

SLIP SHOE LOVEY

You're the cook's understudy
A gentle idiot body.
You are slender like a broom
Weaving up and down the room,
With your dirt hair in a twist
And your left eye in a mist.
Never thinkin', never hopin'
With your wet mouth open.
So bewildered and so busy
As you scrape the dirty kettles,
O Slip Shoe Lizzie
As you rattle with the pans.
There's a clatter of old metals,
O Slip Shoe Lovey,
As you clean the milk cans.
You're a greasy little dovey,
A laughing scullery daughter
As you slop the dish water,
So abstracted and so dizzy,
O Slip Shoe Lizzie!

So mussy, little hussie,
With the china that you break,
And the kitchen in a smear
When the bread is yet to bake,
And the market things are here —
O Slip Shoe Lovey!

You are hurrying and scurrying
From the sink to the oven,
So forgetful and so sloven.
You are bustling and hustling
From the pantry to the door,
With your shoe strings on the floor,
And your apron strings a-draggin',
And your spattered skirt a-saggin'.

You're an angel idiot lovey,
One forgives you all this clatter
Washing dishes, beating batter.
But there is another matter
As you dream above the sink:
You're in love pitter-patter,
With the butcher-boy I think.
And he'll get you, he has got you
If he hasn't got you yet.

For he means to make you his,
O Slip Shoe Liz.
And your open mouth is wet
To a little boyish chatter.
You're an easy thing to flatter

With your hank of hair a-twist,
And your left eye in a mist —
O Slip Shoe Lovey!

So hurried and so flurried
And just a little worried
You lean about the room,
Like a mop, like a broom.
O Slip Shoe Lovey!
O Slip Shoe Lovey!

It is a relief to turn from a poem like that, clever though it is, and a very authentic side of Mr. Masters' talent, to the fine and serious "Autochthon." Here Mr. Masters compares the careers of three famous men, all of whom were born in the same year: Alfred Tennyson, Charles Darwin, and Abraham Lincoln. Space forbids me to give the whole poem, but I will quote two passages about Lincoln, and the reader will remember what I said of Mr. Masters' treatment of Lincoln a few pages back.

This is the year,
You sit in a little office there in Springfield,
Feet on the desk and brood. What are you thinking?
You're forty-one; around you spears are whacking
The wind-mills of the day, you watch and weigh.
The sun-light of your mind quivers about
The darkness every thinking soul must know,
And lights up hidden things behind the door,
And in dark corners. You have fathomed much,

Weighed life and men. O what a spheréd brain,
Strong nerved, fresh blooded, firm in plasmic fire,
And ready for a task, if there be one!
That is the question that makes brooding thought:
For you know well men come into the world
And find no task, and die, and are not known —
Great spheréd brains gone into dust again,
Their light under a bushel all their days!

. . . .

And still in 1860 all the Brahmins
Have fear to give you power.
You are a backwoodsman, a country lawyer
Unlettered in the difficult art of states.
A denizen of a squalid western town,
Dowered with a knack of argument alone,
Which wakes the country school house, and may lift
Its devotees to Congress by good fortune.
But then at Cooper Union intuitive eyes
Had measured your tall frame, and careful speech,
Your strength and self-possession. Then they came
With that dramatic sense which is American
Into the hall with rails which you had split,
And called you Honest Abe, and wearing badges
With your face on them and the poor catch words
Of Honest Abe, as if you were a referee
Like Honest Kelly, when in truth no man
Had ever been your intimate, ever slapped you
With brisk familiarity, or called you
Anything but Mr. Lincoln, never
Abe, or Abraham, and never used
The Hello Bill of salutation to you —

O great patrician, therefore fit to be
Great democrat as well!

Yes, Mr. Masters is the chief poet of our middle era.   Already, in the work of a man so closely allied to him as Mr. Sandburg, we see evidence of a coming change.   Mr. Masters stands up rugged, solid, energetic, clearing his way by stern force of will. Much passes him by, there are notes in our national life too high or too low for him to catch.   He cannot always give back those he does catch.   But what he does give back is resonant with the overtones of personality, with the truth of heart, body, and mind. Whatever America is to become, "Spoon River" will always stand in her libraries, a work of genius and a record of what was.   Already it vanishes, even as it is being written down.   Mr. Masters himself feels this, in "Come, Republic," he exhorts his country to step forward boldly into the new time. He sees it glimmering on the horizon, but too far still for him quite to focus.   Here we will leave him, with the God-speed of his own words sounding in our ears:

It is time to lift yourself, O Republic,
From the street corners of Spoon River.

To turn from Edgar Lee Masters to Carl Sandburg is like crossing the line of a generation.   In actual years, they are not so far apart, but they represent

Carl Sandburg

the two sides of the barrier of change. Mr. Sandburg, although intellectually and poetically in the second stage of our "movement," belongs to the new America which I have called multi-racial. He springs from the strong immigrant class which comes yearly in boat-loads to our shores. It is he and his ilk who are moving us away from our Anglo-Saxon inheritance. It is he and his ilk who bring us the points of view which are working so surely, if insidiously, upon the whole body of the people.

Some day, America will be a nation; some day, we shall have a national character. Now, our population is a crazy quilt of racial samples. But how strong is that Anglo-Saxon ground-work which holds them all firmly together to its shape, if no longer to its colour!

Mr. Sandburg is of Swedish stock. The stock which has given to the world Gustaf Fröding and Selma Lagerlöf. One has only to turn the pages of "Gösta Berling" to see what manner of peasantry Sweden has produced. One has only to read their folk-tales to discover the poetry inherent in these people, who can neither read nor write, but who can watch the procession of the seasons fearlessly, snatching a beautiful joy through the short Summers, and enduring the long dark Winters and their swirling snows with quiet equanimity.

They are dumb for the most part, this peasantry, but give them speech, give them letters, and what do they not become? In the particular instance with which we have to do, they become the American poet, Carl Sandburg.

Mr. Sandburg, no less than Mr. Masters, is at war with himself, and with the customs of the economic world. His Swedish ancestors have given him mysticism and poetry, his American experiences have sown his heart thickly with a strange combination of dissatisfaction and idealism. Many of his theories are built upon false premises, but he has theories, definite theories of reconstruction. And if he is chiefly conscious of this reconstruction from the financial side, his sub-conscious mind is at work upon it also from the æsthetic side.

Mr. Sandburg possesses a powerful imagination, which plays over and about his realistic themes and constantly ennobles them. It is not only that yellow primroses are more than primroses to him; strikes, and factories, and slaughter-houses, and railroad trains, all take on a lyric quality under his touch. It is the force of this imagination which drags him on toward the third stage of our movement. I say "drags him on," because he never quite reaches it. He can never get free of the actual, can never rise entirely above his world on the wings of a certain hope.

The first poem in his volume, "Chicago Poems," will show what I mean. This is no mere bald presentation of a city, but an imaginative conception of real grandeur, and if the grandeur is spattered with coarseness, perhaps that was inherent in the theme — at the angle from which the poet chooses to take it at any rate.

CHICAGO

Hog Butcher for the World,
Tool Maker, Stacker of Wheat,
Player with Railroads and the Nation's Freight Handler;
Stormy, husky, brawling,
City of the Big Shoulders:
They tell me you are wicked and I believe them, for I have seen your painted women under the gas lamps luring the farm boys.
And they tell me you are crooked and I answer: Yes, it is true I have seen the gunman kill and go free to kill again.
And they tell me you are brutal and my reply is: On the faces of women and children I have seen the marks of wanton hunger.
And having answered so I turn once more to those who sneer at this my city, and I give them back the sneer and say to them:
Come and show me another city with lifted head singing so proud to be alive and coarse and strong and cunning.
Flinging magnetic curses amid the toil of piling job on job, here is a tall bold slugger set vivid against the little soft cities;
Fierce as a dog with tongue lapping for action, cunning as a savage pitted against the wilderness,
    Bareheaded,
    Shoveling,

Wrecking,

Planning,

Building, breaking, rebuilding,

Under the smoke, dust all over his mouth, laughing with white teeth,

Under the terrible burden of destiny laughing as a young man laughs,

Laughing even as an ignorant fighter laughs who has never lost a battle,

Bragging and laughing that under his wrist is the pulse, and under his ribs the heart of the people,

Laughing!

Laughing the stormy, husky, brawling laughter of Youth, half-naked, sweating, proud to be Hog Butcher, Tool Maker, Stacker of Wheat, Player with Railroads and Freight Handler to the Nation.

Carl Sandburg's father was a Swedish immigrant whose real name was August Johnson. He came to this country in search of work, and became a construction hand on one of the great Western railroads. He changed his name to Sandburg, because there were so many other August Johnsons in the gang with which he worked that confusion occurred, and after the loss of one pay roll, he adopted this simple method of avoiding such accidents in the future.

August Johnson, or August Sandburg, was an uneducated man. Uneducated as our school curriculums count education, that is. He had been to school for only three months in his life, his wife had been to school for only two. He was obliged to make "his mark," in the good old way, when appending his name to contracts or other legal documents. His son's career proves how arbitrary are our tests of reading and writing to determine mental aptitude. The results of education — character and intellectual vigour — were surely present in this illiterate railroad worker, and these he has left a legacy to his son.

Carl Sandburg was born at Galesburg, Illinois, in 1878.   In due time he was sent to school, but not for long ; when he was thirteen he left to take a job on a milk wagon.   This avocation was abandoned for the more exalted one of porter in a barber shop, which in turn gave way to that of scene-shifter in a theatre, to be followed by working a truck at a brick kiln, and making balls in a pottery.

Nothing could have been better.   The poet was learning modern life through its constructive sources. The pictures which all these trades have left in his mind have greatly enriched his work.

When he was seventeen, Carl Sandburg went West, for Illinois is East if we halve the continent. Here he worked for a time at his father's old trade of railroad construction, but left it to wash dishes in hotels in Denver and Omaha, bursting out of doors again to pitch wheat in Kansas.   These were the poet's *wanderjähre*, a sort appropriate to a big industrial democracy.

At the outbreak of the Spanish War, Carl Sandburg was learning the painter's trade in Galesburg. The war appeared to his imagination as a means of adventure in distant countries, places of mountains, islands, and sea, with possible fighting to challenge his heroism. He enlisted in Company C, Sixth Illinois Volunteers — the first company, as it happened, to set foot on the Island of Porto Rico.

At the end of the war, the poet was mustered out, with one hundred dollars in his pocket for the first time in his life. Here was a chance. His eager mind had been scantily fed hitherto. With his hundred dollars, Mr. Sandburg put himself back to school. The school was Lombard College, in his native town of Galesburg.

At the close of his first college year, the officers and men of his military company voted him a candidate for cadetship at West Point. So to West Point the young man went for his examinations. It is significant that he got ninety-nine per cent in the physical examination; in his studies, he passed every thing but arithmetic, which was a miserable failure, and closed the door of the army definitely upon him. This was probably a fortunate thing for his poetical career.

On his return to Galesburg, his money was spent, but his ambition was not. So he went back to Lombard College, working his way through by tutoring, ringing the college bell, and acting as janitor of the gymnasium. His literary life began to assert itself. He became the editor of the College monthly, and editor and chief writer of an annual, " The Cannibal "; also, Galesburg boasted a local " Daily Mail," and the young man obtained the position of its college correspondent.

Galesburg was an enterprising and ambitious little town in those days. A number of men who have since made some mark in the larger world were active in its affairs. There was a considerable amount of intellectual fermentation constantly going on, and to the young poet it meant the burgeoning of life : moral, æsthetic, economic. It gave him a banner under which to fight; it released his own powers and girded him for action. When Carl Sandburg left college, he was no longer an unskilled labourer, working with his hands. He was a thinking man, with a brain charged with ideas and emotions, determined to do his part in bringing about the millennium. For Carl Sandburg, too, is a revolutionary; he must push the world to where he is convinced it ought to be.

It is perhaps inevitable that a young man of sensitive nature, born with a passionate love of humanity, and seeing life only from the standpoint of the unskilled wage-earner, should find in our whole economic civilization only a vast injustice. As I pointed out, at the beginning of this chapter, the second stage of a movement, the revolutionary one, must always concern itself with material advance. As the outcome

of certain ideas, of course, but still, for immediate purposes, it is the alteration of those abuses in the realm
of fact which chiefly concerns the propagandists.

It is probable that Mr. Sandburg felt very much
as he does now about matters sociological and economic, before he went to Lombard College.   But his
studies focussed his wandering sympathies.   He left
college with a great, burning resolve to better social
conditions.   It must be admitted that any one less
fitted than this generous, spirited young man to
cope with the economic paradoxes of high finance
could hardly be imagined.   But ignorance is ever
foremost in the suggesting of panaceas.   Where Mr.
Masters' greater experience hesitated to suggest, Mr.
Sandburg was ready with a thousand cogent reasons.
The next step in his career was the obvious one for a
man of his tastes and training.   It was the newspaper,
that flamboyant medium for the dissemination of
half-baked ideas.   Surely, over the long-suffering
United States should float the banner of a huge front
page, crinkling its bold-faced headlines in the morning breeze.

So Mr. Sandburg roamed the West as a newspaper
man, salesman, and advertisement writer, and gradually his sociological yearnings took on a more practical turn.   During 1907 and 1908, he worked as a
district organizer for the Social-Democratic party of
Wisconsin.   We can imagine the young man, full of
ardour, persuasion, and personal charm, speaking at

street corners and factory gates, and, in the evenings, writing pamphlets and leaflets to advance the cause.

It will help us to understand what manner of man Mr. Sandburg is to glance for a moment at a little pamphlet entitled "Incidentals," which was issued by the Asgard Press, Galesburg, Illinois, some ten years ago, or about 1907. This is a series of jottings, such as might have been taken from a note-book. They make no didactic claim, seeming rather to be rules and thoughts for the author's own guidance. They reveal a sweet and gentle nature, and also a bold and strong one. This, called "Consolations," is, if not new, at any rate indicative:

I want to do the right thing, but often I don't know just what the right thing is. I am making mistakes and expect to make more. Every day I know I have bungled and blundered and come short of what I would like to have done. Yet as the years pass on and I see the very world itself with its oceans and mountains and plains as something unfinished, a peculiar little satisfaction hunts out the corners of my heart. Sunsets and evening shadows find me regretful at tasks undone, but sleep and the dawn and the air of the morning touch me with freshening hopes. Strange things blow in through my window on the wings of the night-wind and I don't worry about my destiny.

In "Egoism," is the arrogance of youth, but of a youth which harbours the seed of power:

I want the respect of intelligent men but I will choose for myself the intelligent. I love art but I decide for myself what is art. I adore beauty but only my own soul shall tell me what is beauty. I worship God but I define and describe God for myself. I am an individual. The pleasure of my own heart shall be first to inform me when I have done good work.

Already, lyricism is struggling for expression :

OUT OF DOORS

Freedom is found, if anywhere, in the great out-door world of wild breezes and sunshine and sky. To get out into the daylight and fill your lungs with pure air, to stop and watch a spear of grass swaying in the wind, to give a smile daily at the wonder and mystery of shifting light and changing shadow, is to get close to the source of power. Out under the wide dome, amid night odors and silences, you get your size, and breathe, feel, think, and live. Careless winds blow in your face and your eye is keen for things homely and beautiful near by. Stars look at you through tangled tree tops. The rattle of a distant wagon is like subdued laughter. You get a new hold on your own particular problems and the ghosts of despair are put out of business.

There is excellent good sense, too, in "Whimsicalities" :

Sometimes when fate kicks us and we finally land and look around, we find we have been kicked upstairs !

and pathetic fallacies such as the following :

If the working people knew the platitudes of politics as they know the intricacies of base-ball, the kingdom of heaven would fall through the sky and settle impalpably on the earth like a vast air-ship.

but, in the "Prayer for Everyday," is a fine idealism :

O Thou great Spirit of Truth! whose filaments pervade and interfuse all things. Thou whose energy vibrates in passing trolley car and far-swung planet, Thou art neither of the East nor West nor North nor South. Thou art here and everywhere, in all times and all places.

The hot-house rose belongs to Thee and the back-yard cabbage is also Thine. From Thy hands came the blue-bottle flies that buzz on the window pane and by Thy hands took shape sun, moon, star, and worlds that throb and glow in measureless space. Thou art in the pulsations of our brains and the desires of our hearts. Across and through the whole scheme of things as they are, Thy plan and law is at work. For the simple and common things around us, like sunlight and dew and rain and voices and faces, we are thankful.

To Thee belong all the children of men. Give them faith and simplicity in their dealings with each other. Grant that they look on each other as comrades, ready for laughter and love and work and good-will and belief. Amen.

Already, in this leaflet, we see that Mr. Sandburg has caught a fleeting glimpse of a road beyond the stopping-place of materialism. He sees, but cannot quite hit upon the path. It is his desire to get there, to run happily along it followed by a great rejoicing mob of "the people," but he can find no clearer line of approach than through the brambles of economic reform. He does not understand that what to him is merely a means, is to most of his followers an end. He has not grasped the fact that the world needs his

lyricism, his vision of beauty, far more than it needs
his concrete suggestions on material fact.　He is a
poet who constantly flings away the guiding star
of a new order to grub a lump of coal.　And yet Mr.
Sandburg professes to believe in the motive impulse
of ideas.　He has said:

> No man is more startling in action than a dreamer.　Through
> the centuries, the dramatic manœuverings of dreamers have held
> the world's eye and shaped its changing civilizations.　All
> creations of man, be they machines, statues, poems or political
> movements, were at one time mere ideas, dreams and deep
> longings, having no form outside the brains that conceived them.
> To the restlessness and forever active recuperative powers of the
> "seers of visions" is due the world's advance.

Yet, again and again, he deserts the seer's mountain
peak for the demagogue's soap-box.

　Mr. Sandburg has a vision, but it is vague, in-
choate.　"I am an idealist," he exclaims.　"I don't
know where I'm going, but I'm on my way."　This is
a joyous utterance, and Mr. Sandburg believes whole-
heartedly in joy.　It is just this belief in joy in the
midst of a joyless world that makes the paradox of
Mr. Sandburg's writings.　He believes in it, but not
quite enough to confide in its complete saving power,
and he confuses himself with all mankind.　"What
I ask for myself I want you to have on the same terms.
We are made of the same stuff.　We are going the
same way."　Again the fallacy of ardent youth.

It is only experience that teaches of how many varying stuffs mankind is made. "What is one man's
meat is another man's poison," is a truer statement.
Mr. Sandburg's desires no more mirror those of the
great body of the people, than did William Morris's
in an earlier generation. He has yet to discover
how different they are, and the discovery when made
may well be a shattering one.

He admits:

The great body of people is better off to-day than it ever was.
Books, music, pictures, travel, more people are enjoying these
things than ever before. The Roman patrician and the feudal
baron were lacking thousands of advantages to be had to-day for
pennies and dimes.

But farther on is this postulate:

Man does not live by bread alone. He has a soul. This soul
imperiously asks to be fed. It wants art, beauty, harmony.
For sweet sounds and forms of beauty and things that caress
the eye and thrill the touch, it asks and demands.

The people who are without these things are asking for them.
Those who have them in degree are asking for more. Patient as
the stars and unwearied as the earth, they know what they want.
Always and forever the cry has been for more and more and more.
Up from the huts and hovels and sordid bedraggled shanties
comes the cry for more. Let us feed our souls! For Christ's
sake, let us feed our souls! is the cry.

Is that really the great inarticulate cry of the
masses? In face of facts, one may be permitted to

doubt it; and the worst side of the teaching of modern sociology would seem to be its insistence upon material rather than spiritual welfare.   Certainly, our newspapers, which exist by providing the public with what it wants, hardly seem cognizant of such needs. We may agree with Mr. Sandburg in the belief in a better order, and yet feel sure that this better order can best be arrived at through the saving medium of ideas.

The man who makes beauty, constantly, energetically, undauntedly, stands more chance of moulding opinion than he who dims that beauty by turning it to uses for which it is unfitted.   Mr. Sandburg is like a man striving to batter down a jail with balls of brightly coloured glass.   He may well alter points of view by focussing them upon his spheres of iridescent light, but not by shooting these same spheres from a cannon.

We need not follow him minutely through the many changes of job of this period of his life.   After various occupations in various places, he became Secretary to Mayor Seidel of Milwaukee, later joining the staff of the "Milwaukee Journal" as Labour Editor.

A split with the Parliamentary Socialists was the result of his promoting a street car strike.   Since which time he has been a free lance, allied to no party, and passionately believing in the dreams of his own imagination, and in action — the action prompted by these dreams!

During the newspaper lockout and strike of 1912, Mr. Sandburg went on the staff of "The World." Later, upon that paper going into the hands of a receiver, he became its associate editor, on the strength of some articles on Accident Prevention, City Efficiency, and Municipal Accounting, which had been printed in "LaFollette's Weekly." In January, 1914, he became a member of the staff of "The Day Book," a courageous little sheet published in Chicago, which has for its ideal the high resolve to live without the aid of advertisements, and so preserve its freedom from commercial control.

All this is fine, high-minded, pathetically honest. But what has it to do with poetry? Nothing. It is as much the result of Fate as that a man should be born in Iceland or Timbuctoo. But it is inevitable, as is a man's nationality after he has once been born. It is the result of circumstance, and of a book-learning which has no earlier tradition than the present possesses.

During this time, however, the natural poetry of the man was gaining strength and expression. His poem, "Chicago," was printed by "Poetry" early in 1914, and, at the end of the year, was awarded the Helen Haire Levinson prize of two hundred dollars for "the best poem written by a citizen of the United States during the year," which that magazine has in its gift.

Whatever one may think of the advisability of

prizes, however one may balk at any one poem being so confidently labelled "the best," no one could fail to see on reading "Chicago" that here was a poet with a vigorous personality and an original technique.

Mr. Sandburg continued to contribute poems to various periodicals for the next two years, principally to "Poetry," "The Masses," and "Others," and in April, 1916, his collected poems were issued by Messrs. Henry Holt and Company, under the rather forbidding title of "Chicago Poems."

The impression which one gets on reading this book is of a heavy steel-gray sky rent open here and there, and, through the rents, shining pools of clear, pale blue. It is a rare and beautiful combination which we find in this volume, under whatsoever simile we describe it. Seldom does such virility go with such tenderness. There is no bitterness here such as we find in "Spoon River"; there is anger, there is unjust prejudice, but the soul of the poet is wholesome and sane. The reader feels a certain wistfulness coming over him as he looks at so much strength and hope pitting itself against a cruel natural law. Perhaps science was not one of the subjects in Mr. Sandburg's course at Lombard College, for, to him, all cruelty is man-made, he has but to sweep away the man who made it, and behold, it is gone, all study of the lives of wild animals and fishes notwithstanding. If only life were as simple as that! If only one's morality could be measured by one's pocket-book! A man in a well-cut coat — he is an evil thing, shun him; a man in rags begging on a street corner — take him to your heart, he is of the elect. It is but just to say that Mr. Sandburg tries to be fair to his millionaires (all his well-to-do men are millionaires), in fact, a great desire for justice is visible throughout the book; but prejudice is a firmly-rooted thing, and try as he will, Mr. Sandburg cannot help feeling that virtue resides with the people who earn their daily bread with their hands rather than with those who do so with their brains. Doubtless, Mr. Sandburg considers that the brain-workers get more than they need, and the hand-workers less. Perhaps this is true, of certain sorts of brain-work, that is. (For it is not true of poets, scientists, nor of any of the higher kinds of brain-workers.) But this form of doctrine leads to a strange reversion of values. Through pity and sympathy, the poet is led to a re-valuation of human types, in which those least far on the evolutionary road, those least important if we measure by scientific laws, come in for the most attention.

I point this out, not with any desire to belittle the great value of studies of these types, but to mark how invariably a preoccupation tends to blur a man's eyes to the fundamental principle of all human existence, which is advance, evolution. No one will deny that the brutal, unimaginative dinner-eating millionaire is probably one of the lowest forms of animals on our earth. But there is another type, the high-minded, ideal-following, sober-living man, who needs to be considered. He rather spoils the argument, so he is usually left out of it, which is scarcely fair. Not that Mr. Sandburg, or other democratic poets, deny his existence, but they throw the weight of their sympathy and their art into the scale against him. Whether constant preoccupation with disease is a healthy form of literature, whether it acts as a curative, is open to question. But we can surely say that to be curative the disease must be treated unsentimentally and truly. Mr. Sandburg has aimed at doing this, has striven hard to do it. For this, one honours him above his fellows. For this, and the spirit of beauty which pervades his work.

To illustrate: "Fellow Citizens" is a fine poem, true, and with well-balanced values:

FELLOW CITIZENS

I drank musty ale at the Illinois Athletic Club with the millionaire manufacturer of Green River butter one night
And his face had the shining light of an old-time Quaker, he
spoke of a beautiful daughter, and I knew he had a peace
and a happiness up his sleeve somewhere.
Then I heard Jim Kirch make a speech to the Advertising Asso-
ciation on the trade resources of South America.
And the way he lighted a three-for-a-nickel stogie and cocked it
at an angle regardless of the manners of our best people,

I knew he had a clutch on a real happiness even though some of
the reporters on his newspaper say he is the living double of
Jack London's Sea Wolf.

In the mayor's office the mayor himself told me he was happy
though it is a hard job to satisfy all the office-seekers and
eat all the dinners he is asked to eat.

Down in Gilpin Place, near Hull House, was a man with his jaw
wrapped for a bad toothache,

And he had it all over the butter millionaire, Jim Kirch, and the
mayor when it came to happiness.

He is a maker of accordions and guitars and not only makes
them from start to finish, but plays them after he makes
them.

And he had a guitar of mahogany with a walnut bottom he offered
for seven dollars and a half if I wanted it,

And another just like it, only smaller, for six dollars, though he
never mentioned the price till I asked him,

And he stated the price in a sorry way, as though the music
and the make of an instrument count for a million times more
than the price in money.

I thought he had a real soul and knew a lot about God.

There was light in his eyes of one who has conquered sorrow in so
far as sorrow is conquerable or worth conquering.

Anyway he is the only Chicago citizen I was jealous of that
day.

He played a dance they play in some parts of Italy when the
harvest of grapes is over and the wine presses are ready for
work.

But, in "Dynamiter," the values are woefully out
of line :

DYNAMITER

I sat with a dynamiter at supper in a German saloon eating
steak and onions.

And he laughed and told stories of his wife and children and the
cause of labor and the working class.

It was laughter of an unshakable man knowing life to be a rich
and red-blooded thing.

Yes, his laugh rang like the call of gray birds filled with a glory
of joy ramming their winged flight through a rain storm.

His name was in many newspapers as an enemy of the nation
and few keepers of churches or schools would open their
doors to him.

Over the steak and onions not a word was said of his deep days
and nights as a dynamiter.

Only I always remember him as a lover of life, a lover of children,
a lover of all free, reckless laughter everywhere — lover of
red hearts and red blood the world over.

That a man loves children, particularly his own,
is a good and beautiful thing. But to use that fact
as a dazzling screen to obscure the horror of his trade
of blowing other men, who possibly also love their
children, into atoms, because of a difference in opinions, may fairly be stated as faulty vision on the part
of the poet. Now Mr. Sandburg severely handles
the killing in war; a killing again brought about by
a difference of opinions. He does not justify his
dynamiter, it is true, but he looks at him obliquely,
leaving out what he does not wish to see, because of

his sympathy with the opinions the man represents. Propaganda is the pitfall of poets. So excellently endowed a poet as Mr. Sandburg should beware.

Far better, because real and pitiful, are "A Teamster's Farewell," "Fish Crier," "Onion Days," "Mamie," and a host of other poems. But the propaganda seizes him again in "The Right to Grief." What justification can so honest a poet find for sneering at a father's grief over his dead child and calling it "perfumed sorrow"? Is not grief stark and terrible in all its forms, whether it come to rich or poor? The reformers hurt their cause by showing such a lack of knowledge of human nature. But again, Mr. Sandburg wins our sympathy in "Child of the Romans."

I have dwelt so long on the propagandist side of Mr. Sandburg's book, because he challenges us with it upon many pages. But these are poems, and it is as poetry that the work must be judged. "Chicago Poems" is one of the most original books which this age has produced. Mr. Sandburg, in a piece entitled "Style," explains that his style, good or bad, is his own. It is just this fact which is so interesting. Whether the poems are in regular English or in the slang of the streets, they are full of personality. Written, some in *vers libre*, some in a rhythmical prose, some in a cross between the two, they seldom fail to justify their form to the ear. If any one will take the trouble to read the first poem, "Chicago," which I quoted above, aloud, he will find how strangely and musically it beats out its heavy cadences.   Then take the beautiful little sketch, "Fog":

FOG

The fog comes
On little cat feet.
It sits looking
over harbor and city
on silent haunches
and then moves on.

That whispers along as stealthily as the fog itself. It is one of the best of the nature pieces, but there are many others scattered through the book.   For Mr. Sandburg is a true poet, observant of beauty, and quick with new trains of thought in which to express it.

This, with its lovely last line, for instance:

NOCTURNE IN A DESERTED BRICKYARD

Stuff of the moon
Runs on the lapping sand
Out to the longest shadows.
Under the curving willows,
And round the creep of the wave line,
Fluxions of yellow and dusk on the waters
Make a wide dreaming pansy of an old pond in the night.

Often, in his short lyrics, we see Mr. Sandburg approaching the Imagist technique:

WINDOW

Night from a railroad car window
Is a great, dark, soft thing
Broken across with slashes of light.

I have said several times that he is the link leading over from the second stage into the third. The poem I have just given will prove how absolutely this is so, and, in the next chapter, the gap will be found to have been bridged by just these poems.

He has a curiously wide-flying imagination. In "Hydrangeas," the suggestion is so subtle that we feel the poet's meaning rather than see it. Yet is this not a war-poem hidden under a figure: true, tragic, stern?

HYDRANGEAS

Dragoons, I tell you the white hydrangeas turn rust and go soon.
Already mid September a line of brown runs over them.
One sunset after another tracks the faces, the petals.
Waiting, they look over the fence for what way they go.

That poem is not in the section of the book called "War Poems." It is as well. Perhaps it is not of this war, but of any war, all war — Life.

No poet of to-day has touched the present war

more convincingly, more poetically, than Mr. Sandburg. "Killers" is a terrible thing:

KILLERS

I am singing to you
Soft as a man with a dead child speaks;
Hard as a man in handcuffs,
Held where he cannot move:

Under the sun
Are sixteen million men,
Chosen for shining teeth,
Sharp eyes, hard legs,
And a running of young warm blood in their wrists.

And a red juice runs on the green grass;
And a red juice soaks the dark soil.
And the sixteen million are killing . . . and killing and killing.

I never forget them day or night:
They beat on my head for memory of them;
They pound on my heart and I cry back to them,
To their homes and women, dreams and games.

I wake in the night and smell the trenches,
And hear the low stir of sleepers in lines —
Sixteen million sleepers and pickets in the dark:
Some of them long sleepers for always,
Some of them tumbling to sleep to-morrow for always,
Fixed in the drag of the world's heartbreak,

Eating and drinking, toiling . . . on a long job of killing.
Sixteen million men.

In a flash, the poet sets this war apart from former wars. He does not say so, he raises a picture, a dream of fancy, and it is all in that slight, short dream :

STATISTICS

> Napoleon shifted,
> Restless in the old sarcophagus
> And murmured to a watchguard :
> "Who goes there?"
> "Twenty-one million men,
> Soldiers, armies, guns,
> Twenty-one million
> Afoot, horseback,
> In the air,
> Under the sea."
> And Napoleon turned to his sleep :
> "It is not my world answering;
> It is some dreamer who knows not
> The world I marched in
> From Calais to Moscow."
> And he slept on
> In the old sarcophagus
> While the aeroplanes
> Droned their motors
> Between Napoleon's mausoleum
> And the cool night stars.

We notice in these poems an entirely different technique from that employed by Mr. Robinson and Mr. Frost.   Their content, their points of view, were modern;   their form was not.   In Mr. Masters' work, a new style of presentation made its appearance, but the very matter of form seemed to exact certain sacrifices.   The "Spoon River" pieces were mostly bald presentation of fact.   When Mr. Masters essayed the lyrical, he usually felt constrained to return to metrical verse.   A student considering Mr. Masters' practice, might very well be led into supposing that the new forms were essentially non-lyrical.   But here, in the work of Mr. Sandburg, we find such a hypothesis to be untenable.   These poems which I have quoted show the new forms to be as proper a medium for lyrical emotion as is metrical verse.   I shall only note this here, for, in the matter of form, Mr. Sandburg has been surpassed by the poets in the third stage of the New Movement.   In the next chapter, I shall consider at length this vexed and interesting question.

All the poets of the New Movement seem haunted by the visions of history.   It is commonly supposed that they cut themselves off from the past.   Far from it;   they are more concerned with analogies between past and present than is often the case in poetry.   History, to them, is no dry and mouldy document, but both a live and palpitating reality and a legendary touchstone.   I have spoken of the treatment of Lincoln by Mr. Robinson, Mr. Masters, and Mr. Fletcher. A moment ago, in "Statistics," we found Mr. Sandburg occupying himself with Napoleon. In that poem, Napoleon was fact, legend, and symbol; he was many things, but never a dead fragment of a dead world. In "Cool Tombs," Mr. Sandburg again has recourse to history. It is by this analogy with the past that he lights the present. The poem is in Mr. Sandburg's most personal idiom. Serious, beautiful lines alternating with the slang of the day, and all to bring about a grave and moving whole.

COOL TOMBS

When Abraham Lincoln was shoveled into the tombs, he forgot the copperheads and the assassin . . . in the dust, in the cool tombs.

And Ulysses Grant lost all thought of con men and Wall Street, cash and collateral turned ashes . . . in the dust, in the cool tombs.

Pocahontas' body, lovely as a poplar, sweet as a red haw in November or a paw-paw in May, did she wonder? does she remember? . . . in the dust, in the cool tombs?

Take any streetful of people buying clothes and groceries, cheering a hero or throwing confetti and blowing tin horns . . . tell me if the lovers are losers . . . tell me if any get more than the lovers . . . in the dust . . . in the cool tombs.

Not the least of Mr. Sandburg's attributes is irony, a sad, pitying irony :

LIMITED

I am riding on a limited express, one of the crack trains of the
　　nation.
Hurtling across the prairie into blue haze and dark air go fifteen
　　all-steel coaches holding a thousand people.
(All the coaches shall be scrap and rust and all the men and
　　women laughing in the diners and sleepers shall pass to
　　ashes.)
I ask a man in the smoker where he is going and he answers :
　　"Omaha."

That poem seems to me little short of magnificent.
Again, take "Buttons," from the section, "War
Poems":

BUTTONS

I have been watching the war map slammed up for advertising
　　in front of the newspaper office.
Buttons — red and yellow buttons — blue and black buttons
　　— are shoved back and forth across the map.
A laughing young man, sunny with freckles,
Climbs a ladder, yells a joke to somebody in the crowd,
And then fixes a yellow button one inch west
And follows the yellow button with a black button one inch west.
(Ten thousand men and boys twist on their bodies in a red soak
　　along a river edge,
Gasping of wounds, calling for water, some rattling death in
　　their throats.)

Who would guess what it cost to move two buttons one inch on
   the war map here in front of the newspaper office where the
   freckled-face young man is laughing to us?

All these war poems are very strong.

There is one unfortunate slip throughout the
volume. And it is one which Mr. Sandburg shares
with Mr. Masters and with many other modern
American writers. It is an occasional slip in grammar. The constant use of "will" for "shall," and of
"would" for "should," is a torment to the instructed
ear; and the common American blunder of employing "around" quite apart from its true meaning of
"surrounding," confusing it for "round"—about,
hither and thither, etc.—is a constant annoyance in
both these authors.

Of course, language must change; words must be
added as life grows more complex and inventions
increase. But to impoverish a language by forcing
shades of meaning to become confused, is another
matter. The picturesque quality of American slang
shows us to be an imaginative people; but, on the
other hand, this blurring of fine shades of expression
proves that we have some distance to go before we
can be considered a literary people. It is perhaps
inevitable, although to be regretted, that current
speech should exhibit an occasional incorrectness, but
it is strange that an author should permit faults
of grammar to appear in his printed work. The
only answer is—he does not notice them. This is,

of course, unfortunate; but it is a matter which time and cultivation will eradicate. We find few such mistakes in the work of those poets in the first stage of the modern movement, who inherit the traditions of an older practice; or in the work of the poets of the third stage, who have progressed far enough along the road of evolution to have again achieved a culture, at once cosmopolitan and indubitably their own.

Perhaps nothing better illustrates the stages of a movement than this fact of language; and it is perfectly understandable that at a time when life, art, is in a state of flux, those poets most conscious of changing conditions should be swept along on the waves of thought so fast that they have neither time nor inclination to concern themselves with correctness of expression. Of course, it may be objected that this is largely a matter of education, but, in a young country such as America is, nationality must go through the stage of lack of education in its effort to cast aside the leading strings of tutelage. It is only later that it emerges, purged and whole.

"Chicago Poems" is divided into sections of which perhaps "Handfuls" is the least impressive, but seldom does a first book contain so few unsuccessful things.

It will have been observed throughout these poems how the poet's imagination constantly colours and brightens the subject he has in hand. The last line of this little piece is a good illustration of what I would point out:

A FENCE

Now the stone house on the lake front is finished and the work-
men are beginning the fence.
The palings are made of iron bars with steel points that can
stab the life out of any man who falls on them.
As a fence, it is a masterpiece, and will shut off the rabble and all
vagabonds and hungry men and all wandering children looking for a place to play.
Passing through the bars and over the steel points will go nothing
except Death and the Rain and To-morrow.

There is something of Hans Christian Andersen in that poem. A touch of the Scandinavian mysticism which Mr. Sandburg comes by through right of inheritance.

Judged from the standard of pure art, it is a pity that so much of Mr. Sandburg's work concerns itself with entirely ephemeral phenomena. The problems of posterity will be other than those which claim our attention. Art, nature, humanity, are eternal. But the minimum wage will probably matter as little to the twenty-second century as it did to the thirteenth, although for different reasons.

Mr. Sandburg has not the broad outlook to achieve the epic quality of Mr. Masters' work. He is a lyric poet, but the lyrist in him has a hard time to make itself heard above the brawling of the market-place.

It is dangerous to give a final verdict on contemporary art. All that one can safely say of Mr. Sandburg's work is that it contains touches of great and original beauty, and whatever posterity may feel about it taken merely as poetry, it cannot fail to hold its place to students of this period as a necessary link in an endless chain.

"H.D."

THE IMAGISTS:
"H.D." AND JOHN GOULD FLETCHER

THE IMAGISTS:

"H.D." AND JOHN GOULD FLETCHER

WE are now to deal with the work of the small group of poets known as Imagists. Later, I shall explain just what are the tenets of the Imagist School, but before beginning on the work of the two poets whose names stand at the head of this chapter, it is proper to state that they only represent a fraction of the Imagist group. Of course, any one who writes poetry from the same point of view might be said to write Imagistic verse, to be an Imagist, in short; but, in speaking of the Imagists as a group, I shall confine myself to those six poets whose work has appeared in the successive volumes of the annual anthology, "Some Imagist Poets." These poets are exactly divided in nationality, three being American, three English. The English members of the Imagist group are Richard Aldington, F. S. Flint, and D. H. Lawrence, and I regret that this book, being confined to American poets, leaves me no opportunity to discuss the work of these Englishmen. The three American Imagists are the lady who writes under the pseudonym of "H. D.," John Gould Fletcher, and myself. In this chapter, therefore, I shall consider only the work of "H. D." and John Gould Fletcher.

However individual the work of the six Imagist poets is (and any one who has read their anthology cannot fail to have observed it), the poems of "H. D." and Mr. Fletcher are enough in themselves to show the tendencies and aims of the group.

I suppose few literary movements have been so little understood as Imagism. Only a short time ago, in the "Yale Review," Professor John Erskine confessed that he had no clear idea of what was Imagist verse and what was not, and in unconscious proof of his ignorance, spoke of Robert Frost and Edgar Lee Masters as Imagists.

To call a certain kind of writing "a school," and give it a name, is merely a convenient method of designating it when we wish to speak of it. We have adopted the same method in regard to distinguishing persons. We say John Smith and James Brown, because it is simpler than to say: six feet tall, blue eyes, straight nose — or the reverse of these attributes. Imagist verse is verse which is written in conformity with certain tenets voluntarily adopted by the poets as being those by which they consider the best poetry to be produced. They may be right or they may be wrong, but this is their belief.

Imagism, then, is a particular school, springing up within a larger, more comprehensive movement, the New Movement with which this whole book has had to do. This movement has as yet received no convenient designation. We, who are of it, naturally have not the proper perspective to see it in all its historic significance. But we can safely claim it to be a "renaissance," a re-birth of the spirit of truth and beauty. It means a re-discovery of beauty in our modern world, and the originality and honesty to affirm that beauty in whatever manner is native to the poet.

I have shown Edwin Arlington Robinson and Robert Frost as the pioneers of this renaissance; I have shown Edgar Lee Masters and Carl Sandburg plunging forward in quest of change and freedom, hurling themselves against the harshness and materialism of existing conditions, shouting their beliefs, sometimes raucously, but always honestly and with abounding courage. Now, I am to show a condition, not changing, but changed. These poets not only express themselves differently, they see life and the universe from a different standpoint.

It is not over; the movement is yet in its infancy. Other poets will come and, perchance, perfect where these men have given the tools. Other writers, forgetting the stormy times in which this movement had its birth, will inherit in plenitude and calm that for which they have fought. Then our native flowers will bloom into a great garden, to be again conventionalized to a pleasance of stone statues and mathematical parterres awaiting a new change which shall displace it. This is the perpetually recurring history of literature, and of the world.

I have chosen the Imagists as representing the third stage of the present movement advisedly, for only in them do I see that complete alteration of point of view necessary to this third stage. An alteration, let me add, due solely to the beliefs — moral, religious, and artistic — inherent in the characters of these poets. Honest difference of opinion leads to honestly different work, and this must not be confused with the absurd outpourings of those gadflies of the arts who imitate the manners of others without an inkling of their souls; nor with those nefarious persons who endeavour to keep themselves before the public by means of a more or less clever charlatanism.

The spoken word, even the written word, is often misunderstood. I do not wish to be construed as stating that poets in the third stage are better, as poets, than those in the other two. Fundamental beliefs change art, but do not, necessarily, either improve or injure it. Great poetry has been written at every stage of the world's history, but Homer did not write like Dante, nor Dante like Shakespeare, nor Shakespeare like Edgar Allan Poe. So, in literary criticism, one may assign a poet his place in a general movement without any attempt to appraise his individual merit by so doing.

Before taking up the work of "H.D." and John Gould Fletcher in detail, I think it would be well to consider, for a moment, what Imagism is, and for what those poets who style themselves "Imagists" stand.

In the preface to the anthology, "Some Imagist Poets," there is set down a brief list of tenets to which the poets contributing to it mutually agreed. I do not mean that they pledged themselves as to a creed. I mean that they all found themselves in accord upon these simple rules.

I propose to take up these rules presently, one by one, and explain them in detail, but I will first set them down in order:

1. To use the language of common speech, but to employ always the *exact* word, not the nearly-exact, nor the merely decorative word.

2. To create new rhythms — as the expression of new moods — and not to copy old rhythms, which merely echo old moods. We do not insist upon "free-verse" as the only method of writing poetry. We fight for it as for a principle of liberty. We believe that the individuality of a poet may often be better expressed in free-verse than in conventional forms. In poetry a new cadence means a new idea.

3. To allow absolute freedom in the choice of subject. It is not good art to write badly of aeroplanes and automobiles, nor is it necessarily bad art to write well about the past. We

believe passionately in the artistic value of modern life, but we wish to point out that there is nothing so uninspiring nor so old-fashioned as an aeroplane of the year 1911.

4. To present an image (hence the name: "Imagist"). We are not a school of painters, but we believe that poetry should render particulars exactly and not deal in vague generalities, however magnificent and sonorous. It is for this reason that we oppose the cosmic poet, who seems to us to shirk the real difficulties of his art.

5. To produce poetry that is hard and clear, never blurred nor indefinite.

6. Finally, most of us believe that concentration is of the very essence of poetry.

There is nothing new under the sun, even the word, "renaissance," means a re-birth not a new birth, and of this the Imagists were well aware. This short creed was preceded by the following paragraph:

These principles are not new; they have fallen into desuetude. They are the essentials of all great poetry, indeed of all great literature.

It is not primarily on account of their forms, as is commonly supposed, that the Imagist poets represent a changed point of view; it is because of their reactions toward the world in which they live.

Now let us examine these tenets and see just what they mean, for I have observed that their very succinctness has often occasioned misunderstanding.

The first one is : "To use the language of common speech, but to employ always the *exact* word, not the nearly-exact, nor the merely decorative word."

The language of common speech means a diction which carefully excludes inversions, and the *clichés* of the old poetic jargon. As to inversions, we only need to remember Matthew Arnold's famous parody on this evil practice in his essay, "On Translating Homer" :

> Yourself, how do you do,
> Very well, you I thank.

But, until very recently, it persisted in our poetry. One of the tenets in which all the poets of the present movement, Imagists and others, are agreed, however, is this abhorrence of the inversion.

"*Cliché*" is a French word and means "stamped," as a coin, for instance. In other words, it is something in common use, and not peculiar to the author. Old, faded expressions like "battlemented clouds," and "mountainous seas," are *clichés*. Excellent the first time, but so worn by use as to convey no very distinct impression to the reader. As an example of the old poetic jargon, take such a passage as this:

> To ope my eyes
> Upon the Ethiope splendour
> Of the spangled night.

It will at once be admitted that this is hardly the

language of common speech. Common speech does not exclude imaginative language nor metaphor; but it must be original and natural to the poet himself, not culled from older books of verse.

The *exact* word has been much misunderstood. It means the *exact* word which conveys the writer's impression to the reader. Critics conceive a thing to be so and so and no other way. To the poet, the thing is as it appears in relation to the whole. For instance, he might say:

> Great heaps of shiny glass
> Pricked out of the stubble
> By a full, high moon.

This does not mean that the stones are really of glass, but that they so appear in the bright moonlight. It is the *exact* word to describe the effect. In short, the exactness is determined by the content. The habit of choosing a word as unlike the object as possible, much in vogue among the would-be-modern poets, is silly, and defeats its own object. One example of this kind which was brought to my attention some time ago was "a mauve wind." That is just nonsense. It is not *exact* in any sense, it connotes nothing. "Black wind," "white wind," "pale wind," all these are colours and therefore do not exactly describe any wind, but they do describe certain windy effects. "Mauve wind," on the other hand, is merely a straining after novelty, unguided by common-sense or a feeling for fitness.

So much for the first Imagist tenet. The second: "To create new rhythms — as the expression of new moods — and not to copy old rhythms which merely echo old moods. . . . In poetry a new cadence means a new idea."

This, of course, refers to the modern practice of writing largely in the free forms. It is true that modern subjects, modern habits of mind, seem to find more satisfactory expression in *vers libre* and "polyphonic prose" than in metrical verse. It is also true that "a new cadence means a new idea." Not, as has been stated by hostile critics, that the cadence engenders the idea; quite the contrary, it means that the idea clothes itself naturally in an appropriate novelty of rhythm. Very slight and subtle it may be, but adequate. The Imagist poets "do not insist upon free-verse as the only method of writing poetry." In fact, the group are somewhat divided in their practice here.

This brings us to the third tenet: "To allow absolute freedom in the choice of subject." Again, over this passage, misunderstandings have arisen. "How can the choice of subject be absolutely unrestricted?" — horrified critics have asked. The only reply to such a question is that one had supposed one were speaking to people of common-sense and intelligence. To make this passage intelligible to any others, it would be necessary to add "within the bounds of good taste." Of course, what one person might consider good taste another might think the reverse of it; all that the passage intends to imply is that this group restricts itself to no particular kind of subject matter. Old, new, actual, literary, anything which excites the creative faculty in the individual poet, is permissible; they are equally Imagists and poets if they write about ancient Greece, or about a cluster of chimney-stacks seen out of the window.

Number four says: "To present an image (hence the name 'Imagist'). We are not a school of painters, but we believe that poetry should render particulars exactly, and not deal in vague generalities, however magnificent and sonorous."

This paragraph has caused a great deal of confusion. It has been construed to mean that Imagist poetry is chiefly concerned with the presentation of pictures. Why this should have come about, considering that the words, "we are not a school of painters," were intended to offset any such idea, I do not know. The truth is that "Imagism," "Imagist," refers more to the manner of presentation than to the thing presented. It is a kind of technique rather than a choice of subject. "Imagism" simply means — to quote from the second anthology, "Some Imagist Poets, 1916"—"a clear presentation of whatever the author wishes to convey. Now he may wish to convey a mood of indecision, in which case the poem should be indecisive; he may wish to bring before his reader the constantly shifting and changing lights over a landscape, or the varying attitudes of mind of a person under strong emotion, then his poem must shift and change to present this clearly." Imagism is presentation, not representation. For instance, Imagists do not speak of the sea as the "rolling wave" or the "vasty deep," high-sounding, artificial generalities which convey no exact impression; instead, let us compare these two stanzas in a poem of Mr. Fletcher's called "The Calm":

> At noon I shall see waves flashing,
> White power of spray.
>
> The steamers, stately,
> Kick up white puffs of spray behind them.
> The boiling wake
> Merges in the blue-black mirror of the sea.

That is an exact image; but here is another from "Tide of Storms," in which the exactness of the image is augmented by powerful imaginative connotations:

> Crooked, crawling tide with long wet fingers
> Clutching at the gritty beach in the roar and spurt of spray,
> Tide of gales, drunken tide, lava-burst of breakers,
> Black ships plunge upon you from sea to sea away.

This vivid "presentation of whatever the author wishes to convey" is closely allied to the next tenet of the Imagist manifesto, which is: "To produce poetry which is hard and clear, never blurred nor indefinite." It must be kept in mind that this does not refer to subject but to the rendering of subject. I might borrow a metaphor from another art and call it "faithfulness to the architectural line." Ornament may be employed, so long as it follows the structural bases of the poem. But poetical jig-saw work is summarily condemned. That is why, although so much Imagist poetry is metaphorical, similes are sparingly used. Imagists fear the blurred effect of a too constant change of picture in the same poem.

The last rule is very simple, it is that "concentration is of the very essence of poetry." A rule, indeed, as old as art itself, and yet so often lost sight of that it can hardly be too often affirmed. How many works of art are ruined by a too great discursiveness! To remain concentrated on the subject, and to know when to stop, are two cardinal rules in the writing of poetry.

We see therefore that these canons boil down into something like the following succinct statements: Simplicity and directness of speech; subtlety and beauty of rhythms; individualistic freedom of idea; clearness and vividness of presentation; and concentration. Not new principles, by any means, as the writers of the preface admit, but "fallen into desuetude."

One characteristic of Imagist verse which was not mentioned in this preface, is: Suggestion — the implying of something rather than the stating of it, implying it perhaps under a metaphor, perhaps in an even less obvious way.

This poem of Mr. Fletcher's is an excellent example of Imagist suggestion :

THE WELL

The well is not used now
Its waters are tainted.

I remember there was once a man went down
To clean it.
He found it very cold and deep,
With a queer niche in one of its sides,
From which he hauled forth buckets of bricks and dirt.

The picture as given is quite clear and vivid. But the picture we see is not the poem, the real poem lies beyond, is only suggested.

Of the poets we have been considering in these essays, Mr. Robinson is most nearly allied to the Imagists in the use of suggestion ; but the technique he employs is quite unlike theirs. In Mr. Sandburg's "Limited," which I quoted in the last chapter, suggestion again is the poem, and his treatment of it there is almost Imagistic.

It must not be forgotten that however many rules and tenets we may analyze, such mechanical labour can never give the touchstone to style. That must lie in a sense which is beyond reason. As Matthew Arnold said of the grand style, "one must feel it." It is possible to determine the work of different painters by their brush strokes, but such knowledge is for the expert alone, and then only for purposes of authenticity. The layman who had no way of telling the work of Titian from that of Watteau by any other method than that of brush strokes, would make a poor connoisseur.

I could go minutely into the work of these poets and show how each differs from the other — the varying modes of expression, the individual ways of using words, the changing progression of the phrases, the subtle originality of rhythms — but any one who could intelligently follow such an analysis would have no difficulty in determining Imagist work *per se;* and those who could not tell it at a glance, would find such hair-splitting dissection totally incomprehensible.

A few broad lines, then, shall serve us here, and I trust that, before I have finished, the reader will be incapable of making the blunder of that recent critic, who placed Mr. Frost and Mr. Masters in the Imagist group.

I have shown certain aspects of the Imagist idiom, but we must not lose sight of the fact that all these barriers are arbitrary, and fade somewhat into each other. Much of this idiom is applicable to the other poets whom we have been considering, as well; some of it is peculiar to the Imagists. But it is principally in their manner of dealing with the idiom that we shall find the difference to lie. Let me insist once more that Imagism is only one section of a larger movement to which the six poets of these essays all belong.

So much, then, for the idiom, at present. As to the forms, principally *vers libre* and "polyphonic prose," I shall take them up later. Now we must return to the poets themselves. The first of whom I wish to speak is "H.D."

"H.D.," as I have already said, is a pseudonym; but a very simple and natural one. It consists merely of the inititals of the lady in question — before she was married, that is. For "H.D."'s name was Hilda Doolittle, and she is the daughter of Professor Charles L. Doolittle, for many years Director of the Flower Astronomical Observatory of the University of Pennsylvania.

Professor Doolittle has been twice married. His second wife was Miss Helen Eugenia Wolle, a name which hints of a German ancestry. Probably Mrs. Doolittle comes from that fine, undeviating people, known for more than two hundred years as the Pennsylvania Dutch.

Mrs. Doolittle married her husband before he was

called to the University, and Hilda Doolittle was born in Bethlehem, Pennsylvania, on September 10, 1886. Before she was old enough to go to school, however, Professor Doolittle accepted the position of Director of the Flower Observatory, and the family moved to a suburb of Philadelphia. Here the little girl went to the public school in the village, being sent later to a private school, the Gordon School, in West Philadelphia. Hilda Doolittle stayed at the Gordon School until 1902, when she left to be prepared for college at the Friends' Central School. She entered Bryn Mawr College in the Autumn of 1904.

A good student she must have been, and excellently grounded, since she reads Greek and Latin as easily as most people do French ; but eagerness often defeats its own object, and Hilda Doolittle was obliged to give up her college course in her sophomore year, as her health had completely broken down.

We can imagine the next few years, although we know very little about them. The slow recovery of health ; the trial flights of literature ; the loneliness of surrounding, from which all the poets of this generation have suffered. The interest in poetry was not yet. Each of our six poets has fought the demons of indifference and despair, fought through to freedom in his or her way ; and, in so doing, each apparently alone and all, unconsciously, together, they have made this poetic renaissance, this new movement, of which I have been speaking. Not that Hilda Doolittle wrote poetry in those days; she had not yet found out her possibilities in that line. She wrote stories, and mostly stories for children, some of which appeared in a Presbyterian paper in Philadelphia.

It is hard to conceive of these little tales, in view of the exquisite work of "H.D."'s maturity; it is hard to figure the shy, reticent girl plodding up and down the straight Philadelphia streets, bitterly suppressing a desire for beauty which nothing about her satisfied. "H.D." has a strange, faun-like, dryad-like quality, she seems always as though just startled from a brake of fern; and if this is so now that she has written and justified her longings, what must it have been when it was all beyond the dim horizon of the future and she herself alone believed.

In 1911, Miss Doolittle went abroad, on what, at the time, was intended to be merely a Summer trip. But, as was natural, she found in Italy and France solace for that desire for beauty which had been torturing her for so many years. London, too, supplied her with the stimulus of literary companionship. As I pointed out in speaking of Robert Frost, London at that time was a very El Dorado for young poets, and Hilda Doolittle had at last found her true niche in the world of art, she was indubitably a poet. She had known Ezra Pound years before, when he was still living in Philadelphia, and she soon became a member of that small band of insurgent poets of which he was one.

It only needed the spark of sympathy and competition to start the smouldering poetry in Miss Doolittle to bright flame. She began to write, and what she wrote was as perfect as a clear intaglio. Mr. Pound, with that rare instinct for good work which is undeniably his, at once perceived her remarkable talent. Acting as the London agent for "Poetry," he accepted some of her poems, and, using them as an example of a kind of writing in which he and others were becoming interested, he persuaded her to appear under the banner of the new school. Her poems were printed in the January, 1913, number of "Poetry," over the pseudonym "H.D.," followed by the word "Imagist."

The work of "H.D." (as she prefers to be called, and as I shall speak of her in future) is so homogeneous, and shows so little change, except for a slight widening and deepening as she proceeds, that I shall abandon my usual custom in mentioning it. Instead of interlarding criticism with biography, I shall first set down the few facts of her life, and reserve all consideration of her work until after they are disposed of.

"H.D.'"s life is that of a true artist. It is one of internal mental and emotional experiences, not of external events.

One of the little band of poets with whom " H.D."

now identified herself was Richard Aldington, the well-known Imagist. Like "H.D.," Mr. Aldington was fascinated by Greek culture; the flawless purity of Greek models was a perpetual source of delight to him. Mr. Pound, in his life of the young Vorticist sculptor, Gaudier Brzeska, has told of the long discussions between these two; Brzeska wishing to cut away all bonds with the past, Richard Aldington firmly insisting that the Hellenic outlook was more needed to-day than ever.

In this age of pedantic learning, or no learning at all, it is strange to find two young people reading Greek "for fun." But this was just what "H.D." and Mr. Aldington did. The Imagists seem to have a natural *flair* for languages. The so-called dead languages are very living to most of them, and modern languages they all know well, some one, some two, most of them three. There is nothing bookish about this. It comes as easily to them as slang comes to some people.

"H.D." and Richard Aldington were married on October 18, 1913.

During the Winter of 1913, Mr. Pound collected a number of poems illustrating the Imagist point of view, and they were printed together in a little volume entitled: "Des Imagistes," in April, 1914. The book was brought out by Messrs. Albert and Charles Boni, of New York. The work of both "H. D." and Mr. Aldington was excellently represented in this collection. But the publishers were young men, only just starting, they had not much money to spend on advertisements, the point of view was a departure from accepted standards, and, to add to the confusion, the volume had no explanatory preface. It was much, but very ignorantly, reviewed. It found only a handful of admirers. Truly, the Imagists have had an exceedingly hard struggle.

When I returned to London in the Summer of 1914, the great preoccupation of all the group was how to make people understand what they were trying to do. How get past prejudiced editors and reviewers and appeal intelligently to the reading public. It was decided, after much discussion, that we should again appear together, and continue doing so until people at least understood our kind of poetry. Mr. Pound withdrew from the group and joined the Vorticists, and other contributors were excluded for various reasons, but we were joined by Mr. John Gould Fletcher and Mr. D. H. Lawrence. It was agreed that the authors should be arranged alphabetically according to their names, so that there should be no question of precedence ; and our desire for democracy went to even greater lengths: each author was permitted to make his own selection of his own poems, but any poem could be excluded by one veto, and everyone had a right to veto whatever they chose. It speaks well for the poets' devotion to the cause, when I say that no one was permitted to grumble when his pet contribution was vetoed; and for their confidence in one another's integrity, when I add that no suspicion of professional jealousy has ever come between them. I returned to America in September, 1914, and I brought with me the manuscript of "Some Imagist Poets."

I soon found a publisher in Messrs. Houghton, Mifflin and Company to whose cordial sympathy the group owes much. In the name of my *confrères*, I signed a contract with them for three years, or rather for three separate anthologies to be issued at yearly intervals. The first appeared in the Spring of 1915, and the next two in 1916 and 1917, respectively.

There will be no more volumes of "Some Imagist Poets." The collection has done its work. These three little books are the germ, the nucleus, of the school; its spreading out, its amplification, must be sought in the published work of the individual members of the group.

There is very little more to record about "H. D.'"s life. During the Winter of 1915 and 1916, she and her husband, with the collaboration of one or two other poets, and under the auspices of "The Egoist" (a London paper of which Mr. Aldington was associate editor), published a number of translations from the Greek and Latin poets, in small unpretentious pamphlets. The series was called, "The Poets' Translation Series." So beautiful were these translations, particularly "H.D."'s "Choruses from Iphigeneia in Aulis," that the well-known scholar, Professor Mackail, wrote an article in praise of them in the London "Times."

The series was successful from every point of view, and a new series was planned, but had to be abandoned on Mr. Aldington's joining the army. Since his departure for "somewhere in France," "H.D." has taken his position on the staff of "The Egoist."

It is now time to consider "H.D."'s work.

On the first appearance of these short, concentrated poems, many "smart" critics likened them to carved cherry-stones, and dismissed them as something too inconsiderable to be taken seriously. But since when has bulk been the touchstone of art? "Cherry-stones" was a poor simile; "exquisite cameos and intaglios," would have been a more exact definition. These poems are fragile as shells, and as transparent, but their modelling is as carefully done as that of a statue of Parian marble.

Writing in a highly and most carefully wrought *vers libre*, "H.D."'s poems achieve a beauty of cadence which has been surpassed by no other *vers libriste*. Indeed, her subtly changing rhythms are almost without an equal. Never, in her verse, do we find a prose suggestion. Hers are not, as some of her husband's are, the piquant paradoxes of romance springing out of plain fact. Her poems are kept to a key; the key of haunted woodland, of nymph-bearing sea. Reading them, we hear pipe strains lost in the mists of forests, we hear voices calling through the wash of waves. They remind me of a story I once read by a French author, in which an ancient shell preserved within it a few moments of a siren's song. I seem to hear in "H. D."'s work echoes of a beauty long departed.

Not that these poems, as has been so often asserted, are copies of the Greek. Often employing Greek names, still the poems have no real Hellenic prototype. Rather is it that "H.D." dwells in a world of her own longings, builded of remembered things, or things read of and delighted in. With this, with that, she makes her picture; and, when finished, it resembles nothing but itself.

To this poet, beauty is a thing so sharp as to be painful, delight so poignant it can scarcely be borne. Her extreme sensitiveness turns appreciation to exquisite suffering. Yet, again and again, she flings herself bravely upon the spears of her own reactions.

Here is a poem which shows her shrinking from this piercing appreciation of the beauty of nature:

ORCHARD

I saw the first pear
as it fell —
the honey-seeking, golden-banded,
the yellow swarm
was not more fleet than I,

(spare us from loveliness)
and I fell prostrate
crying:
you have flayed us
with your blossoms,
spare us the beauty
of fruit-trees.

The honey-seeking
paused not,
the air thundered their song,
and I alone was prostrate.

O rough-hewn
god of the orchard,
I bring you an offering —
do you, alone unbeautiful,
son of the god,
spare us from loveliness:

these fallen hazel-nuts,
stripped late of their green sheaths,
grapes, red-purple,
their berries
dripping with wine,
pomegranates already broken,
and shrunken figs
and quinces untouched,
I bring you as offering.

This next one again gives the ache of weariness

which comes when one has been stretching the cords
of wonder for a long time :

SHELTERED GARDEN

I have had enough.
I gasp for breath.

Every way ends, every road,
every foot-path leads at last
to the hill-crest —
then you retrace your steps,
or find the same slope on the other side,
precipitate.
I have had enough —
border-pinks, clove-pinks, wax-lilies,
herbs, sweet-cress.

O for some sharp swish of a branch —
there is no scent of resin
in this place,
no taste of bark, of coarse weeds,
aromatic, astringent —
only border on border of scented pinks.

Have you seen fruit under cover
that wanted light —
pears wadded in cloth,
protected from the frost,
melons, almost ripe,
smothered in straw?

Why not let the pears cling
to the empty branch?
All your coaxing will only make
a bitter fruit —
let them cling, ripen of themselves,
test their own worth,
nipped, shrivelled by the frost,
to fall at last but fair
with a russet coat.

Or the melon —
let it bleach yellow
in the winter light,
even tart to the taste —
it is better to taste of frost —
the exquisite frost —
than of wadding and of dead grass.

For this beauty,
beauty without strength,
chokes out life.
I want wind to break,
scatter these pink-stalks,
snap off their spiced heads,
fling them about with dead leaves —
spread the paths with twigs,
limbs broken off,
trail great pine branches,
hurled from some far wood
right across the melon-patch,

break pear and quince —
leave half-trees, torn, twisted
but showing the fight was valiant.

O to blot out this garden
to forget, to find a new beauty
in some terrible
wind-tortured place.

The poet is, like Robert Frost, suffering from a too minute and impressing observation — observation and its correlative, imagination ; and the very hair-strokes of her ordered art force a cry for rest and disorder.   She desires :

. . a new beauty
in some terrible
wind-tortured place.

But the "new beauty" which "H.D." is to make is not that of wind-tortured places.   Hers is an art of balance, of repose, of mellowness and charm.   Limitations are hard things to submit to, and yet every poet, no less than every person, must bow to them. We have watched Mr. Masters rebelling against his. That poet is happy indeed who can express himself in divers moods, and ease the strain of one by his ability to experience another.

In both these poems, notice the beautiful curves of the cadences.   "H.D."'s cadences are always very marked, yet never is there a hint of a metrical line. Her practice, and that of her husband, Mr. Aldington, is absolutely to abandon the rhythms of metre when writing cadenced verse. Some *vers libristes* permit themselves occasional lines which might be timed by the old scansion, if only such lines also fall within the circle of their cadence, but "H.D." and Mr. Aldington never do. Free verse within its own law of cadence has no absolute rules, it would not be "free" if it had. I do not say which of these two methods is the best. I am only pointing out a peculiarity in the rhythms of these two poets.

Perhaps I cannot do better than pause here and explain just what is *vers libre*, just what I mean by calling it "cadenced verse." In the chapter on Mr. Masters, I said that "*vers libre* was a verse-form based upon cadence." In the preface to "Some Imagist Poets, 1916," there is an explanation of cadence which I will quote:

Now cadence in music is one thing, cadence in poetry quite another, since we are not dealing with tone, but with rhythm. It is the sense of perfect balance of flow and rhythm. Not only must the syllables so fall as to increase and continue the movement, the whole poem must be as rounded and recurring as the circular swing of a balanced pendulum. It can be fast or slow, it may even jerk, but this perfect swing it must have, even its jerks must follow the central movement. To illustrate: Suppose a person were given the task of walking, or running, round

a large circle, with two minutes given to do it in.   Two minutes
which he would just consume if he walked round the circle
quietly.   But in order to make the task easier for him, or harder,
as the case may be, he was required to complete each half-circle
in exactly a minute.   No other restrictions were placed upon
him.   He might dawdle in the beginning, and run madly to reach
the half-circle mark on time, and then complete his task by
walking steadily round the second half to goal.   Or he might
leap, and run, and skip, and linger in all sorts of ways, making
up for slow going by fast, and for extra haste by pauses, and vary
these movements on either lap of the circle as the humour
seized him, only so that he were just one minute in traversing
the first half-circle, and just one minute in traversing the second.
Another illustration which may be employed is that of a Japanese
wood-carving, where a toad in one corner is balanced by a
spray of blown flowers in the opposite upper one.   The flowers
are not the same shape as the toad, neither are they the same
size, but the balance is preserved.

The unit of *vers libre* is not the foot, the number of syllables,
the quantity, or the line.   The unit is the strophe, which may
be the whole poem, or may be only a part.   Each strophe is a
complete circle;   in fact, the meaning of the Greek word
"strophe" is simply that part of the poem which was recited
while the chorus was making a turn round the altar set up in
the centre of the theatre.   The simile of the circle is more than
a simile, therefore;   it is a fact.   Of course, the circle need not
always be the same size, nor need the times allowed to negotiate
it be always the same.   There is room here for an infinite number
of variations.   Also, circles can be added to circles, movement upon movement to the poem, provided each movement
completes itself, and ramifies naturally into the next.

Let us illustrate with this little poem of "H. D."'s:

OREAD

Whirl up, sea —
Whirl your pointed pines,
Splash your great pines
On our rocks,
Hurl your green over us,
Cover us with your pools of fir.

It will quickly be seen that this poem is made up of five cadences: "Whirl up, sea —" is one cadence; "Whirl your pointed pines," is another; "Splash your great pines on our rocks," is a third; "Hurl your green over us," a fourth; and the fifth, "Cover us with your pools of fir."

Now these cadences are made up of time units which are in no sense syllabic. I mean that the number of syllables to each unit is immaterial. The words must be hurried or delayed in reading to fill out the swing, that is all. The time units are also an irregular measurement within the main cadences. Some of the cadences are made up of two such units, some of three, and, in the fourth line, the last two syllables are in the nature of a feminine ending, in that they are really an unaccented or suppressed part of the first time unit of the fifth line.

Whirl up / sea — /
Whirl / your pointed pines /
Splash / your great pines / on our rocks /
Hurl / your green over us /
Cover us / with your pools / of fir. /

How nearly identical these time units are, is shown by the following table. In January, 1917, I made some experiments in reading *vers libre* aloud into a sound-photographing machine, through the courtesy of Dr. William M. Patterson of Columbia University. The results of the reading of "Oread," as recorded on the film and afterwards measured by Dr. Patterson, are here given. The measurements are of the intervals between the chief accents.

"The Oread:" (intervals between chief accents given in tenths of a second, roughly estimated) 13 — 22 — 15 — 24 — 13 — 13 — 19 — 13 — 15 — 13.

It will here be seen that the greatest variation of time length of unit is 11/10, or that between a 13/10 second and a 24/10. While, as Dr. Patterson pointed out, the interval 13/10 appears five times in this short poem.

Of course, no one in reading the poem would have such measurements in mind. They were recorded by a scientific instrument while the poem was being read in a perfectly simple and natural manner, but they are interesting for purposes of analysis.

The cadences of *vers libre* are not all so simple as this. But for that very reason I selected this to illustrate upon. No matter how changing and subtle, it is upon this principle that all *vers libre* is constructed.

"H.D." has published only one book as yet— "Sea Garden," issued by Messrs. Constable and Company, London, during the Autumn of 1916. "Sea Garden" is a charming name for a book, and the sea flower poems scattered through this garden are extremely beautiful. Also, they show the changed point of view of which I have spoken. What careful observation is here; and yet, rather an observation by the imagination than by the physical eye, although the imaginative impulse never jars upon our sense of truth. I will give a few of these flower poems.

SEA IRIS

I

Weed, moss-weed,
root tangled in sand,
sea-iris, brittle flower,
one petal like a shell
is broken,
and you print a shadow
like a thin twig.

Fortunate one,
scented and stinging,

rigid myrrh-bud,
camphor-flower,
sweet and salt — you are wind
in our nostrils.

II

Do the murex-fishers
drench you as they pass?
Do your roots drag up colour
from the sand?
Have they slipt gold under you —
Rivets of gold?

Band of iris-flowers
above the waves,
you are painted blue,
painted like a fresh prow
stained among the salt weeds.

SEA LILY

Reed,
slashed and torn
but doubly rich —
such great heads as yours
drift upon temple-steps,
but you are shattered
in the wind.

Myrtle-bark
is flecked from you,

scales are dashed
from your stem,
sand cuts your petal,
furrows it with hard edge,
like flint
on a bright stone.

Yet though the whole wind
slash at your bark,
you are lifted up,
aye — though it hiss
to cover you with froth.

It is difficult to analyze the delicate art of these flower-pieces. I think it consists largely in the crispness and accuracy of vision of the poet, combined with clear, sharp consonant sounds in the verse; again, of an original imaginative insight, kept unsentimentally strong and incisive by a satisfying but astringent cadence.

Of all "H.D.'"'s flower poems, the following is to my mind probably the finest. It is a part of a longer poem, "Sea Gods." These violets are the offering brought to the gods:

SEA GODS

But we bring violets,
great masses — single, sweet,
wood-violets, stream-violets,
violets from a wet marsh.

Violets in clumps from hills,
tufts with earth at the roots,
violets tugged from rocks,
blue violets, moss, cliff, river-violets.

Yellow violets' gold,
burnt with a rare tint —
violets like red ash
among tufts of grass.

We bring deep-purple
bird-foot violets.

We bring the hyacinth-violets,
sweet, bare, chill to the touch —
and violets whiter than the in-rush
of your own white surf.

The repetition of the word " violets," is a daring and dangerous thing, but the poet has so managed this repetition that it is a beauty not a torment. The masses of violets are heaped one upon another until the sheer music of the poem almost obscures the picture, fine though that is. Take the first stanza, and note the word "violets," and the beautiful qualifying words set to it:

But we bring violets,
great masses — single, sweet,

> wood-violets, stream-violets,
> violets from a wet marsh.

For pure loveliness of adjective, listen to the last line of the second stanza:

> blue violets, moss, cliff, river-violets.

"H.D." is a great artist — repetitions where the effect is enhanced by them, but never a repetition where most poets would be forced to repeat from a paucity of imaginative images, or an ill-furnished vocabulary.

"H.D." is peculiarly a poet of flowers, and in the very manner in which she uses her flowers, we have hints of that changed technique of which I have been speaking. Compare the violet poem I have just quoted, with Keats's "I Stood Tiptoe upon a Little Hill," for instance. Almost all the effects in Keats's poem are got by the use of similes and metaphors:

> Sweetpeas on tiptoe for a flight.
>
> .   .   .   .
>
> The clouds were pure and white as flocks new-shorn.
>
> .   .   .   .
>
> Bloomy grapes laughing from green attire.
>
> .   .   .   .
>
> .   .   .   clumps of woodbine taking the soft wind
> Upon their summer thrones.

Now take these lines from "H.D.":

> We bring deep-purple
> bird-foot violets.
>
> We bring the hyacinth-violets,
> sweet, bare, chill to the touch —
> and violets whiter than the in-rush
> of your own white surf.

There is one simile here, but it is employed more as a statement than as a simile. That whole passage illustrates most excellently what Imagists mean by verse that is hard and clear.

"H.D." is not a poet of great breadth of mood nor of many moods. All her effects are delicate rather than broad. She is also essentially a lyric poet. Even in those poems which aim at a sort of narrative suggestion like "The Helmsman," "The Shrine," "Pursuit," "The Cliff Temple," and "Sea Gods," the poems succeed rather by their lyricism than by anything else.

THE HELMSMAN

> O be swift —
> we have always known you wanted us.
>
> We fled inland with our flocks,
> we pastured them in hollows,

cut off from the wind
and the salt track of the marsh.

We worshipped inland —
we stepped past wood-flowers,
we forgot your tang,
we brushed wood-grass.

We wandered from pine-hills
through oak and scrub-oak tangles,
we broke hyssop and bramble,
we caught flower and new bramble-fruit
in our hair: we laughed
as each branch whipped back,
we tore our feet in half buried rocks
and knotted roots and acorn-cups.

We forgot — we worshipped,
we parted green from green,
we sought further thickets,
we dipped our ankles
through leaf-mould and earth,
and wood and wood-bank enchanted us —

and the feel of the clefts in the bark,
and the slope between tree and tree —
and the slender path strung field to field
and wood to wood
and hill to hill
and the forest after it.

We forgot — for a moment
tree-resin, tree-bark,
sweat of a torn branch
were sweet to the taste.

We were enchanted with the fields,
the tufts of coarse grass
in the shorter grass —
we loved all this.

But now, our boat climbs — hesitates — drops —
climbs — hesitates — crawls back —
O be swift —
we have always known you wanted us.

Yes, it is the lyric touch in that poem which delights the reader. Such passages as:

We fled inland with our flocks,
we pastured them in hollows,
cut off from the wind
and the salt track of the marsh.

How apt and perfect is that expression, "the salt track of the marsh," any one who has seen a wide swath of rank marsh grass cutting into arable land will instantly appreciate.

"We parted green from green" is a beautiful line. The reader sees the variously tinted leaves and grasses, and almost the shapes of them, one and

another, growing thicker and darker to the lushness
and dimness of :

> We sought the further thickets,
> we dipped our ankles
> through leaf-mould and earth,
> and wood and wood-bank enchanted us.

The last stanza is an example of that elusive thing,
movement, which can be given more subtly in *vers
libre* than in any other form.   Read it aloud, and
notice how the lines creep and waver, until

> O be swift —

starts the boat darting toward land on the crest of a
sudden breaker.   Yet, in this last stanza, lyricism
gives place to drama, and this is so rare with "H.D."
as to be noted the more carefully when it does occur.
    The sea shares "H.D."'s interest with flowers, and
her descriptions of it are no less accurate and vivid :

> where rollers shot with blue
> cut under deeper blue.

Of a cliff, she says :

> But you — you are unsheltered,
> cut with the weight of wind —
> you shudder when it strikes,
> then lift, swelled with the blast —
> you sink as the tide sinks,

> you shrill under hail, and sound
> thunder when thunder sounds.

of a shore:

> Wind rushes
> over the dunes,
> and the coarse, salt-crusted grass
> answers.

"H.D."'s work deals entirely with those things which are constant and eternal. She seems quite unaffected by the world about her. Cliffs, and sea, and flowers, have always been the same; in one poem, "Cities," where she deserts nature for man and his activities, it is in a pathetic endeavour to believe in the beauty and use of a modernity in which she feels she has no part.

Strange paradox! To be the prophet of a renewing art, and to spend one's life longing for a vanished loveliness. It is only in the things which were and still are that "H.D." finds beauty. It is not to her that we must look for a revaluation of the terms of beauty. Other poets are possessed of a vision which can perceive a new beauty in the modern world; we shall see Mr. Fletcher doing this. But "H.D." has no such insight. The everyday world startles her as though she really were the dryad to which I likened her at the beginning of this essay.

There are people who find this poetry cold. In

one sense it is, for in it is something of the coolness of marble, something of the clarity of fresh water. But it is a mistake to suppose that this coolness, this clearness, covers no feeling. The feeling is there, but the expression chastens it. Let me mix my similes, let me liken "H.D.'"'s poetry to the cool flesh of a woman bathing in a fountain — cool to the sight, cool to the touch, but within is a warm, beating heart. Nothing could point out more aptly what I mean than this poem:

CIRCE

It was easy enough
to bend them to my wish,
it was easy enough
to alter them with a touch,
but you
adrift on the great sea,
how shall I call you back?

Cedar and white ash,
rock-cedar and sand plants
and tamarind,
red cedar and white cedar
and black cedar from the inmost forest,
fragrance upon fragrance
and all of my sea-magic is for naught.

It was easy enough —
a thought called them

from the sharp edges of the earth;
they prayed for a touch,
they cried for the sight of my face,
they entreated me
till in pity
I turned each to his own self.

Panther and panther,
then a black leopard
follows close —
black panther and red
and a great hound,
a god-like beast,
cut the sand in a clear ring
and shut me from the earth,
and cover the sea-sound
with their throats,
and the sea-roar with their own barks
and bellowing and snarls,
and the sea-stars
with the swirl of the sand,
and the rock-tamarinds
and the wind resonance —
but not your voice.

It is easy enough to call men
from the edges of the earth.
It is easy to summon them to my feet
with a thought —
it is beautiful to see the tall panther
and the sleek deer-hounds
circle in the dark.

It is easy enough
to make cedar and white ash fumes
into palaces
and to cover the sea-caves
with ivory and onyx.

But I would give up
rock-fringes of coral
and the inmost chamber
of my island palace
and my own gifts
and the whole region
of my power and magic
for your glance.

How sad that is! The loneliness of it! An en-
chantress, mistress of transforming spells, poet of
submissive words, wielding power lightly, almost
with ease, but of what use is it when she is constantly
longing for one who is not there. "H.D." has set
this poem very far away. She has overlaid it with
plates and plates of wrought and beaten gold, but
still, in the final count, it is just the desire of a woman,
a simple, human woman, for the man she loves.
Cold indeed! Cold as the words of cut marble upon
a tombstone recording the anguish of a soul.

To appreciate this poetry needs a certain knowledge. "H.D." is indubitably a poet for poets. It
is doubtful if the great mass of poetry lovers will

ever fully appreciate work of such a delicate perfection, but it is no less important for that. Few books better repay study than "Sea Garden," not only can any poet learn much from "H.D."'s method, the poems themselves reveal new meanings as they become more familiar.

The faults of such poetry are not in its treatment, but in its very texture. This is a narrow art, it has no scope, it neither digs deeply nor spreads widely. Not that it is superficial; it is quite the reverse. But merely that "there are more things in Heaven and Earth" than such poetry takes cognizance of. "H.D." is not a great poet, but she is a rarely perfect poet. It is true that she employs the same technique throughout her work, and that is perhaps monotonous to those who are not concerned with its excellence. It also bears with it the seeds of over-care, of something bordering on preciosity. There is a certain thinness in the original conception, and only the lustre of its polish saves it. But this is a lustre known to no one else. The secret is "H.D."'s peculiar possession. Her poems are native, personal, to a marked degree. They show no slightest trace of those influences which until recently ruled American art. Deeply affected by classic literature, still it is only as a blush of colour that we perceive it in her work. The tricks of her manner occasionally recall the Greek, but her thoughts are perfectly her own. Here is a fresh flower, sprung out of a new graft upon an old stock. Here is the frank, unartificial paganism of a new world. Neither in point of view, nor in technique, does this art resemble any preceding English art, yet it is cosmopolitan in that it is a fusion of much knowledge, all melted and absorbed in the blood of a young and growing race. She takes her good where she finds it, and the perfect singleness of her aim has resulted in releasing all her forces to concentrate them upon the simple fact of beauty. There is no clipping her pattern to a traditional mode; there is no staining it for ulterior ends. It is completely personal, completely sincere. Meticulous, at times, undoubtedly, "H. D."'s faults are obvious enough, because they are also her greatest virtues; but, in the narrow compass in which she works, she has achieved a rare and finely-wrought beauty.

Nothing could better illustrate the wide latitude within the bounds of Imagism than to turn from the work of "H.D." to that of John Gould Fletcher. Where she holds her work in the check of a faultless taste, Mr. Fletcher gives his full range and so obtains a grandeur akin to that of mountains and winds. Both poets have a compelling need for beauty, but where "H.D." retires within herself and finds it in her own soul, Mr. Fletcher goes out from himself and wrests it from the entire world before him.

John Gould Fletcher.

"H.D."'s colours are clear and single, like Fra Angelico's; Mr. Fletcher's are turgid, and imposed one upon another, like Turner's. Turner is not a bad prototype for Mr. Fletcher, each takes the everyday world and colours it to iridescent romance. I can easily imagine Mr. Fletcher having painted "Rain, Steam and Speed," for instance.

John Gould Fletcher was born in Little Rock, Arkansas, on January 3, 1886. His father was of Scotch-Irish stock, the son of a pioneer who went to Arkansas from Tennessee in the early part of the nineteenth century. From pre-Revolutionary days, the family had lived in Tennessee, but Mr. Fletcher's grandfather was caught in the great romantic Western exodus, and his son, the poet's father, was born in a log cabin in the then scarcely settled country of Arkansas.

At that time, Little Rock was only a settlement of a few dozen houses, and Mr. John Gould Fletcher, senior, had only a backwoods education, but it seems to have sufficed. Again and again, in the history of our country, we are struck with the extraordinary results of this apparently insufficient schooling. At the outbreak of the Civil War, this gentleman volunteered in the Confederate Army, serving until 1863. He was promoted captain after the Battle of Chickamauga, and after being mentioned in despatches for bravery, was wounded at the Battle of Murfreesboro, in January, 1862.

It should be noticed that all the poets whom we have studied come of sturdy forbears, and this is particularly the case of those of the second and third stages of the movement. The energy which led their ancestors to war with physical conditions has enabled them to war with mental.

After the war, Mr. Fletcher, senior, kept a small general shop in Little Rock, of which he made such a success that he was able to save enough money to become a cotton buyer. In this business, he also prospered, and with the proceeds took a pleasure trip to Europe in 1873. A trip to Europe meant more in those days than it does now, and it speaks much for Mr. Fletcher's desire for culture that he should have chosen to spend his hardly earned money in this way. Returning to Little Rock, he married, in 1877, Adolphine Krause. This lady was the daughter of a Danish father and a German mother. Her father had come to America in 1839, and became a naturalized citizen; her mother, a Hanoverian by birth, had emigrated to this country in 1835. In the tracing of racial traits, it is interesting to note a certain strain of sentiment in John Gould Fletcher's work, which he undoubtedly inherits from his German and Danish forbears. We can also see a love of the fantastic, a sort of allegorical, elfin quality which links him to these Northern, Teutonic nations.

When the little boy was four years old, the family,

consisting of his father, his mother, his two sisters, and himself, moved into a large square white house; one of those high mansions, with pillared front, so common in the South. It had been built by one of the first settlers of Little Rock, and was old, as Arkansas counts old, when the Fletcher family bought it. It already had memories, not theirs, to be speculated about. Layers of wall-paper upon the walls, four and five deep, lent a suggestion of romance to its faded rooms. This house is the background of the poet's childhood. Mr. Fletcher is fortunate in having one place which he has always looked upon as "home." Americans lose much in depth of character and mellowness of mind by their nomadic habit of life. A person whose childhood has been a series of rapid arrivals and departures from hired lodgings never gains the peculiar tenderness that comes from roots long nourished in one soil.

The profound impression which this house made upon the poet is shown in his "Ghosts of an Old House." Reading this series of short poems, one sees the house, one feels it, and one knows very well the imaginative child who lived in it.

This is the house:

PROLOGUE

The house that I write of, faces the north:
No sun ever seeks

Its six white columns,
The nine great windows of its face.

It fronts foursquare the winds.

Under the penthouse of the veranda roof,
The upper northern rooms
Gloom outwards mournfully.

Staring Ionic capitals
Peer in them:
Owl-like faces.

On winter nights
The wind, sidling round the corner,
Shoots upwards
With laughter.

The windows rattle as if some one were in them wishing to get
    out
And ride upon the wind.

Doors lead to nowhere:
Squirrels burrow between the walls.
Closets in every room hang open,
Windows are stared into by uncivil ancient trees.

In the middle of the upper hallway
There is a great circular hole
Going up to the attic.
A wooden lid covers it.

All over the house there is a sense of futility;
Of minutes dragging slowly
And repeating
Some worn-out story of broken effort and desire.

Here is the little boy in his nursery, teased, even then, by a desire for something beyond what even his fancy could reach:

OLD NURSERY

In the tired face of the mirror
There is a blue curtain reflected.
If I could lift the reflection,
Peer a little beyond, I would see
A boy crying
Because his sister is ill in another room
And he has no one to play with:
A boy listlessly scattering building blocks,
And crying,
Because no one will build for him the palace of Fairy Morgana.
I cannot lift the curtain:
It is stiff and frozen.

This poem is the very nostalgia of remembered childhood:

THE TOY CABINET

By the old toy cabinet,
I stand and turn over dusty things:
Chessmen — card games — hoops and balls —

Toy rifles, helmets, swords,
In the far corner
A doll's tea-set in a box.

Where are you, golden child,
Who gave tea to your dolls and me?
The golden child is growing old,
Further than Rome or Babylon
From you have passed those foolish years.
She lives — she suffers — she forgets.

By the old toy cabinet,
I idly stand and awkwardly
Finger the lock of the tea-set box.
What matter — why should I look inside,
Perhaps it is empty after all!
Leave old things to the ghosts of old;

My stupid brain refuses thought,
I am maddened with a desire to weep.

Those three poems are so vivid, so full of personality, that, after reading them, one knows the wistful little boy, avid of impressions, who read " The Ancient Mariner" in the shadow of the Ionic columns.   Mr. Fletcher tells us that he did not understand the poem, but we can imagine how greatly its weird images and uncanny music must have affected him.

Mrs. Fletcher was musical, with artistic interests, and she loved to buy books.   So the little boy had plenty to feed upon, particularly as he was encouraged to read by presents of books. He says that he was very fond of "Tom Sawyer," and that the scenes in the graveyard "sent shivers up and down my spine and gave me an unquenchable taste for the uncanny and weird." We shall see the truth of this when we come to consider his work.

He was taught to read and write by his mother, learning the former out of "Webster's Blue Back Spelling Book," of which he has keen recollections. When he was about seven or eight, teachers were engaged for him, and he says that he began the studies of Latin and German when he was only eight years old. Certainly, Mr. Fletcher must have been a very precocious little boy, for he distinctly remembers "revelling" in Schiller and Uhland at this period.

When he was eleven years old, in 1897, he was sent to school for the first time, and here he fell in love with Longfellow, Scott, and Tennyson. At this time, too, he began to write verses.

In 1899, Mr. Fletcher entered the High School, graduating in 1902. Some time in 1900 or 1901, he was given a set of Poe, and the effect of such reading upon the sensitive boy can be imagined. He was even then enough of a serious artist to read, not only the poems and stories, but the essays, and it was quite natural that, to use his own words, he "swallowed all Poe's theories wholesale."

In 1902, he was sent to Phillips Academy, Andover, to prepare for Harvard. Here, under a system of compulsory gymnastic training, he gained in vigour and physical strength, and from being a puny boy, developed into a man whose body is strong enough to bear the strain of an unusually fecund creative faculty.

At Phillips Academy, he became interested in chemistry, once more proving that true science and true art are never far apart. Entering Harvard in 1903, Mr. Fletcher started for the first time to learn French. His knowledge of Latin made the reading of French easy to him, and he was soon embarked upon a course of Gautier and Baudelaire. In Mr. Fletcher, as in the other Imagists, we see the great value of lingual studies. Who was it who said that with each new language learnt one acquires a new brain? This is certainly true if, for " brain," we substitute "habit of thought." There is no better training for the mind, there is no better method of gaining vicarious experience, than the study of languages.

Mr. Fletcher is peculiarly sensitive to the *nuances* of tongues. (I shall show how sensitive in a moment, when we come to consider his Japanese poems.) The French language was just what he needed to give his work that severe grounding in technique without which no poet can ever be sure of mastery. Words are stubborn things, it requires much training to make them docile to one's purpose. No modern nation has achieved so perfect a control of words as has the French. It was a happy thought which turned Mr. Fletcher's attention to French.

In the Summer of 1905, the young man took a trip to the West, to California and the Yosemite Valley. The West fascinated him. Again and again he returns to it, most notably in his Arizona poems.

Mr. Fletcher, senior, died in 1906. He had not sympathized in his son's literary aspirations, but had wanted him to study law or go into a bank. To this end, he had wished him to have a Harvard degree. But the poet was too original, too restive under mental control, to be happy learning in a prescribed curriculum. He was too young to appreciate that college courses are not designed for the education of geniuses, but for "l'homme sensuel moyen." Inheriting a small competence from his father, he promptly left college and moved into Boston, intent upon devoting himself wholly to writing.

But Boston suited his needs at that time as little as did Harvard. He, like "H.D.," needed the stimulus of a more mellow surrounding. Realizing this, Mr. Fletcher sailed for Europe in August, 1908. He went straight to Venice, with a sure instinct for what his life had lacked hitherto. Perhaps his mind was too new a field for such impressions to allow of their becoming immediately transferable to poetry. However that may be, I can recall no poem of his which has Venice for a background.

Leaving Venice in November, he passed the Winter in Rome, drinking in history, scenery, colour; and reading as usual, in great thirsty gulps, first Shelley, and then, perhaps more fortunately for him, Browning.

He stayed in Rome until May, 1909, and then moved to London, which greatly intrigued his imagination. It is from this moment that his real career as a poet begins. By October, 1909, he was definitely settled in London, and working hard. When I first met him, he was living in Adelphi Terrace, a place full of literary associations, past and present. I remember thinking that it was an ideal habitat for a poet. There we sat in the large, quiet room, with its hard-wood floor, great writing-table, and overflowing bookcases, and outside, through the trees, the green Thames rolled slowly along, with its constantly shifting pictures of lighters, steamboats, barges, and puffing river craft.

Mr. Fletcher lived in Adelphi Terrace until the Spring of 1914, when he moved to Sydenham, close to the Crystal Palace, and it was during this time that he sowed his literary wild oats, as he insists they are, in the shape of five little books of poems, which, with careless indifference to ridicule, were all published in the same year, 1913, and from the presses of four different firms. These little volumes are out of print, with the exception of one, "The Book of Nature," issued by Messrs. Constable and Company.

I think Mr. Fletcher is hardly fair to his early work in his consideration of these books. With much that was jejune, they nevertheless contained some very interesting things. An attempt, in which he followed the French poet, Arthur Rimbaud, to render the sounds of vowels in colour, achieves, to my mind, a more satisfactory result than Rimbaud's poem. Still, of course, it was something of an imitation.

Let us compare the two :

VOYELLES

A noir, E blanc, I rouge, U vert, O bleu, voyelles,
Je dirai quelque jour vos naissances latentes.
A, noir corset velu des mouches éclatantes
Qui bombillent autour des puanteurs cruelles,

Golfe d'ombre ; E, candeur des vapeurs et des tentes,
Lance des glaciers fiers, rois blancs, frissons d'ombelles ;
I, pourpres, sang craché, rire des lèvres belles
Dans la colère ou les ivresses pénitentes ;

U, cycles, vibrements divins des mers virides,
Paix des pâtis semés d'animaux, paix des rides
Que l'alchimie imprime aux grands fronts studieux ;

O, suprême clairon plein de strideurs étranges,
Silences traversés des Mondes et des Anges:
— O l'Oméga, rayon violet de Ses Yeux.

It is strange how tortured and exaggerated Rimbaud's images seem. They bear only the most distant relation to the letters. Although the open sound of A, may be made, by a slight stretching, to connote black when it is the French "noir" which is used, there is no such approximation in the other colour analogies, with the possible exception of O, for blue. Now, observe how he has worked them out — arbitrarily, for the most part, with very little phonetic effect to relate his colours and images to his vowels. With the exception of "éclatantes" and "puanteurs," we have not a single A sound in the whole clause devoted to A, unless we include the questionable "noir"; while "golfe d'ombre" instantly throws a weight on O, which is quite out of place in the A, section. E, begins better with "candeur" and "vapeurs" and "tentes," but falls entirely out of key in the next line where no E sound appears, except in the unimportant second syllable of "ombelles." I, has "rire" and "ivresses" to hold it in place, and these words may mitigate such singularly unlike vowel sounds as those of "pourpres" and "sang craché," if one has enough imagination to keep the red of the lips and the wine before one, which is the more difficult as "ivresses pénitentes" may refer to intoxications which have no connection with wine. In fact, one has a shrewd suspicion that "pénitentes" is simply used because of the rhyme. We have been told that U, is green, and if we are willing to grant it, the lines which detail that fact would be well enough in any poem which had no phonetic end in view. As it is, one cannot help smiling a little at a technique which was unable to think of a single word with a single U, in it, except "animaux," in which the U, being a compound, loses its original pronunciation entirely. O, is the most successful of these vowel analogies. "Clairon" is such a strong word that it easily dominates "strideurs étranges," and, in the same way, "Mondes" takes precedence over "Anges" and completely suppresses "Silences traversés." The last line is distinctly good until we get to "Ses Yeux," but these words entirely upset the excellent sound weight of the rest of the line.

This is Mr. Fletcher's presentation of the same subject:

THE VOWELS

(To Leon Bakst)

A light and shade, E green, I blue, U purple and yellow, O red,
All over my soul and song your lambent variations are spread.
A, flaming caravans of day advancing with stately art
Through pale, ashy deserts of grey to the shadowy dark of the
     heart;

Barbaric clangor of cataracts, suave caresses of sails,
Caverned abysms of silence, assaults of infuriate gales;
Dappled vibrations of black and white that the bacchanal val-
    leys track;
Candid and waxlike jasmine, amaranth sable black.

E, parakeets of emerald shrieking perverse in the trees,
Iridescent and restless chameleons tremulous in the breeze,
Peace on the leaves, peace on the sea-green sea,
Ethiopian timbrels that tinkle melodiously:
I, Iris of night, hyacinthine, semi-green,
Intensity of sky and of distant sea dimly seen,
Chryselephantine image, Athena violet-crowned,
Beryl-set sistra of Isis ashiver with infinite sound:
Bells with amethyst tongues, silver bells, E and I,
Tears that drip on the wires, Æolian melody!

U, torrid bassoons and flutes that murmur without repose,
Butterflies, bumblebees, buzzing about a hot rose;
Upas-flower bursting, thunder, furnaces, sunset, lagoon;
Muted tunes of the autumn, ruby, purple, maroon:
O, orange surface of bronze, topaz spotted brocade,
Sorrow and pomp of the Orient, colour and odour and shade,
Ebony and onyx corollas opening to the sun;
O, lotus-glory Olympian, glory of God that is One!
O, crimson clarion horn that echoes on in the bold
Old omnipotence of power; O, rosy glow of gold!
These are the miracles and I make them day and night:
O red, U purple and yellow, I blue, E green, A black and
    white.

It is a purely arbitrary thing to give vowels colour values, unless the colours can be made to spring naturally from words containing these vowels. In the piquant charm of such unexpected relations lies the whole reason for such a suggestion in a work of art. Mr. Fletcher is a more original poet than Arthur Rimbaud, and has a finer ear. He justifies his colours at the very outset in

> Flaming caravans of day advancing with stately art

and holds it admirably throughout. Those vowel sounds which are unlike the particular letter in question are so managed as either to remain subordinate :

> O, crimson clarion horn that echoes on in the bold
> Old omnipotence of power ;

or else to accord so perfectly that they enhance the effect rather than detract from it :

> U, torrid bassoons and flutes that murmur without repose.

The poem is a properly rounded whole, the ends join to make a complete conception. The vowels have a use in themselves as building material, and as such the poet leaves them.

Undoubtedly, the initial suggestion of Mr. Fletcher's poem came from Arthur Rimbaud's. But poets have ever been a light-fingered gentry in this respect, and Time, with a complete indifference to moral considerations, invariably awards the spoils to the victor.

It is possible to trace the influence of various poets in all these early volumes, as is natural in the work of a young man. The fault lay, not in writing them, but in publishing them. Mr. Fletcher is curiously unselective always. He is constantly progressing, and has scant sympathy for the phase just left behind.

The years in London were full of mental experiences. In 1909, he made a close study of Walt Whitman, and it is strange that, in spite of this, the one poet who seems never to have affected his work in the slightest degree is Whitman.

In 1910, Mr. Fletcher paid his first visit to Paris, and through reading a poem of Verhaeren's made the acquaintance of the great body of contemporary French literature. He plunged into it with his usual ardour. When I first went to London, it used to be said that Mr. Fletcher made a point of reading a new French book every day. Certainly he has done an unusual amount in that field.

But literature was not the only art which claimed the poet's attention. He was much interested in music, and also in painting. Not a concert of any importance, not an art exhibition, took place in London to which Mr. Fletcher did not go. His knowledge of both music and painting is extraordinary in a layman. But he is too wise to dabble in the production of either. One art is enough for one man. Still, it is true also, that his poetry would not be what it is, without its musical and artistic connotations.

Mr. Fletcher says that it was the Post-Impressionist Exhibition of 1912 that finally demolished his conservatism. He realized that both music and painting were employing a new idiom; he felt that poetry too must break the old bonds. This knowledge freed him, as the knowledge of *vers libre* freed Mr. Masters. He determined to write as he felt, with no regard to old rules or canons. The result was his volume, "Irradiations," all written in May, 1913.

But publishers were wary, this poetry was too new for them, and not a single London firm could be found to undertake it. All through that Winter the poems remained in manuscript, except for a few published in "Poetry" and in the London "Egoist." Mr. Fletcher was undaunted, however, and continued writing to please himself; among other things done at this time was his sea symphony, "Sand and Spray," some extracts of which I quoted at the beginning of this chapter.

When Mr. Fletcher read me these poems in London, I was very much struck by them. They seemed to me to open a door which had always remained closed, I felt that the publication of the book was a prime necessity, and when I returned to America in the Autumn of 1914, I brought the manuscript with me, together with the manuscript of "Some Imagist Poets," which contained Mr. Fletcher's "Blue Symphony" and "London Excursion."

I had no difficulty in finding a publisher. Mr. Ferris Greenslet, of the firm of Messrs. Houghton, Mifflin and Company, a man of much literary acumen and with a rare sympathy for good work in all manners, instantly saw the value of these poems. He accepted the book at once, and the volume was published under the title, "Irradiations — Sand and Spray," in April, 1915.

In a very interesting preface, the poet argued in favour of *vers libre*, and for the first time in recent years, made an attempt to analyze it.   He says:

The basis of English poetry is rhythm, or, as some would prefer to call it, cadence.   This rhythm is obtained by mingling stressed and unstressed syllables.   Stress may be produced by accent.   It may — and often is — produced by what is known as quantity, the breath required to pronounce certain syllables being more than is required on certain others.   However it be produced, it is precisely this insistence upon cadence, upon the rhythm of the line when spoken, which sets poetry apart from prose, and not — be it said at the outset — a certain way of printing, with a capital letter at the beginning of each line, or an insistence upon end-rhymes.

Now this rhythm can be made the same in every line of the poem.   This was the aim of Alexander Pope, for instance.   My

objection to this method is that it is both artificial and un-
musical. In the case of the eighteenth century men, it gave
the effect of a perfectly balanced pattern like a minuet or fugue.
In the case of the modern imitator of Kipling or Masefield, it
gives the effect of monotonous rag-time. In neither case does
it offer full scope for emotional development.

I maintain that poetry is capable of as many gradations in
cadence as music is in time. We can have a rapid group of
syllables — what is called a line — succeeded by a slow heavy
one; like the swift scurrying of the wave and the sullen dragging
of itself away. Or we can gradually increase or decrease our
tempo, creating accelerando and rallentando effects. Or we can
follow a group of rapid lines with a group of slow ones, or a single
slow, or vice versa. Finally, we can have a perfectly even and
unaltered movement throughout if we desire to be monotonous.

The good poem is that in which all these effects are properly
used to convey the underlying emotions of its author, and that
which welds all these emotions into a work of art by the use of
dominant motif, subordinate themes, proportionate treatment,
repetition, variation, — what in music is called development,
reversal of rôles, and return. In short, the good poem fixes a
free emotion, or a free range of emotions, into an inevitable and
artistic whole. The real secret of the greatest English poets lies
not in their views on life, — which were, naturally, only those
which every sane man is obliged to hold, — but in their profound
knowledge of their craft, whereby they were enabled to put forth
their views in perfect form. Each era of man has its unique and
self-sufficing range of expression and experience, and therefore
every poet must seek anew for himself, out of the language
medium at his disposal, rhythms which are adequate and forms
which are expressive of his own unique personality.

This was at once an explanation and a challenge. It was taken as both, but now that the opposition has largely died away, we can read it quietly and perceive its excellent logic and sensible exegesis.

For the book itself, it is very difficult to classify these poems, even to describe them. Here is imagination only, the quintessence of it. Mr. Fletcher has a fertility and vigour which is wholly remarkable.

I can conceive of an unimaginative person saying that they can make neither head nor tail of these poems. I say that I can conceive of such a thing. But for me, and for many like me, they must stand as inspiring interpretations of moods. Possibly that is their best analysis: Mr. Fletcher's poems are moods, expressed in the terms of nature, plus a highly fanciful point of view. I admit that that confuses rather than explains, but Mr. Fletcher's poems have an organic quality which defies explanation. They are as refreshing as an October wind, and as elusive.

That is it. Go out on a windy Autumn morning and try to describe the wind. It will slap you and push you, it will flap away in front of you and scurry over the sky above you. You can feel all this, you can experience the wind, so to speak, but describe it you cannot. Well, Mr. Fletcher can. Does he do so by analogy? A little. Does he name things directly? Seldom. How does he do it? I do not know. I can show you, but I cannot define. This is a description of rain. "Description" is not the right word, of course ; it is really an expressing of the effect of a rainy day upon him.

VII

Flickering of incessant rain
On flashing pavements :
Sudden scurry of umbrellas :
Bending, recurved blossoms of the storm.

The winds come clanging and clattering
From long white highroads whipping in ribbons up summits :
They strew upon the city gusty wafts of apple-blossom,
And the rustling of innumerable translucent leaves.

Uneven tinkling, the lazy rain
Dripping from the eaves.

Could anything be better? We see the rain, we feel it, and we smell the earthiness which all Spring rain has. The first three lines, with the flickering rain on the pavements and the scurrying umbrellas, are exact description, of course. But the " bending, recurved blossoms of the storm " is a wild imaginative flight. And how well it makes us see those round, shining umbrella-tops! The next line is straightforward poetry — " clanging " and " clattering " are good words for the wind. But what about it coming " whipping in ribbons up summits "?

That is certainly not descriptive, unless we assume that the city is built upon a series of hill-tops. No, it is another imaginative leap, and an absolutely original one, for the effect is got in a new way.

The same thing is true of the next two lines, for obviously no apple-blossoms are really blown into the city from the distant orchards, but in this way the poet has got the earthy smell into his wind. The last two lines are a marvel of exact description, with only the adjective "lazy" to unite them to the imaginative treatment of the middle of the poem.

I have said enough, I think, to show Mr. Fletcher's unusual technique. But let us make no mistake, this is more than technique; it is a manner of seeing and feeling. I chose the rain poem because it was a simple one to use for illustration, but there are others which have a greater imaginative intensity. This is a day of whirling cloud-shadows:

V

Over the roof-tops race the shadows of clouds;
Like horses the shadows of clouds charge down the street.

Whirlpools of purple and gold,
Winds from the mountains of cinnebar,
Lacquered mandarin moments, palanquins swaying and
    balancing
Amid the vermilion pavilions, against the jade balustrades.
Glint of the glittering wings of dragon-flies in the light:

Silver filaments, golden flakes settling downwards,
Rippling, quivering flutters, repulse and surrender,
The sun broidered upon the rain,
The rain rustling with the sun.

Over the roof-tops race the shadows of clouds;
Like horses the shadows of clouds charge down the street.

What a movement that has! We get all the effect of horses galloping without the usual recourse to anapestic metre. It is true that anapestic rhythm appears every now and then, but so come upon and again deserted, that its effect is psychological rather than actual. There, also, are the imaginative leaps:

Lacquered mandarin moments, palanquins swaying and
    balancing

for instance. What have mandarins and palanquins to do with the rest of the poem? Nothing, if we are seeking the relations of fact; but the Oriental connotations of these words throw a splendour and brilliance into his clouds which no other words could achieve. The lines:

The sun broidered upon the rain,
The rain rustling with the sun

might serve as an epitome of the poet's work. It is lyric truth in its highest form.

Mr. Fletcher's observation is very minute and

exact. This is the more remarkable when we think how often he must have to subdue his imagination to let reality print itself upon him with the force which it does. He sees a sea-fog creeping up a river:

> In the grey skirts of the fog seamews skirl desolately,
> And flick like bits of paper propelled by a wind
> About the flabby sails of a departing ship
> Crawling slowly down the low reaches
> Of the river.

The poet must have watched the inconsequential flutterings of gulls about a boat very carefully to think of that simile of blown bits of paper.

In the poems I have quoted, there is a great variation of rhythms. No one is more absolute master of the rhythms of *vers libre* than is Mr. Fletcher. So much is this true, indeed, that an Englishman has written a paper upon this side of his work alone.

The following is a most beautiful translation into a scene of that vague feeling of unrest which French eighteenth century physicians called " la maladie de l'après-midi":

I

> The spattering of the rain upon pale terraces
> Of afternoon is like the passing of a dream
> Amid the roses shuddering 'gainst the wet green stalks
> Of the streaming trees — the passing of the wind

Upon the pale lower terraces of my dream
Is like the crinkling of the wet grey robes
Of the hours that come to turn over the urn
Of the day and spill its rainy dream.
Vague movement over the puddled terraces;
Heavy gold pennons — a pomp of solemn gardens
Half hidden under the liquid veil of spring:
Far trumpets like a vague rout of faded roses
Burst 'gainst the wet green silence of distant forests:
A clash of cymbals — then the swift swaying footsteps
Of the wind that undulates along the languid terraces.
Pools of rain — the vacant terraces
Wet, chill and glistening
Toward the sunset beyond the broken doors of today.

The slow, languorous rhythm of that poem greatly
heightens its mood of futile melancholy. It is all
in the choice of words, and the reader will note that
Mr. Fletcher pays as much attention to his verbs
as to his adjectives. The use of "spattering," in
the first line, gives at the very start the note of
desolation, heightened by the adjective "pale." For
this matter of verbs: the wet, grey robes "crinkle,"
the trumpets "burst," the wind "undulates," and
this last is again strengthened by an adjective, when
the poet speaks of "languid" terraces. There are
beautiful, still lines, like

.   .   .   the wet green silence of distant forests.

and this marvel of dignified gloom:

> .   .   .   a pomp of solemn gardens
> Half hidden under the liquid veil of Spring.

Slow, stately, the movement holds to the end.

This next poem is picture and movement in one, so closely connected that they seem to melt together. Notice the rising and falling of the verse, like the thrown-up water column, to relapse, dropping, like it, at the end.

VIII

> The fountain blows its breathless spray
> From me to you and back to me.
>
> Whipped, tossed, curdled,
> Crashing, quivering:
> I hurl kisses like blows upon your lips.
> The dance of a bee drunken with sunlight:
> Irradiant ecstasies, white and gold,
> Sigh and relapse.
>
> The fountain tosses pallid spray
> Far in the sorrowful, silent sky.

One is tempted to quote a great many of these poems, but it is hardly necessary, the ones I have given sufficiently illustrate the poet's peculiar method. Still, there are two more sides of this original imagination which must not be passed by. This is sheer fancy, but one so apt as to strike the reader as inevitable:

X

The trees, like great jade elephants,
Chained, stamp and shake 'neath the gadflies of the breeze;
The trees lunge and plunge, unruly elephants:
The clouds are their crimson howdah-canopies,
The sunlight glints like the golden robe of a Shah.
Would I were tossed on the wrinkled backs of those trees.

That is one of the most completely successful things
that Mr. Fletcher has done. It is extraordinarily
pictorial and imaginative. The trees, stamping,
shaking, lunging and plunging, but always "chained,"
is a beautiful truism. Here, too, is one of Mr.
Fletcher's unique touches — the rhymes, "lunge and
plunge," coming in with startling effect in the middle
of an un-rhymed poem. But perhaps the best touch
is the "wrinkled" backs of the trees, in the last
line.

Another fancy, less joyous, more serious, is the
following:

XV

O, seeded grass, you army of little men
Crawling up the long slope with quivering, quick blades of steel:
You who storm millions of graves, tiny green tentacles of
    Earth,
Interlace yourselves tightly over my heart,
And do not let me go:
For I would lie here forever and watch with one eye
The pilgrimaging ants in your dull, savage jungles,

The while with the other I see the stiff lines of the slope
Break in mid-air, a wave surprisingly arrested,
And above them, wavering, dancing, bodiless, colourless, unreal,
The long thin lazy fingers of the heat.

It cannot be doubted by any one reading that poem that here we have a new idiom, a new manner of seeing, a new method of interpretation. The old thoughts and attitudes are irrevocably departed. There is no ancient animus here to cause bitterness and regret. Mr. Fletcher is conscious of no necessity to be other than he is. This is strong, nervous work, untiring in its creative vision. For its technical effects, there are so many that I shall only ask the reader to notice carefully the last two lines.

Mr. Fletcher is a virtuoso of sound effects. These passages from the poems just read will prove what I mean :

Amid the vermilion pavilions, against the jade balustrades

.   .   .   .

The clouds are their crimson howdah-canopies.

He is exceedingly fond of internal rhymes, and in his hands these effects are more than "un bijou d'un sou," as Verlaine called rhyme.

This is very strange, as in regular metrical verse his rhymes are often far from happy. It is as if the knowledge that he had to rhyme took away the faculty. Where it is not imperative, it is often most

cunningly accomplished. But his sound effects
are frequently got without the aid of rhyme, for
instance:

> A clash of cymbals — then the swift swaying footsteps
> Of the wind.

I will quote one more poem from this book, for it
shows a new preoccupation on the part of the poet.
A more human interest. It is not expressed in the
terms of an imagined landscape, but directly, and it is
a side which is growing upon him; as though more
and more overtones were deepening a beautiful,
individual note.

XXVIII

> I remember, there was a day
> During which I did not write a line of verse:
> Nor did I speak a word to any woman,
> Nor did I meet with death.
>
> Yet all that day I was fully occupied:
> My eyes saw trees, clouds, streets, houses, people;
> My lungs breathed air;
> My mouth swallowed food and drink;
> My hands seized things, my feet touched earth,
> Or spurned it at my desire.
>
> On that day I know I would have been sufficiently happy,
> If I could have kept my brain from bothering at all
> About my next trite poem;

About the tedious necessities of sex;
And about the day on which I would at last meet death.

All the poems in the volume are not so good as these. Mr. Fletcher has eminently the faults of his qualities. Such a fecundity of creation naturally leads to the production of much that is below the level of his best, and one of his marked traits is the uncritical, unselective habit of mind I have already mentioned. He has a curious desire to write in series. As we examine his work, we shall constantly observe this tendency. The method has certain advantages, but its disadvantages are peculiarly unfortunate in his case, for, when it comes to publication, he wishes to include all of any given series, good and bad together. The result is a volume in which the plums are scattered and lost in packing. I think it is largely for this reason that his work has not yet received the recognition it deserves.

Mr. Fletcher returned to this country in December, 1914, driven home by the war. After short sojourns in New York and Little Rock, he settled in Boston, and remained there, except for Summer trips to the West, until May, 1916, when he returned to England and was married on July 5, 1916, to Florence Emily Arbuthnot.

In April, 1916, Messrs. Houghton, Mifflin and Company published "Goblins and Pagodas." This book contains the "Ghosts of an Old House" of which I have already given extracts, and a series of eleven symphonies.

In this volume, even more than in "Irradiations," the longing for poems in sequence leads to a plethora of one sort of thing, and numbs the reader's interest by an over-sameness of effect. In a long and intricate preface, Mr. Fletcher explained his method. One interesting passage will condense it for us:

A book lies on my desk. It has a red binding and is badly printed on cheap paper. I have had this book with me for several years. Now, suppose I were to write a poem on this book, how would I treat the subject?

If I were a poet following in the main the Victorian tradition, I should write my poem altogether about the contents of this book and its author. My poem would be essentially a criticism of the subject-matter of the book. I should state at length how that subject-matter had affected me. In short, what the reader would obtain from this sort of poem would be my sentimental reaction towards certain ideas and tendencies in the work of another.

If I were a realist poet, I should write about the book's external appearance. I should expatiate on the red binding, the bad type, the ink stain on page sixteen. I should complain, perhaps, of my poverty at not being able to buy a better edition, and conclude with a gibe at the author for not having realized the sufferings of the poor.

Neither of these ways, however, of writing about this book possesses any novelty, and neither is essentially my own way. My own way of writing about it would be as follows: —

I should select out of my life the important events connected with my ownership of this book, and strive to write of them in terms of the volume itself, both as regards subject-matter and appearance.   In other words, I should link up my personality and the personality of the book, and make each a part of the other.   In this way I should strive to evoke a soul out of this piece of inanimate matter, a something characteristic and structural inherent in this inorganic form which is friendly to me and responds to my mood.

In this preface, also, he maps out his series of symphonies as the stages in the life of an artist. This idea is not new, and we need not pause upon it here; in fact, these poems seem rather forced into the design than written in accordance with it.   The symphonies themselves are the arresting thing, each one in itself, and each built upon a dominant colour.

This is what I have called, in the preface to my own book, "Men, Women and Ghosts," the unrelated method.   As linked to the programme of the artist's life, these colour symphonies cease to be unrelated, but taken each by itself they for the most part follow it.

By the unrelated method, I mean a description which takes trees, houses, people, all the many parts of a landscape, merely as they appear to the eye or ear, or both, and with no hint of the "pathetic fallacy" intruding itself.   Already, in "London Excursion," Mr. Fletcher had experimented with this method.   In these symphonies, it finds much fuller expression.   This "Green Symphony" is a riot of Spring:

GREEN SYMPHONY

I

The glittering leaves of the rhododendrons
Balance and vibrate in the cool air;
While in the sky above them
White clouds chase each other.

Like scampering rabbits,
Flashes of sunlight sweep the lawn;
They fling in passing
Patterns of shadow,
Golden and green.

With long cascades of laughter,
The mating birds dart and swoop to the turf:
'Mid their mad trillings
Glints the gay sun behind the trees.

Down there are deep blue lakes:
Orange blossom droops in the water.

In the tower of the winds,
All the bells are set adrift:
Jingling
For the dawn.

Thin fluttering streamers
Of breeze lash through the swaying boughs,
Palely expectant
The earth receives the slanting rain.

I am a glittering raindrop
Hugged close by the cool rhododendron.
I am a daisy starring
The exquisite curves of the close-cropped turf.

The glittering leaves of the rhododendron
Are shaken like blue-green blades of grass,
Flickering, cracking, falling:
Splintering in a million fragments.

The wind runs laughing up the slope
Stripping off handfuls of wet green leaves,
To fling in people's faces.
Wallowing on the daisy-powdered turf,
Clutching at the sunlight,
Cavorting in the shadow.

Like baroque pearls,
Like cloudy emeralds,
The clouds and trees clash together;
Whirling and swirling,
In the tumult
Of the spring,
And the wind.

II

The trees splash the sky with their fingers,
A restless green rout of stars.

With whirling movement
They swing their boughs

About their stems:
Planes on planes of light and shadow
Pass among them,
Opening fanlike to fall.

The trees are like a sea;
Tossing;
Trembling,
Roaring,
Wallowing,
Darting their long green flickering fronds up at the sky,
Spotted with white blossom-spray.

The trees are roofs:
Hollow caverns of cool blue shadow,
Solemn arches
In the afternoons.
The whole vast horizon
In terrace beyond terrace,
Pinnacle above pinnacle,
Lifts to the sky
Serrated ranks of green on green.

They caress the roofs with their fingers,
They sprawl about the river to look into it;
Up the hill they come
Gesticulating challenge:
They cower together
In dark valleys;
They yearn out over the fields.

Enamelled domes
Tumble upon the grass,
Crashing in ruin
Quiet at last.

The trees lash the sky with their leaves,
Uneasily shaking their dark green manes.

III

Far let the voices of the mad wild birds be calling me,
I will abide in this forest of pines.

When the wind blows
Battling through the forest,
I hear it distantly,
The crash of a perpetual sea.

When the rain falls,
I watch silver spears slanting downwards
From the pale river-pools of sky,
Enclosed in dark fronds.

When the sun shines,
I weave together distant branches till they enclose mighty circles,
I sway to the movement of hooded summits,
I swim leisurely in deep blue seas of air.

I hug the smooth bark of stately red pillars
And with cones carefully scattered

I mark the progression of dark dial-shadows
Flung diagonally downwards through the afternoon.

This turf is not like turf:
It is a smooth dry carpet of velvet,
Embroidered with brown patterns of needles and cones.
These trees are not like trees:
They are innumerable feathery pagoda-umbrellas,
Stiffly ungracious to the wind,
Teetering on red-lacquered stems.

In the evening I listen to the winds' lisping,
While the conflagrations of the sunset flicker and clash behind
    me,
Flamboyant crenellations of glory amid the charred ebony
    boles.

In the night the fiery nightingales
Shall clash and trill through the silence:
Like the voices of mermaids crying
From the sea.

Long ago has the moon whelmed this uncompleted temple.
Stars swim like gold fish far above the black arches.

Far let the timid feet of dawn fly to catch me:
I will abide in this forest of pines:
For I have unveiled naked beauty,
And the things that she whispered to me in the darkness,
Are buried deep in my heart.

Now let the black tops of the pine-trees break like a spent wave,
Against the grey sky :
These are tombs and memorials and temples and altars sun-
kindled for me.

If we remarked a new, and quite personal idiom in "Irradiations," "The Green Symphony" carries that idiom still another step away from tradition. If we had no other poems at hand to prove that these poets of the third stage are doing something quite new and original, that one alone would suffice. It is too long to analyze. But the reader who has followed the analysis of the shorter poems, will have no difficulty in tracking its effects in detail.

Throughout these poems, no attempt is made to follow regular symphonic form, the title seems to have been given merely to indicate a certain musical, rhapsodic treatment.

These symphonies are not all of equal excellence. Each has interesting passages, but those most certainly successful are "Blue Symphony," "Solitude in the City (Symphony in Black and Gold)," "Poppies of the Red Year (A Symphony in Scarlet)," and the "Green Symphony" I quoted above. In the less contained of these poems, the poet occasionally loses himself in vagueness, his words run into a bright mist, and cloud over the articulateness of his thought. Mannerism rides him at times to the detriment of his work, but the four poems I have named are singularly free from this fault.

I have not space to pursue the course of these symphonies at greater length. Mr. Fletcher is so rich in original conceptions and treatments that I can only indicate his work by outlines.

The anthology, "Some Imagist Poets, 1916," contained a group of Arizona poems — they are the burgeoning of that charm which the West has for him — and a little vignette of skaters:

THE SKATERS

To A. D. R.

Black swallows swooping or gliding
In a flurry of entangled loops and curves;
The skaters skim over the frozen river.
And the grinding click of their skates as they impinge upon the
    surface,
Is like the brushing together of thin wing-tips of silver.

Contrast that bright little picture with this grotesque from "Ghosts from an Old House":

AN OAK

Hoar mistletoe
Hangs in clumps
To the twisted boughs
Of this lonely tree.

Beneath its roots I often thought treasure was buried:
For the roots had enclosed a circle.

But when I dug beneath them,
I could only find great black ants
That attacked my hands.

When at night I have the nightmare,
I always see the eyes of ants
Swarming from a mouldering box of gold.

Or with this other, whimsical and weird, full of
strange suggestion :

THE YARDSTICK

Yardstick that measured out so many miles of cloth,
Yardstick that covered me,
I wonder do you hop of nights
Out to that still hill-cemetery,
And up and down go measuring
A clayey grave for me?

The poet's German and Danish ancestry is inter-
estingly in evidence in that little piece. Here is the
goblin quality of Hoffmann's "Die Serapionsbrüder."
We feel a background of folk-lore, of gnomes and
pixies, and fused with it is the allegorical seriousness
of Hans Christian Andersen. This Teutonic and
Scandinavian mysticism persists long, as we noted

in reference to Mr. Sandburg. But it is an even more remarkable atavism in Mr. Fletcher, enduring, as it has, through nearly a hundred years of changed environment.

No study of Mr. Fletcher's work would be complete without a consideration of his "polyphonic prose." "Polyphonic prose" is not a prose form, although, being printed as prose, many people have found it difficult to understand this. It is printed in that manner for convenience as it changes its character so often, with every wave of emotion, in fact. The word "polyphonic" is its keynote. "Polyphonic" means — many-voiced — and the form is so called because it makes use of all the "voices" of poetry, viz. : metre, *vers libre*, assonance, alliteration, rhyme, and return. It employs every form of rhythm, even prose rhythm at times, but usually holds no particular one for long. It is an exceedingly difficult form to write, as so much depends solely upon the poet's taste. The rhymes may come at the ends of the cadences, or may appear in close juxtaposition to each other, or may be only distantly related. It is an excellent medium for dramatic portrayal, for stories in scenes, as it permits of great vividness of presentation.

Mr. Fletcher has written some remarkable poems in "polyphonic prose." He uses it principally in those pieces which are a sort of epic of place, and he has achieved extraordinary effects with it in giving not only an atmosphere, but a whole historical epoch. A series of poems on American subjects is done in this way. One is of the Mississippi River; another entitled "The Old South," is, as its name implies, a sort of condensation of the feeling aroused by our Southern States, particularly Louisiana; a third is wound about the catafalque of Jefferson Davis preserved in a museum in New Orleans. Perhaps the best one which he has done is this of the clipper-ship era. It illustrates his method of synthesizing a whole period in a single poem, instead of allowing it to be implied by one concrete example, as is the old and usual way. The particular ship which comes in from time to time is merely symbolic, and soon merges into the whole. Throughout the poem, Mr. Fletcher brings in snatches of well-known chanties sung by the sailors of all sailing ships the world over, but dating from the period in question:

CLIPPER–SHIPS

(In Memoriam — Ship *W. P. Frye*, sunk by converted cruiser *Eitel Friedrich*, 1915)

Beautiful as a tiered cloud, skysails set and shrouds twanging, she emerges from the surges that keep running away before day on the low Pacific shore. With the roar of the wind blowing half a gale after, she heels and lunges, and buries her bows in the smother, lifting them swiftly and scattering the glistening spray-drops from her jibsails with laughter. Her spars are cracking, her royals are half splitting, her lower stunsail booms are bent aside, like bowstrings ready to loose, and the water is roaring into her scuppers, but she still staggers out under a full press of sail, her upper trucks enkindled by the sun into shafts of rosy flame.

Oh, the anchor is up and the sails they are set, and it's 'way Rio; round Cape Stiff and up to Boston, ninety days hauling at the ropes: the decks slope and the stays creak as she lurches into it, sending her jib awash at every thrust, and a handful of dust and a thirst to make you weep are all we get for being two years away to sea.

Topgallant stunsail has carried away! Ease the spanker! The anchor is rusted on the deck. Men in short duck trousers, wide-brimmed straw hats, with brown, mahogany faces, pace up and down, spinning the worn-out yarns they told a year ago. Some are coiling rope; some smoke; Chips is picking oakum near the boats. Ten thousand miles away lies their last port. In the rigging climbs a hairy monkey, and a green parakeet screams at the masthead. In the dead calm of a boiling noonday near the line she lifts her spread of shining canvas from heel to truck, from jib o' jib to ringtail, from moonsails to watersails. Men have hung their washing in the stays so she can get more way on her. She ghosts along before an imperceptible breeze, the sails hanging limp in the crosstrees and clashing against the masts. She is a proud white albatross skimming across the ocean, beautiful as a tiered cloud. Oh, a Yankee ship comes down down the river: blow, boys, blow: her masts and yards they shine like silver: blow, my bully boys, blow: she's a crack ship, a dandy clipper, nine hundred miles from land; she's a down-Easter from Massachusetts, and she's bound to the Rio Grande!

Where are the men who put to sea in her on her first voyage?

Some have piled their bones in California among the hides; some died frozen off the Horn in snow-storms; some slipped down between two greybacks when the yards were joggled suddenly. Still she glistens beautifully, her decks snow-white with constant scrubbing, as she sweeps into some empty, sailless bay which sleeps all day where the wild deer skip away when she fires her eighteen-pounder, the sound reverberating about the empty hills. San Francisco? No. San Francisco will not be built for a dozen years to come. Meanwhile she hums with the tumult of loading. The mutineers, even, are let out of their irons and flogged and fed. Every day from when the dawn flares up red amid the hills to the hour it drops dead to westward, men walk gawkily, balancing on their heads the burden of the cargo. Now the anchor is up and the sails they are set, and it's 'way, Rio. Boston girls are pulling at the ropes: only three months of trouble yet: time for us to go!

Beautiful as a tiered cloud she flies out seaward, and on her decks loaf and stumble a luckless crowd, the filthy sweepings of the stews. In a week, in a day, they have spent a year's wages, swilling it away and letting the waste of it run down among the gutters. How are these dead-beats bribed to go? Only the Ann Street runners know. Dagos, Dutchmen, Souwegians, niggers, crimp-captured greenhorns, they loaf up on the after-deck, some of them already wrecks; so sick they wish they had never been born. Before them all the "old man" calls for a bucket of salt water to wash off his shore face. While he is at it, telling them how he will haze them till they are dead if they try soldiering, but it will be good grub and easy work if they hand, reef and steer and heave the lead, his officers are below, rummaging through the men's dunnage, pulling out heavers, prickers, rum bottles, sheath knives, and pistols. On each grizzled, half-

cowed face appears something between a sheepish grin, a smirk
of fear, a threat of treachery, and the dogged resignation of a
brute. But the mate — Bucko Douglas is his name — is the
very same who booted three men off the masthead when they
were shortening sail in the teeth of a Cape Horn snorter. Two
of them fell into the sea, and the third was tossed still groaning
into the water. Only last night the captain stuck his cigar butt
into one poor swabber's face for not minding the compass, and
gave Jim Baines a taste of ratline hash for coming up on deck
with dirty hands. Meanwhile under a grand spread of canvas,
one hundred feet from side to side, the ship rides up the parallels.
From aloft through the blue stillness of a tropic night, crammed
with stars, with thunder brewing on the horizon, a mournful
echo rises and swells:

> "Oh, my name is hanging Johnny,
>   Away-i-oh!
> Oh, my name is hanging Johnny,
>   So hang, boys, hang."

The *Great Republic*, launched before thirty thousand people,
her main truck overlooking the highest steeple of the town, the
eagle at her bows, and colors flying, now in her first and last
port, is slowly dying. She is a charred hulk, with toppling
masts, seared gilding, and blistered sides. The *Alert* no more
slides pertly through the bergs of the Horn. The desolate
barrens of Staten Land, where no man was ever born, hold her
bones. The Black Baller *Lightning*, that took eighty thousand
dollars' worth of cargo around the world in one quick trip, was
hurled and ripped to pieces on some uncharted reef or other.
The *Dreadnought* disappeared in a hurricane's smother of foam.
The *Sovereign of the Seas*, that never furled her topsails for ten
years, was sheared clean amidships by the bows of an iron steamer

as she left her last port. The slaver *Bald Eagle* cut an unlucky career short when she parted with her anchor and piled up on the Paracels where the pirate junks are waiting for every ship that swells out over the horizon. The *Antelope* was caught off the Grande Ladrone in the northeast monsoon; she's gone. The *Flying Cloud*, proud as she was of beating every ship that carried the Stars and Stripes or the St. George's flag could not race faster than a thunderbolt that fell one day on her deck and turned her to a cloud of flame — everything burned away but her fame! No more will California hear the little *Pilgrim's* parting cheer. The crew took to an open boat when their ship was scuttled by a privateer. So they die out, year after year.

Sometimes the lookout on a great steamer wallowing and threshing through the heavy seas by night, sees far off on his lee quarter something like a lofty swinging light. Beautiful as a tiered cloud, a ghostly clipper-ship emerges from the surges that keep running away before day on the low Pacific shore. Her upper works are kindled by the sun into shafts of rosy flame. Swimming like a duck, steering like a fish, easy yet dry, lively yet stiff, she lifts cloud on cloud of crowded stainless sail. She creeps abeam, within hail, she skips, she chases, she outpaces like a mettlesome racer the lumbering teakettle that keeps her company. Before she fades into the weather quarter, the lookout cries: "Holy jiggers, are you the Flying Dutchman, that you go two knots to our one?" Hoarsely comes back this answer from the sail: "Challenge is our name: America our nation: Bully Waterman our master: we can beat Creation."

> "And its 'way Rio;
> 'Way — hay — hay, Rio;
> O, fare you well, my pretty young girl,
> For we're bound to the Rio Grande."

What a splendid thing that is! Full of movement, so bright as to be almost dazzling, rough, lively, vigorous. The true epic of the fast-vanishing sailing ship.

Sometimes this sense of historical significance, this poignant feeling for the romance of a time, finds an even higher expression, and rises into pure symbolism. I have referred several times to Mr. Fletcher's "Lincoln." If the reader will recall what I said in regard to the treatment of Lincoln by three such different poets as Mr. Robinson, Mr. Masters, and Mr. Fletcher, he will remember that I spoke of Mr. Fletcher's treatment as raising Lincoln to the veiled awe of a national legend. This is the poem:

LINCOLN

I

Like a gaunt, scraggly pine
Which lifts its head above the mournful sandhills;
And patiently, through dull years of bitter silence,
Untended and uncared for, starts to grow.

Ungainly, labouring, huge,
The wind of the north has twisted and gnarled its branches;
Yet in the heat of midsummer days, when thunderclouds ring
    the horizon,
A nation of men shall rest beneath its shade.

And it shall protect them all,
Hold everyone safe there, watching aloof in silence;

Until at last one mad stray bolt from the zenith
Shall strike it in an instant down to earth.

II

There was a darkness in this man; an immense and hollow
    darkness,
Of which we may not speak, nor share with him, nor enter;
A darkness through which strong roots stretched downwards
    into the earth
Towards old things;

Towards the herdman-kings who walked the earth and spoke
    with God,
Towards the wanderers who sought for they knew not what
    and found their goal at last;
Towards the men who waited, only waited patiently when all
    seemed lost
Many bitter winters of defeat;

Down to the granite of patience
These roots swept, knotted fibrous roots, prying, piercing, seeking,
And drew from the living rock and the living waters about it
The red sap to carry upwards to the sun.

Not proud, but humble,
Only to serve and pass on, to endure to the end through
    service;
For the axe is laid at the roots of the trees, and all that bring
    not forth good fruit
Shall be cut down on the day to come and cast into the fire.

III

There is a silence abroad in the land to-day,
And in the hearts of men, a deep and anxious silence;
And, because we are still at last, those bronze lips slowly open,
Those hollow and weary eyes take on a gleam of light.

Slowly a patient, firm-syllabled voice cuts through the endless
    silence
Like labouring oxen that drag a plow through the chaos of rude
    clay-fields:
" I went forward as the light goes forward in early spring,
But there were also many things which I left behind.

Tombs that were quiet;
One, of a mother, whose brief light went out in the darkness,
One, of a loved one, the snow on whose grave is long falling,
One, only of a child, but it was mine.

Have you forgot your graves?   Go, question them in anguish,
Listen long to their unstirred lips.   From your hostages to
    silence,
Learn there is no life without death, no dawn without sunsetting,
No victory but to him who has given all."

IV

The clamour of cannon dies down, the furnace-mouth of the
    battle is silent.
The midwinter sun dips and descends, the earth takes on afresh
    its bright colours.

But he whom we mocked and obeyed not, he whom we scorned
and mistrusted,
He has descended, like a god, to his rest.

Over the uproar of cities,
Over the million intricate threads of life wavering and
crossing,
In the midst of problems we know not, tangling, perplexing,
ensnaring,
Rises one white tomb alone.

Beam over it, stars,
Wrap it round, stripes — stripes red for the pain that he bore
for you —
Enfold it forever, O flag, rent, soiled, but repaired through your
anguish;
Long as you keep him there safe, the nations shall bow to your
law.

Strew over him flowers:
Blue forget-me-nots from the north, and the bright pink
arbutus
From the east, and from the west rich orange blossom,
But from the heart of the land take the passion-flower;

Rayed, violet, dim,
With the nails that pierced, the cross that he bore and the
circlet,
And beside it there lay also one lonely snow-white magnolia,
Bitter for remembrance of the healing which has passed.

I think that is the finest poem on Lincoln which has
been written. It has the emotional seriousness of
prayer. It was written in the Winter of 1916, before
the United States had entered the war, and it is
instinct with the anxiety of waiting, the anguished
desire for guidance. Lincoln stands before us, at
once a man and an aspiration, a recollection and a
goal. He is the symbol of our possibilities, the
reason for our courage. Gravely, like a funeral
march, with serene steadfastness, like the hope of
resurrection, the poem moves along, and the great
darkness of the opening lines yields gradually to the
lyric close.

Mr. Fletcher's later work shows a growing interest
in humanity. He is delving deeper into life, developing more knowledge and more tenderness. Hitherto,
he has seldom attempted the expression of human
emotions, but in these later poems are moments of
real understanding and poignancy.

It is, however, always in connection with some
scene or some historical event. He seems little
interested in persons for their own sake. He tells
no stories; his dramas are epics of time, not of people.
Some critics will aver that this is the weak spot in
the Imagistic method, that this very manner of presentation precludes the more intimate note of drama.
But I see no reason why that should be so. I should
say, rather, that it is mere coincidence which has
caused the Imagist poets to be markedly lyrists,

It is quite true that neither "H.D." nor Mr. Fletcher can approach the other poets of whom we have been speaking in either narrative or dramatic pieces, that they are both deficient in portraying human feeling. But, granted this, I cannot find it to reflect upon the method as a whole. It is wiser to consider it as a limitation in the work of these two poets. Where they have laboured to make a clearing, others are at liberty to plant what seeds they will.

These Imagist poets achieve much; they point the way to more. But they seldom touch on human relations. There is a certain aloofness about both of them, yet to the artist they hold more gifts than do the other poets we have been considering. The third stage is still in its infancy. It will be a long time before its possibilities are exhausted.

Of course, to say that a poet is a lyric and not a dramatic poet, is in no sense an adverse criticism. For most people, lyric poetry is the truest sort of poetry. It is, however, interesting to note, that the other four poets of this volume are mainly narrative and dramatic poets. I have called Mr. Masters' work epic, and so it is; an epic compounded of short, incisive dramas. I have shown Mr. Sandburg as a lyrist partly obscured by a propagandist, but he, also, is often intensely dramatic. In the work of the Imagists, we find romantic lyricism, and this, and their approach to their art, is their contribution to

the time. And it is necessary to remember that
Mr. Fletcher, while in no sense either narrative or
dramatic, is occasionally epic, as we have seen.
The real point to be noted of both his work and that
of "H.D." is not that they are lyrists, but that
their lyricism is so seldom a record of the reactions
of one personality upon another. Nature needed
to be affirmed, and they affirm it; it will be for
other poets once more to knit man into nature
in a changed relation, and that is primarily the
road along which the movement would seem to be
travelling.

Some time ago, I spoke of Mr. Fletcher as being
peculiarly sensitive to the *nuances* of tongues. He
is a veritable mirror of the atmosphere of peoples,
periods, and places. Language is more than language; it is the key by which we enter the race-soul.
To this poet, the race-soul can be read, not only in
books, but in the running brooks as well. He deduces a race-consciousness from his reading, but he
deduces it from his observation also. No man can
construct a personality from a landscape better than
can Mr. Fletcher.

I do not know if Mr. Fletcher reads Spanish. I
do not know whether he is familiar with Mexican or
South American literature. It may well be so, for
he is an omnivorous reader. But certain it is, that,
in his Arizona poems, we have the whole spirit of
Colonial Spain:

MEXICAN QUARTER

By an alley lined with tumble-down shacks
And street-lamps askew, half-sputtering,
Feebly glimmering on gutters choked with filth and dogs
Scratching their mangy backs:
Half-naked children are running about,
Women puff cigarettes in black doorways,
Crickets are crying.
Men slouch sullenly
Into the shadows:
Behind a hedge of cactus,
The smell of a dead horse
Mingles with the smell of tamales frying.

And a girl in a black lace shawl
Sits in a rickety chair by the square of an unglazed window,
And sees the explosion of the stars
Softly posed on a velvet sky.
And she is humming to herself: —
"Stars, if I could reach you,
   (You are so very clear that it seems as if I could reach you)
   I would give you all to Madonna's image,
   On the grey-plastered altar behind the paper flowers,
   So that Juan would come back to me,
   And we could live again those lazy burning hours
   Forgetting the tap of my fan and my sharp words.
   And I would only keep four of you,
   Those two blue-white ones overhead,
   To hang in my ears;
   And those two orange ones yonder,
   To fasten on my shoe buckles."

A little further along the street
A man sits stringing a brown guitar.
The smoke of his cigarette curls round his head,
And he, too, is humming, but other words:
"Think not that at your window I wait;
New love is better, the old is turned to hate.
Fate! Fate! All things pass away;
Life is forever, youth is for a day.
Love again if you may
Before the stars are blown out of the sky
And the crickets die;
Babylon and Samarkand
Are mud walls in a waste of sand."

I have heard it objected in connection with this
poem that tamales are never fried. And, as a matter
of fact, that is, of course, so. Mr. Fletcher is often
inexcusably careless about such details. But in
spite of this unimportant trifle, is not the soul of
Spain in that poem, the Spain of a debased and
deserted colony?

Here is another of these Arizona poems, and now
we have the atmosphere of an old, past civilization
engulfed in a new, wild land.

RAIN IN THE DESERT

The huge red-buttressed mesa over yonder
Is merely a far-off temple where the sleepy sun is burning
Its altar-fires of pinyon and of toyon for the day.

The old priests sleep, white-shrouded,
Their pottery whistles lie beside them, the prayer-sticks closely
    feathered;
On every mummied face there glows a smile.

The sun is rolling slowly
Beneath the sluggish folds of the sky-serpents,
Coiling, uncoiling, blue-black, sparked with fires.

The old dead priests
Feel in the thin dried earth that is heaped about them,
Above the smell of scorching oozing pinyon,
The acrid smell of rain.

And now the showers
Surround the mesa like a troop of silver dancers:
Shaking their rattles, stamping, chanting, roaring,
Whirling, extinguishing the last red wisp of light.

Suggestion is beautifully managed in that poem.
The desert is scarcely mentioned, and yet the whole
is hot and arid with the smell of scorched earth.
Notice the contrast between the stillness of the beginning and the movement of the end, an end of
clatter, but under which there remains always, silent
and imperishable, the recollection of a pre-historic
civilization.

Now let us turn to Mr. Fletcher's latest volume,
"Japanese Prints," shortly to be issued by The Four
Seas Company, Boston. In the preface to this

book, Mr. Fletcher analyzes the Japanese *tanka* and *hokku* forms, and sketches lightly the history of Japanese prosody, and then analyzes that chief quality of all Japanese verse — psychological suggestion. The modern poets are becoming more and more indebted to the Japanese for a realization of the value of this effect. To quote a moment from Mr. Fletcher's preface:

Let us take an example. The most famous hokku that Basho wrote, might be literally translated thus:

An old pond / And the sound of a frog leaping / Into the water.

This means nothing to the Western mind. But to the Japanese it means all the beauty of such a life of retirement and contemplation as Basho practised. If we permit our minds to supply the detail Basho deliberately omitted, we see the mouldering temple enclosure, the sage himself in meditation, the ancient piece of water, and the sound of a frog's leap — passing vanity — slipping into the silence of eternity. The poem has three meanings. First, it is a statement of fact. Second, it is an emotion deduced from that. Third, it is a sort of spiritual allegory. And all this Basho has given us in his seventeen syllables.

It is perhaps hardly necessary to state here that Japanese prosody is based upon alternate lines of five and seven syllables. The *tanka* is a poem of thirty-one syllables arranged as follows: 5, 7, 5, 7, 7. The *hokku* is a truncated *tanka* in which the last two lines are suppressed; it consists, therefore, of seventeen syllables : 5, 7, 5. Mr. Fletcher explains the peculiar adaptability of the *hokku* to suggestion in this manner :

> It must always be understood that there is an implied continuation to every Japanese hokku. The concluding hemistich, whereby the hokku becomes the tanka, is existent in the writer's mind, but never uttered.

Understanding very well the method by which the Japanese obtained these effects, he nevertheless realizes that a purely syllabic form is not well adapted to a highly accented language such as English. It should be said also that Japanese words, being capable of more than one construction, make it possible to convey more than one meaning by a single word. This leads to a sort of serious punning, and by these double meanings a poem of seventeen syllables can be made to contain many more. Mr. Fletcher says: "Good hokkus cannot be written in English. The thing we have to follow is not a form, but a spirit." Speaking of the volume itself, he adds: "As for the poems themselves, they are not Japanese at all, but all illustrate something of the charm I have found in Japanese poetry and art."

Mr. Fletcher is right in saying that these poems are not written absolutely in the Japanese idiom, but still they have a distinct perfume of Japan about them, and once again prove the poet's sensitiveness

to atmosphere. This, to an occidental mind, has
certainly the charm of Japan :

THE YOUNG DAIMYO

When he first came out to meet me,
He had just been girt with the two swords ;
And I found he was far more interested in the glitter of their
　　hilts
And did not even compare my kiss to a cherry-blossom.

Another, the most beautiful in the volume, is, if
not specifically Japanese, full of Oriental splendour :

YOSHIWARA FESTIVAL

The green and violet peacocks
With golden tails
Parade.

Beneath the fluttering jangling streamers
They walk
Violet and gold.

The green and violet peacocks
Through the golden dusk
Showered upon them from the vine-hung lanterns,
Stately, nostalgically,
Parade.

Not the least interesting quality of that poem is its

stately rhythm, moving slowly, itself "parading," with the Oirans whom it portrays.

Sometimes the poet's conception is more Chinese than Japanese:

AN OIRAN AND HER KAMUSO

Gilded hummingbirds are whizzing
Through the palace garden,
Deceived by the jade petals
Of the Emperor's jewel-trees.

That is almost distinctly Chinese. "Yoshiwara Festival" was neither the one nor the other, but elusively both. The difference is not hard to distinguish, once one has learnt to understand the psychology of the two nations, to feel the subtle divergencies of their literary practice.

Where these poems sometimes fail is exactly in this matter of feeling. Mr. Fletcher loses sight of the fact that only the most simple language, the clearest image, is in keeping with the *hokku* form. The poem must be of the most limpid clarity to gain the full effect of the underlying suggestion. It is the contrast which gives the *hokku* its piquancy. So, when Mr. Fletcher writes:

LOVERS EMBRACING

Force and yielding meet together
An attack is half repulsed:

Shafts of broken sunlight dissolving
Convolutions of torpid cloud.

he sacrifices the peculiar Japanese atmosphere.
That poem is in Mr. Fletcher's most personal idiom,
but it is not in the least in the idiom of Japan.
From this point of view, the most successful poem in
the book is

MOODS

A poet's moods:
Fluttering butterflies in the rain.

That is at once Mr. Fletcher and Japan. It is
brief and clear, and the suggestion never becomes
statement, but floats, a nimbus, over the short,
sharp lines.

Chief among Mr. Fletcher's contributions to
"Some Imagist Poets, 1917," which included three
excellent lyrics, "Blackberry Harvest," "Moonlight," and "Dawn," and one interesting war poem,
"Armies," was the "Lincoln" I have already quoted.
And we may leave it as the evidence of the deepening
and broadening of his art. It is an earnest of the
future, and, crushing as the war seems now, hard and
bitter the weight it imposes upon the brains and
hearts of men, it is in such poems as these that we
feel the renewing power of art, rising even upon the
wings of despair. Mr. Fletcher has needed just this
violent concussion between imagination and fact.

Without it, he would always have been an extraordinarily original and suggestive poet; with it, he may well become a great one. Mr. Fletcher is a virtuoso of words, and sometimes this faculty runs away with him. Some of his symphonies, some of the poems in "Irradiations," are heaped too full of words, the changes he rings are too heavy, he confuses too many colours, too many sounds. His enormous fecundity is responsible for this. It is hard for him to curb his exuberance. Nature has given him much, and it is difficult for him to put himself to school. His books would gain by being pruned; but, as I said in the beginning, he lacks the selective instinct. It is largely for this reason that he is not yet esteemed as he should be. But, for the discerning eye, no living poet has more distinction of vision or of style. In him, indeed, we see the beginning of that new order of which I have so often spoken. To the poet, he is a real teacher, indicating new directions, opening up untrodden ways of thought.

Throughout the pages of this book, I have tried to point out that, in speaking of a "new movement," we do not speak idly; that there is a new spirit permeating the work of American poets. Each of the poets of whom I have been speaking represents a tendency, which is in no way altered by their position in one or the other stages of the advance. Among them, they represent all the trends in evidence in modern verse. Which of them will most influence the future, it is impossible now to say. But, different as each is from the others, together they constitute a marching order, from the old into the new. They are the proof of the re-creative energy of the poetic impulse, which, always changing, is nevertheless a permanent possession of the human race.

Professor Dowden, in an article on Heinrich Heine in his "Essays — Modern and Elizabethan," says: "He swam with the current of romantic art, and he headed round and swam more vigorously against the current, so anticipating the movement of realism which was to meet and turn the tide; but Heine's ideal of art, at once realistic and romantic, is still unattained."

This was written in 1910, and already in 1917 we see this ideal, expressed in terms quite other than those of Heine, well on the road to attainment. "At once realistic and romantic," this would seem to be the goal toward which the New Movement in Modern American Poetry is aiming.

BIBLIOGRAPHY

BIBLIOGRAPHY

EDWIN ARLINGTON ROBINSON

THE CHILDREN OF THE NIGHT. Charles Scribner's Sons, New York, 1897.

CAPTAIN CRAIG. Charles Scribner's Sons, New York, 1902; reprint, with new poems, The Macmillan Company, New York, 1915.

THE TOWN DOWN THE RIVER. Charles Scribner's Sons, New York, 1910.

VAN ZORN. The Macmillan Company, New York, 1914.

THE PORCUPINE. The Macmillan Company, New York, 1915.

THE MAN AGAINST THE SKY. The Macmillan Company, New York, 1916.

MERLIN. The Macmillan Company, New York, 1917.

ROBERT FROST

A BOY'S WILL. David Nutt and Company, London, 1913; Henry Holt and Company, New York, 1915.

NORTH OF BOSTON. David Nutt and Company, London, 1914; Henry Holt and Company, New York, 1915.

MOUNTAIN INTERVAL. Henry Holt and Company, New York, 1916.

EDGAR LEE MASTERS

A BOOK OF VERSES.   Way and Williams, Chicago, 1898.

MAXIMILIAN.   (A play in verse.) Richard G. Badger, Boston, 1902.

THE NEW STAR CHAMBER AND OTHER ESSAYS.   The Hammersmark Publishing Company, Chicago, 1904.

THE BLOOD OF THE PROPHETS.   (Under pseudonym: Dexter Wallace.)   The Hammersmark Publishing Company, Chicago, 1905.

THE SPOON RIVER ANTHOLOGY.   The Macmillan Company, New York, 1915.

SONGS AND SATIRES.   The Macmillan Company, New York, 1916.

THE GREAT VALLEY.   The Macmillan Company, New York, 1916.

CARL SANDBURG

CHICAGO POEMS.   Henry Holt and Company, New York, 1916.

"H.D."

SEA GARDEN.   Constable and Company, London; and Houghton Mifflin Company, Boston, 1916.

In collaboration:

DES IMAGISTES.   Albert and Charles Boni, New York, 1914.

SOME IMAGIST POETS.   Houghton Mifflin Company, Boston; and Constable and Company, London, 1915.

SOME IMAGIST POETS, 1916.   Houghton Mifflin Company, Boston; and Constable and Company, London, 1916.

SOME IMAGIST POETS, 1917.   Houghton Mifflin Company, Boston; and Constable and Company, London, 1917.

JOHN GOULD FLETCHER

FIRE AND WINE. Grant Richards, Ltd., London, 1913.

FOOL'S GOLD. Max Goschen, London, 1913.

THE DOMINANT CITY. Max Goschen, London, 1913.

THE BOOK OF NATURE. Constable and Company, London, 1913.

VISIONS OF THE EVENING. Erskine McDonald, London, 1913.

IRRADIATIONS: SAND AND SPRAY. Houghton Mifflin Company, Boston, 1915; and Constable and Company, London, 1915.

GOBLINS AND PAGODAS. Houghton Mifflin Company, Boston, 1916.

In collaboration:

DES IMAGISTES. Albert and Charles Boni, New York, 1914.

SOME IMAGIST POETS. Houghton Mifflin Company, Boston; and Constable and Company, London, 1915.

SOME IMAGIST POETS, 1916. Houghton Mifflin Company, Boston; and Constable and Company, London, 1916.

SOME IMAGIST POETS, 1917. Houghton Mifflin Company, Boston; and Constable and Company, London, 1917.